Permission and regu

This book examines the period that we still colloquially refer to as 'the permissive age': the 1960s. Perhaps more than any other period in our recent history, that decade has been the source of some apparently imperishable myths. This book attempts to separate the myths from the realities. It focuses upon a series of legislative changes that are commonly held to illustrate the permissive or liberal character of the era. These central case studies – of the law, in relation to abortion, obscenity, homosexuality and prostitution – cast doubt on the view propounded by politicians and moralists that such changes indicated moral relaxation and increasing sexual licence.

The book argues that the ideology of permissiveness requires close examination, and analyses the campaigns of Mary Whitehouse to try and pinpoint how this ideology was constructed, applied and challenged. The final chapter compares the permissive era to the moral politics of the Thatcher decade.

Challenging and informative, the book will be of interest to students of social history, sociology, gender studies and politics.

Tim Newburn is Research Co-ordinator of the Hillsborough Project, National Institute for Social Work, London.

Permission and regulation
Law and morals in post-war Britain

Tim Newburn

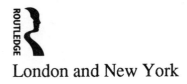

London and New York

176
NEW

1059470 1

First published 1992
by Routledge
11 New Fetter Lane, London EC4P 4EE

Simultaneously published in the USA and Canada
by Routledge
a division of Routledge, Chapman and Hall, Inc.
29 West 35th Street, New York, NY 10001

© 1992 Tim Newburn

Typeset by LaserScript, Mitcham, Surrey
Printed and bound in Great Britain by
Biddles Ltd, Guildford and King's Lynn

British Library Cataloguing in Publication Data
Newburn, Tim *1959*–
Permission and regulation: law and morals in post-war Britain.
1. Great Britain. Social life, history, 1960–1970
I. Title
941.0856

Library of Congress Cataloging in Publication Data
Newburn, Tim.
Permission and regulation: law and morals in post-war Britain/
Tim Newburn.
p. cm.
Includes bibliographical references and index.
1. Sex and law – Great Britain. 2. Criminal law – Social aspects –
Great Britain. 3. Law and ethics. 4. Sexual ethics – Great
Britain – Case studies. 5. Great Britain – Moral conditions – Case
studies. I. Title.
KD7975.N49 1991
345.41′027–dc20   91-10288
[344.10527]   CIP

ISBN 0–415–04639–4
ISBN 0–415–04640–8 (pbk)

(31/07 /92 (0)

Contents

Preface

The research on which this book is based was supported initially by a grant from the Economic and Social Research Council for which I was and I remain grateful. The work has mutated on several occasions, both changing its focus and altering in style and approach. The original intention was to look at a much broader span of history and to consider the disjunctures and continuities in the moral politics of the twentieth century. Before long, however, it became clear that not only do the 1960s appear to occupy an unrivalled position as a source of myth and propaganda about our moral–sexual history but as a decade it has also attracted more critical attention than possibly any other this century.

In addition, the term 'permissiveness', which is generally held to apply either to the 1960s or to some period which includes the 1960s, has been used as a powerful and resonant tool by politicians and social commentators despite its apparent vacuousness. The emerging intention of this work, therefore, became to consider both the reality and the ideology of the 'permissive age'. It is constructed around three case studies which focus upon the major legislative changes during this period – those in the areas of obscenity, abortion and prostitution/homosexuality – changes which are often either assumed to have been or which are presented as being unproblematically and straightforwardly 'permissive'. As is explored in some detail, such a simplistic approach typifies the ideological position adopted by the moral right – particularly those like Mary Whitehouse from the early 1960s onwards, and by the Thatcherite 'new right' in the 1980s. What I have sought to do is to 'unpack' this notion of permissiveness, to demystify it, and to identify the realities that lie behind it and which form the basis for its apparently continuing ideological force.

There are precious few opportunities to acknowledge the debt one owes to friends, family and colleagues for the help and support they provide in alleviating the often unnecessarily lonely life of the researcher. All the more so in this case, as I have been involved in work related to this book in some sense – often no more than guilt-ridden avoidance – for ten years now. I should like to record my thanks to my parents, also to David, Cathy and Nain – and to Bee and Hartley – for their support, encouragement and love. I owe much to friends and ex-colleagues at the University of Leicester: John Williams, Ivan Waddington, Pat Murphy and Ilya Neustadt, and particularly to Professor Eric Dunning who had the ability to exert a crucial influence at the most important moments. My thanks also to my erstwhile colleagues from HORPU for putting up with my whinging and whining, and especially to George Mair for the regular therapeutic visits to the Town and Country Club, and to the late Derek 'VAX' Clifford and David Mann who nursed the text. The staff of the libraries at Leicester University and the Home Office were not only helpful but also put up with a constant flow of overdue books with greater patience than I'm sure I deserved. Finally my love and thanks to Mary, Gavin and Robin. Mary has not only been a tremendous source of support and encouragement, but also applied her expertise to much of the text and saved me from many errors. As ever, any remaining faults are my responsibility alone.

Tim Newburn

Introduction

The cultural critic Robert Hewison has argued[1] that each decade appears to have its own myth. Such myths seem to capture the feeling of the decade. He suggests that, in the 1940s, it was the sense of community engendered by the Blitz, in the 1950s the aggressive ambitiousness of the 'Angry Young Men' and in the 1960s 'Swinging London'. Swinging London and what it was supposed to represent formed the heart of our major 'sustaining image'[2] of that period: 'permissiveness'.

The 1960s have probably attracted more critical attention than any other decade of the twentieth century. Sociologists and social historians, particularly the new breed whose major concerns appear to be popular culture and style, have documented the rise of the affluent teenager, the growth of mass consumption and the spread and proliferation of working-class subcultural styles, all of which have become closely associated with that particular historical period. Contemporary politicians have singled out the 1960s as the source of almost all our current social ills. According to these ideologues, what we have failed to recover from is a period of moral decline, or permissiveness, that they suggest characterised 1960s society. The Conservative MP and ex-headmaster, Rhodes Boyson, has suggested, for example, that:

> Children were brought up in a pathless desert where the world was to be explored, not served ... there was a cheapening of human life and young people were brought up to be selfish, pleasure-seeking or irresponsible. In schools we had child-centered education which led to deprived children, lower standards, disorderly classrooms, and defenceless and disillusioned teachers. Our present ills are the ripened and bitter crop of those seeds of the 1960s.[3]

'Permissiveness', or the historical period that was supposed to be characterised by it, forms the subject-matter of this book.

Whilst there is little agreement as to what permissiveness means or on what characterised its purported growth in the 1960s and what the ensuing results have been, few have come forward to challenge the idea, or to suggest that permissiveness may be a product of our historical imaginations. Several questions immediately arise. Firstly, what is the permissiveness of the 1960s supposed to have consisted of? Secondly, can a process of growing permissiveness – however it is defined – be said to have occurred in post-war British society? Thirdly, what was it about whatever was happening in Britain at this time that allowed the period to be plausibly described as permissive?

This book aims to tackle some of these questions. It does so by focusing, in three separate case studies, on a number of changes in the criminal law in this period. It begins, however, by taking a critical look at the notion of 'permissiveness' itself. Chapter one concentrates upon the accounts of the period provided by sociologists, journalists, politicians and other commentators. By examining their accounts and their explanations for the changes they identify, an attempt is made to build up a composite picture of the idea of permissiveness.

Chapter two builds on this composite. Whether or not the changes discussed in Chapter one may be described as permissive, it is clear that many commentators believed (many continue to believe) that Britain was in the grip of something called 'permissiveness'. Chapter two takes as its focus one of the central characters of the debates over morality and the law in the 1960s. Mrs Whitehouse is used as an example of a position adopted by moral entrepreneurs in this period, not, by any means, because she is the only one, but because her views in this regard are ideal–typical. A close look at her concerns makes visible the preoccupations that underlay the debates over permissiveness.

Having discussed the concept of permissiveness in the first two chapters, Chapter three, the first of the case studies, considers the various ways in which the relationship between the criminal law and morality has been theorised, taking as its starting-point the Wolfenden Report and the legislation in the two areas that it covered: homosexuality and prostitution. Two basic relationships are identified, these being themselves based upon the respective positions adopted by Patrick Devlin and H.L.A. Hart in their famous debate on jurisprudence in the early 1960s. The function of this discussion is to enable a critical appraisal of both the legislative changes described in the case studies, and the concept of permissiveness to be undertaken.

Chapters four and five look at the obscenity laws and their operation, and Chapter six considers the change in the legal position of abortion. Each of the case-studies seeks not only to describe in detail the debates surrounding each of the legislative changes, to relate the changes identified to the debates outlined in Chapter three (and to each other), but also to look at the concerns that underpinned each. That is, it seeks to uncover what appear to be the hidden agendas or subtexts of the debates in the areas under consideration.

Chapters seven and eight return to the questions outlined in the introduction. It is argued that, whilst a one-dimensional concept such as 'permissiveness' is of limited value for sociologists, it nevertheless appears to have strong ideological resonance. Thus, despite its limitations, the term 'permissiveness' has become an accepted and seemingly self-explanatory tool for many commentators on the 1960s. 'Permissiveness' has become an all-embracing term covering a series of analytically separable concerns. It has come to refer to what has been perceived to be one major social transformation. Here, however, it will be argued that three distinct processes – changing balances of power between men and women; changing balances of power between adults and youth; and the declining influence and centrality of the Church – were the major components of the processes of social change which gave rise to the series of concerns eventually subsumed under the generic term 'permissiveness'. Finally, it is suggested that, as a result of these processes, post-war British society must be described as morally pluralistic, and that, consequently, it has become increasingly difficult to sustain the argument – although Mrs Whitehouse and Mrs Thatcher amongst others occasionally still attempt to do so – that we live in an age of moral consensus.

1 Permissiveness

Accounts, discourses and explanations

Post-War Sexual Morality

There are essentially five broad approaches to the subject of permissiveness that may be identified. For present purposes these are termed the 'conservative-historical', the 'liberal-historical', the 'Marxist-Gramscian'/ Foucauldian, the feminist and the 'Eliasian'. The categories are neither intended to be mutually exclusive nor all-embracing. Not every author who has something to say on the subject of post-war sexual morality is included in the following discussion of each of the five categories, but rather those who are considered to be most representative of each genre are discussed.

At its crudest the conservative-historical approach to permissiveness is but a mourning for a lost 'golden age', an expression of grief for the passing of a time when questions of morals supposedly appeared much simpler, more straightforward and certainly less contentious and open to question. The liberal-historical approach by contrast is more forward-looking in character. The tone is different; it is more optimistic, more likely to assume that the process of historical change being viewed has at least some positive attributes, and less likely to dwell on social 'ills' or problems. It is, in a word, more *modernist*. It would be dangerous to assume from this simplification, however, that the two perspectives can be easily separated by the ideological position each adopts, the former tending to see 'permissiveness' as bad, the latter seeing it as good. This tends not to be the case. Whilst the liberal-historians are less likely to be openly damning of the social changes they identify than are the conservative-historians, this should not be read as a sign of their approval. Permissiveness is used almost universally as a pejorative term.

At the core of the conservative-historical position is the suggestion that the constitution of British society underwent a radical transformation in the 1950s and 1960s, and that this transformation included a significant alteration in the society's moral code. The use of the singular 'code' is important as will become clear. The position is most clearly illustrated by John Selwyn Gummer.[1] The essence of his argument is that, during the course of the twentieth century, British society has been characterised by increasing economic regulation and increasing moral licence. We are, he suggests, much less economically permissive than the Victorians, constraining business enterprise, terms and conditions of employment, advertising and so on, whilst morally and sexually becoming less restrictive. Indeed '[w]e are as restrictive materially as the Victorians were morally', he argues.[2] Gummer takes this argument one step further. The new permissive society differs from its Victorian predecessor not only by virtue of its sexual and moral freedom, but also because it is characterised by lack of agreement over questions of morality, and over the role of the state in the enforcement of morals. This is in direct contrast, he argues, to Victorian society:

> In the nineteenth century, men had few such worries. They accepted that the state had a duty to uphold morality and that private morality ought to be subject to the law as it affected society. They then experienced little difficulty in deciding of what private morality consisted. There was a consensus – at least among the articulate. People knew what standards were and when they and, more particularly, others were falling short of them.[3]

For this author, the crucial change has been the break-up of consensus. Even though in the passage above Gummer undermines his own argument (through his use of the phrase 'at least among the articulate', he implies that this consensus is confined to a certain section of society) it is crucial to his thesis that the changes to be identified under the rubric of permissiveness should be viewed against the backcloth of an alleged Victorian moral consensus.

To anyone familiar with the writings of authors such as Gummer, who are critical of the changes that have taken place in post-war Britain, the characteristics he highlights will be similarly familiar. Firstly, he identifies 'a lack of respect for authority' resulting from the decline of moral consensus or firm moral guidelines. For such authors this generally means one of two things: diminishing respect by the young for adults, or diminishing respect by the working class for traditional, i.e. middle-class, values (religion, sobriety, hard work, etc.). Gummer's attention is focused upon the young:

> Thus youth, singled out as important by the commentators and advertising men, is increasingly unfettered by the conventional sanctions which a balanced community imposes. It doesn't matter what Mrs Jones thinks because Mrs Jones doesn't know or care. What is more, because this youthful community has little contact with the older generation it has increasingly little reason to see why it should defer to the older

generation's judgement. It is here that the oft discussed breakdown of authority becomes most apparent.[4]

The result of lack of respect for authority can be seen in higher, and ever increasing, crime rates, in increased drug use and sexual promiscuity. One must add to this the spread and easier availability of pornography, television which not only normalises such changes, but on occasion appears to be in support of them, and the lack of a firm moral grounding in sex education. All this, it is suggested, was met by very little resistance from the Church or other parts of the Establishment, and yet it would be wrong, he argues, to feel that there was popular support for permissive morality.

Gummer makes no pretence of objectivity in his text. Although he suggests he is not wholly against the permissive society, all that he can find to say in its favour is that it points to the continual necessity to make traditional values relevant to contemporary society, to the fact that the importance of the family, 'the very principles of order itself...are not... accepted by all'.[5] Gummer calls for the reassertion of the importance and centrality of the religiously sanctioned, monogamous heterosexual relationship to our culture. Within such an institutional arrangement there is, by implication, little room for alternative practices, including those possibilities opened up by the women's and gay liberation movements of the period, and it is such an arrangement that constituted, for Gummer, the previously existing moral consensus.

Although the authors in this 'school' focus on different aspects of permissive Britain, they are all united by their acceptance of the idea that previously existing moral consensus has given way to confusion and uncertainty. For the conservative-historians it was the Profumo affair that most forcefully illustrated the altered circumstances that 1960s Britain found itself in. Christopher Booker's thoughts on the subject are worth quoting in full for he manages to incorporate a good quota of folk devils in his account, and provides almost a blueprint of the conservative-historical position:

The events of the following weeks and months had little real connection with the personal indiscretion of two summers before which was nominally their occasion. The Profumo affair was merely the focus and catalyst for the coming to a head of that revolution in the mood and character of English life which had begun to show itself in the late summer of 1955. It was the end of a trail which had had its beginnings in those first rumblings of Henry Fairlie against the Establishment and Malcolm Muggeridge against the Monarchy; a trail that had led on through the Angry Young Men and all the resentments sown by Suez, through the heyday of affluence, through all the mounting impatience with convention, tradition and authority that had been marked by the teenage revolution and the CND and the New Morality, through the darkening landscape of security scandals and What's Wrong With Britain and the rising aggression and bitterness of the satirists, in ever more violent momentum. And now, in that wet and windy June, the climax had arrived. Not one ingredient was missing. With Profumo's admission of guilt, all the swelling tide of scorn and resentment for age, tradition and authority, all the poisonous fantasy of limitless corruption and decay into which it had ripened, were finally unleashed in their full fury.[6]

In Booker's eyes Profumo set the seal on the long process of British moral decline, the essence of which was a 'lack of respect for authority' in all its guises – the Establishment, the monarchy, political leaders, the Church and so on. The essence of this constitutional malaise was the changing attitude of the young towards those in authority. It was not that this could be attributed to a weakening of moral fibre on their part, but rather that they had grown up in a society in which there were few straightforward moral guidelines, and into 'a community which is thoroughly confused about morals, and ... their behaviour reflects that confusion'[7].

Confusion and uncertainty are the major characteristics of the permissive society according to the conservative-historians. Pamela Hansford Johnson (1967) suggested that modern Britain was 'affectless'. It was a society, she felt, which was emotionless, in which people committed the most vicious crimes seemingly without motive or purpose, lacking all regard for human worth or dignity.[8] Johnson's book was written in response to the Moors Murders and the ensuing trial. Although Johnson does not go so far as to claim that the affectless society was responsible for the Moors Murders, she does feel able to argue that the general atmosphere in society at the time had 'infected' the social system, and that 'Brady possibly, Hindley almost certainly, have been victims of fallout'.[9]

Beginning with the publication of *Lady Chatterley's Lover*, she argues, the floodgates to total permissiveness were opened and a society in which 'the permissive intellectual's anything goes' was created. A series of murders of young children were, she implies, the corollary of the disintegration of moral rules characteristic of 1960s Britain:

> It seemed to us that April that we were seeing one of the results of total permissiveness in a rather comely young man and woman, ill-educated, but neither of them stupid, on trial at Chester Assizes for multiple murder. A wound in the flesh of our society had cracked open, we looked into it, and we smelled its sepsis.[10]

It is no distance from this position to that adopted by Rhodes Boyson, quoted in the introduction. Such commentators have argued that the breakdown of morality in the 1960s has had lasting effects on the social landscape. As Brian Masters stated succinctly, 'the generation of the sixties inherited such a[n] [established moral] code and rejected it; that of the eighties has had no firm code to inherit'.[11]

By contrast, 'moral collapse' or synonyms for such a phrase rarely find their way into the accounts of the period provided by 'liberal-historians'. Much of this is because the changes identified in the 1960s are viewed through different historical lenses. From this perspective the previously existing moral order is not seen as being wholly positive, and consequently its destruction – for both the conservative- and liberal-historians identify such a process – is not necessarily perceived as being problematic. More particularly, different aspects and different consequences of this previous moral order are identified. Bridget Pym (1974) emphasises the 'joyless morality's' concentration on the integrity of the family and monogamy as the only available form of sexual expression. Fear of promiscuity and perversion, she argues, found expression in laws against abortion and homosexuality, and restrictive attitudes towards contraception. Despite this very different interpretation of pre-permissive morality, there are nevertheless distinct parallels between the conservative- and liberal-historical analyses of cultural change in post-war Britain. Both involve the identification of a previously existing, now largely defunct, set of moral imperatives which have given way to a new order in which control, particularly of sexual conduct, has diminished. Both suggest that in the area of sexual morality the change has been towards less restraint, less control and more choice. Writing in 1972, McGregor suggested that: 'the last two decades have witnessed the cumulative removal of restraints both of custom and law upon behaviour, and upon their public portrayal in print or in the visual arts'.[12]

For McGregor, as for Pym, the major changes centred around the family system which prescribed the conditions for sexual relationships, changes which resulted in loosened bonds of matrimony, increased choice and reduced frustration and suffering. In this manner certain aspects, at least, of the process of permissive change are presented as having been positive and beneficial, in direct contrast to the view of the conservative-historians.

Marwick, like McGregor, looks at legislative change in the period, and describes it generally as both liberal and 'civilising'.[13] Although he comes across exceptions to the rule, such as drug control, most legislation in the period, he argues, removed restraints, undermined fears and 'encouraged the active sexual life as normal'.[14] He views the changes as involving the destruction of Victorian hypocrisy, quite unlike, say, Gummer's mourning

of the passing of Victorian consensus. It is by no means all good news for
the liberal-historians though. Marwick, for example, highlights the rising
crime rate from the mid-1950s onward, which included such highly
publicised events as the Moors Murders, the Great Train Robbery, the
Shepherds Bush police murders, and the arrest and trial of the Kray twins.
Although with regard to young offenders he cites possible mitigating
factors such as the temptations of the affluent society and the frustrations of
dead-end jobs, he nevertheless lays the blame at the door of the 'new
aggressiveness and hostility to authority'. As has been argued above, there
are certainly differences between the conservative- and liberal-historians
on the question of 'permissiveness', but there are similarities as well.
Marwick himself illustrates the point well:

> Perhaps the standards of civic loyalty and respect for law and order have
> never been as high as conservative romantics affected to believe. There
> is no easy way of rooting out deviants in society; but certainly the special
> conditions of the late fifties onwards gave deviants full rein.[15]

Coming from the critical position that they do, the conservative-historians
have little difficulty in deciding whether or not the changes they have
identified in either post-war sexual morality, or legislation relating to
sexual morality, can be plausibly described as 'permissive'. The liberal-
historians, on the other hand, tend to find themselves in a somewhat more
tricky position. Whilst they usually dismiss the more extreme claims made
by the conservative-historians, they are, by and large, convinced that
something approaching 'permissive morality' could be found in 1960s
Britain.[16]

For both the conservative- and liberal-historians legislative change is of
central importance to an understanding of the permissive society. The
conservative-historical analysis takes certain legislative changes as being
fundamentally permissive in outlook, and even suggests that the reforms of
the law can be used as a barometer of the times. Bernard Levin, for
example, argued that 'the sixties in Britain produced an extraordinary
number of legislative reforms, which carried to extraordinary lengths the
new spirit of tolerance and its codification in the law'.[17] The law is viewed
as an index of wider social changes. Christie Davies probably presents this
argument at its starkest:

> One demonstrable sign of the growth of permissiveness in British
> society has been the consistent tendency over the last twenty years for
> Parliament to alter laws governing moral conduct in a permissive
> direction. Activities, which society had previously disapproved of and
> banned, are now permitted and can be freely indulged in.[18]

The liberal-historians, on the other hand, whilst being generally more sceptical of the extent of permissiveness, nevertheless argue that 1960s Britain was characterised by a greater degree of freedom, the limited nature of which is nonetheless guaranteed by law. Thus for both groups the major legislative changes of the period – the Obscene Publications Act, the Sexual Offences Act, the Street Offences Act, the Abortion Act, the Theatres Act – are significant for their 'permissive' or 'liberalising' character. Although interpretations differ, particularly ideologically, they share a common thrust.

This is also true of the Marxist, or more strictly, Gramscian approach to the question of permissiveness, taken by Stuart Hall and others, as well as what might be termed the 'Foucauldian' position. It is a considerably more sophisticated approach though, as should become clear, not without its flaws. The authors of *Policing the Crisis*,[19] although concerning themselves primarily with the 'mugging panic' of the 1970s, also focus on what they take to be the changing moral climate in 1960s Britain. The fundamental change is conceived of in terms of the 'crisis of hegemony' that is experienced by the modern capitalist state when the basis of its cultural authority becomes contested. As the ability of the state to mould popular consensus diminishes, so the argument goes, the method by which hegemony is achieved moves from consent to coercion. This can be seen, they argue, in ever more direct forms of state intervention. More particularly, Hall *et al.* suggest that the discrete moral panics associated with the permissive age, e.g. those around abortion, VD, drugs and pornography, form the backdrop to the 'general crisis of the state' which was identified in panics around violent conduct like 'mugging'. Little evidence is presented that would support the claim that the moral panics associated with permissiveness were linked to the latter panic over street crime. Having suggested that the 1960s were characterised by a series of discrete panics around moral issues, there is neither an account – other than an essentially economistic one – of the aetiology of such panics, nor an explanation of the way(s) in which they can be considered to be discrete.

Hall *et al.* do bring into play Becker's notion of 'moral entrepreneurship'[20] and Gusfield's 'moral indignation'[21] to explain why certain social groups were prime movers in the development of moral panics over permissiveness in the 1960s. The brief history of the National Viewers' and Listeners' Association in the following chapter suggests that this is, however, an incomplete conceptualisation.

The key point in the development of a general moral panic was, for Hall *et al.*, not the watershed year cited by moral entrepreneurs and historians alike – 1963 – but rather 1966, when such diverse subjects as the dissemination of pornography, the capture of Harry Roberts, and the Moors

Murders all hit the headlines. From this point moral indignation became more than simply a grassroots phenomenon. Rather, 'in these campaigns, politicians, Chief Constables, Judges, the press and media joined hands and voices with the moral guardians in a general crackdown on "youth" and the permissive society'.[22] Moral regulation was now more often brought about through coercion rather than consent. Laws which, in the early 1960s, had been 'liberally interpreted and allowed to lapse' were applied with increased rigour. The liberal interlude, as they call it, where laws such as those over obscene publications were allowed to lie fallow, soon came to an end. The laws, they argue, were soon dusted off and exercised to the full.

Stuart Hall employs a rather more sophisticated approach in an article for the National Deviancy Conference on 'consenting legislation'.[23] In this he suggests that description in terms of either permissiveness or control would be too simple and too binary, and thus it is to the nature of reformism that one must look.[24] In the 1960s, moral reformism, he argues, was aimed most specifically at sexual practices, and particularly those of women. The role of women from the 1950s on contained an inherent contradiction, he suggests, a contradiction between what have been termed 'the ideologies of consumption and domesticity'.[25] For the new post-war ideology of consumption to be stimulated it was necessary for women to remain in the home, yet at the same time to enter the labour market to supplement the 'main income' to sustain the family's purchasing power. During the 1960s, however, this traditional role was partially disarticulated, and replaced with a recognition of women's sexual pleasure and satisfaction. This shift was largely made possible by the breaking of the tie between female sexuality and reproduction, particularly through new contraceptive techniques. Women, Hall suggests, were the key interpellated subject of the new legislation:

> Overwhelmingly, it was the position of women in the field of sexual practice, which provided the legislation with its principal object/subject. What is proposed, in sum, was a measure of relaxation in the social and legal control of selected aspects of female sexual practice. It meant, in effect, a new 'modality' of control over these aspects – a more privatised and 'person-focused' regulation.[26]

This 'legislative moment' incorporating all the major changes which Hall places under the title 'legislation of consent', lasted roughly from 1959 (Wolfenden, and the Obscene Publications Act) to 1968 (end of theatre censorship and the Wootton Report on drugs). This was followed, the authors of *Policing the Crisis* (Hall *et al.* 1978) suggest, by two 'waves' of social reaction. The first wave was organised around social, cultural and moral issues, the second around the politicisation of the counter-culture.

The major contrast between the two is that in the latter, 'youth' had become more than mere 'agents' of change, and were identified as 'subversive'.[27] In terms of concrete events, the first wave of the backlash was associated with Mrs Whitehouse, *The Longford Report*, the Festival of Light and the Society for the Protection of the Unborn Child (SPUC). The second wave included such 'events' as the prosecutions of *OZ*, *IT* and *The Little Red Schoolbook*. Whilst this is a generally convincing thesis, closer examination reveals some historical inaccuracies. The first wave of reaction is described by Clarke *et al.* (1976) as an 'organised anti-permissive backlash'.[28] Whilst what is meant by 'organised backlash' is never made clear, it is probably not unreasonable to infer that it implies that it occurred after 1968 and within a limited historical period. Looking at the specific people and events mentioned, the degree to which one might talk of 'organisation' seems somewhat open to question. Mary Whitehouse's 'moral crusade' began in 1963–4 with the setting-up of the Clean-up TV Campaign. SPUC took off in 1966–7. The Festival of Light was launched in September 1971, and *The Longford Report* was published in September 1972. The earliest date at which these four could have formed part of an 'organised backlash' would have been at least eighteen months after what Hall *et al.* (1978) describe as the 'full repressive closure' of 1970.[29] Furthermore if the idea of a first and second wave is to be sustained, then – in Clarke's, Hall's and others' formulations – it must be shown that one wave in some senses follows the other. The three major trials mentioned by the authors as being part of the second wave – those of *International Times* (November 1970), *The Little Red Schoolbook* (March 1971) and *OZ* 28 (June 1971) all occurred before the publication of *The Longford Report* or the launch of the Festival of Light, put forward as being part of the first wave. Whilst it is not incorrect to identify all of these as sources, or illustrations, of moral indignation of one sort or another – indeed there are significant connections between them – attempting to fit them into a historical framework which appears to allow only for movements in one direction, i.e. permissiveness followed by control, results in a degree of historical inaccuracy.

A slight reorientation of the approach taken by Hall and colleagues is to be found in the writings of authors like Jeffrey Weeks. Weeks' approach is influenced by the French philosopher Michel Foucault and, whilst much of it is as essentially economistic as that of the Gramscians, it has a somewhat different slant.

For the Foucauldians sexuality is made meaningful through the discourses which shape it. Sexuality is 'organised' by the state as a technique of social control. Weeks argues that recent history has seen an explosion of speech surrounding sex and that the 1960s in particular 'experienced a decisive, qualititative escalation of the volume'.[30] Looking at the age of the sexual revolution he isolates a set of changes that he views as having been particularly significant in shaping the period.

The first and most important of these (and the one that ties him most clearly to Hall *et al.*) is the 'commercialisation and commodification of sex'. Although he avoids arguing that capitalism created a sexual morality to serve its own imperatives – it has no master plan – 'the best we can do at this stage is to suggest that the articulation between sexual mores and capitalism occurs through complex mediations – through moral agencies, political interventions, diverse social practices'.[31] What has happened, he suggests, is that capitalism's tendency to colonise and penetrate segments of social existence has led to the commercialisation and commodification of sexuality, particularly via the shift from production to consumption. He gives as an example of this the growth of a 'pornocracy' and through the break-up of the sex–procreation nexus has come the increasing commodification of pleasure – the developing range of sex–pleasure items on the market.

As to sexual behaviour itelf, Weeks argues in tandem with both Marxist and feminist theorists that the so-called sexual liberation of women occurred within the well-circumscribed limits of both the capitalist labour market and male-dominated and defined notions of sexual pleasure. There was, however, he suggests, a shift away from legal moralism, and through the reformist legislation of the 1960s a certain amount of 'piecemeal moral engineering' [32] was achieved. Finally, he argues, none of the changes went unchallenged, and the transformations in regulation and domination that occurred in the period themselves resulted in new forms of resistance and, in particular, in the women's and gay movements of the 1970s and 1980s. The consequence of this has been the incorporation into the political sphere of issues which were previously barely regarded as political at all.

Although a number of feminist authors have tended to view some of the 1960s legislation as 'liberalising', they have sought to distinguish the identification of such a trend from any notion of 'liberation'. Whilst legislative reforms such as changes in the abortion laws and the law governing homosexuality are viewed as essentially liberal measures, we are not to assume therefore that this was indicative of a period of unproblematically increasing sexual liberation.

For critics such as Sheila Jeffreys the so-called 'sexual revolution' was in fact a counter-revolution. It was a smokescreen behind which the reconstitution of male domination was hidden:

Behind the baloney of liberation, the naked power-politics of male supremacy were being acted out. The high priests of sexalogic, helped by the pornographers, progressive novelists and sex radicals continued to orchestrate woman's joyful embrace of her oppression through the creation of her sexual response.... The 1960s was a period when greater opportunities were open to women and the 'sexual revolution', rather than being liberating, helped to diffuse the potential threat to male power.[33]

It was not until the feminist movement re-emerged with vigour in the early 1970s that a critique of 'permissiveness' was constructed. As feminist writers began to question male sexuality and, particularly, to consider male violence against women, so they questioned the nature of the revolution. The authors who began to write about rape[34] and related it to male power, male supremacy and male sexuality, questioned what they saw to be the essentialist constructions of female sexuality which continued to predominate within the age of sexual revolution.

The critique of male sexuality which originally focused on rape, developed through analyses of child sexual abuse[35] and non-stranger rape[36] – and later pornography.[37] Such work hit at the heart of the institution which the conservative-historians took to be so much under threat – the nuclear family. Ironically, whilst such a group took the very existence of the family to be in danger from permissiveness, the developing radical-feminist position argued that the 'talk' of permissiveness was a means of disguising the threat that such an institution posed to women's real chances of liberation: 'Rather than posing a threat to traditional patriarchal marriage the sexual revolution strengthened the institution'.[38]

Feminist authors such as Jeffreys, like the conservative historians, are almost unremittingly critical of permissiveness and its products. Although there is little of essence in common between the two approaches, it is perhaps not hard to see how on occasion unlikely alliances between radical-feminist anti-pornography campaigners and moral entrepreneurs such as Mrs Whitehouse might have been countenanced. Of all the recent authors it is perhaps Jeffreys who has developed the most thorough analysis of permissiveness or what she refers to as the 'sexual revolution'. She looks in some detail at the process by which the counter-revolutionary attack on women's liberation took place. Focusing *inter alia* on the work of the sex radicals Reich and Marcuse, and the sexologists of *Forum* magazine and manuals such as *Joy of Sex*, she details the prescription of male dominance and female submission. As she acidly puts it, 'the liberation was not intended to liberate (women) from anything but their common-sense and their instinct for self-protection'.[39]

An element which is largely missing from both the Marxist and feminist accounts, in contrast to either the conservative- or liberal-historical approaches, is reference to the role of religion in contemporary society. For both the conservative- and liberal-historians, the process of 'secularisation' is identified as a necessary if not sufficient condition for the rise of the permissive society. From the Marxist point of view, a process such as secularisation takes a more secondary role in relation to features more closely associated with the functioning of a capitalist economy, and particularly changes in the class structure. As an example, as has already been suggested, the authors of *Policing the Crisis* (Hall *et al.* 1978) explain the existence of moral entrepreneurial groups in the 1960s by reference firstly to their common location in the class structure, and only secondly by reference to their religious views, and their perception of the modern 'secular' world. The following chapter on the role of the National Viewers' and Listeners' Association (NVALA) in the 1960s, and the following case studies, will consider evidence which casts doubt on this order of priority.

The Eliasian approach, as adapted by Cas Wouters, places even less emphasis on changing religious influences on contemporary moral codes than does the Marxist. Indeed notions of moral indignation, moral panic or moral conflict are not used in this perspective at all. The major focus is upon human interdependency, its levels of organisation, and the concomitant balance of social and self-controls that results. That there have occurred changes which may be described as permissive is not doubted: 'We have experienced a change in standards of conduct which one might also describe by reversing Caxton's quotation. One might say: "Things formerly forbidden are now allowed". These changes have popularly become known by the name permissiveness.'[40]

Wouters refers to this process as 'informalisation'. The major example that he gives of informalisation is what he takes to be the decrease of social restraints, particularly in the middle classes, imposed upon sexual behaviour and other connected spheres of conduct. As a result of these changes it has become possible, among other things, to show more of the male and female body. It has become possible to talk more freely and openly both about sexual experiences and other bodily functions such as menstruation. In essence, he argues, certain forms of conduct which were once forbidden are now allowed, and are regulated much less formally than they once were. These areas of conduct have become more subject to self-constraint and less subject to external constraint.

Having suggested the predominant direction in which the movement has gone, i.e towards informalisation, Wouters sets out to explain it. In his first article on the subject[41] the focus was on what he, following Elias, termed the 'changing balance of power between the classes'. Specifically he referred to the changing balance between the middle and working classes, but he suggests that the balance of power between the generations within the middle class also changed. It is not clear from the article to what extent it was Dutch society that he was basing his analysis on, but given that he appears to be making a general point about changes within Western Europe, it is important to point out that most of the literature on youth, adolescence and relations between the generations in Britain has tended to concentrate on, to use Elias' term again, the changing balance of power between the generations *within* the working class.[42] Wouters' more recent writings on the process of informalisation begin to plug another gap in his early conceptualisation by focusing on the changing balance of power between the sexes.[43]

Wouters' project is to build upon Elias' theory of the 'civilising process', and to show how informalisation, far from contradicting Elias' thesis, can actually be incorporated within it. Elias' theory of the civilising process has also been described as a history of manners, in which changing patterns of living are documented, and within which what he refers to as 'affect' becomes increasingly regulated. Emotion becomes ever more constrained by feelings of shame, repugnance or propriety. Changes in standards of conduct in Europe since the Middle Ages have so far generally proceeded, he argues, in the direction of increased civilisation:

> Whatever may be the differences in detail, the overall direction of change in behaviour, the trend in the civilising movement is everywhere the same. The change always presses toward a more or less automatic self-supervision, the subordination of short-term impulses to the commandment of a habitual long-term perspective, and the cultivation of a more stable and differentiated super-ego apparatus.[44]

Wouters' dilemma is that the changes identified as being part of the process of informalisation appear to involve declining rather than increasing levels of 'affect control'. Informalisation or permissiveness is seen as involving increasingly less regulation and less formality over rules of conduct, a relaxation in standards that seems at odds with the civilising movement identified by Elias. However, Wouters suggests that Elias was in fact aware that the process he had identified was not unidimensional:

> One has the impression that in the time that followed the war, compared with the pre-war period, there occurred a change which might be called a loosening of manners. A number of restraints imposed upon conduct before the war became weaker or have even disappeared. Many things previously forbidden are now allowed. Thus the movement, seen from close by, appears to go into reverse gear. It appears to lead to a lessening of the constraints imposed upon the individual by the social way of life. On closer inspection, however, it is not difficult to see that this is a rather

mild counter-movement, one of those smaller eddies that spring up again and again from the many-layered structure of historical change within every stage of more comprehensive processes.[45]

In defending the theory of the civilising process, Wouters argues that informalisation is not inimical to civilisation, but can in fact be integrated into the overall theory. He uses an example to explain how this is to be done. Comparisons of pre- and post-First World War parent–child relationships show that such relations have become more informal, and that parents put, or intend to put, fewer formal restraints on their children. In order to illustrate such an example he gives another example. If children are beaten with a stick by their parents when they transgress, he suggests that they will tend to avoid transgressing on those occasions when their actions are not concealed from their parents. They will not in this way learn to control those impulses which lead them to transgress. Being governed more by fear than by guilt they will be unable to control their impulses when their parents – or other authorities – are absent. Through this example, he suggests that, although a lessening of power inequalities – a concomitant of informalisation – involves a lessening of formal restraints, it also induces and requires more deeply built-in self-restraints. In this way, it is justifiable to talk not only about changes in the pattern or type of self-controls, but also in the level of self-control:

> Thinking of the almost natural way in which particularly young middle-class girls, but by no means only they, repressed all behaviour and thoughts concerning sex, one could say, that in many respects the preceding middle-class generations *had to* restrain their sexual – and possibly other – urges and inclinations, because these controls functioned quite blindly, beyond the conscious control of the individuals concerned…. In comparison, many people today have learned to a far greater extent to express these urges and emotions in a controlled way, that is also socially accepted.[46]

Thus it would be wrong to suggest that the young can behave uninhibitedly in contemporary society. They are, rather, expected to express their impulses in certain ways, ways that do not transgress against the more lenient standards of modern times.

At this point, one encounters two similarities between Wouters' analysis and those of the conservative- and liberal-historians. First of all, he accepts that standards are more lenient than those of the preceding periods. Thus, whilst he has rebutted the charge that permissiveness represents a simple diminution in control, he nevertheless asserts that within the new control structure there are greater possibilities for the expression of emotion. The second point of similarity emerges from the point of his analysis where he talks of changing codes of conduct. With the changing balance of power between the working and middle class, it is suggested that we have witnessed the destruction of traditional codes which have yet to be replaced by a similarly coherent new set:

> One cannot quite understand the process of informalisation in European countries if one does not take into account that here too one can observe upward movements of working-class traditions and downward movements of middle-class traditions of conduct, although it is not possible to speak of the emergence of a new more firmly established code of conduct. It is precisely because such a code does not exist, that we live in a period of uncertainty and experimentation.[47]

The essence of his argument is that changes in behavioural codes reflect changes in the power and dependency relations they are rooted in. The most recent wave of informalisation reflects a change in the balances of power between classes, the generations and the sexes. As higher levels of self-restraint have been achieved, so the social regulation of behaviour has become more lenient, more flexible and more differentiated. In this process of informalisation 'dominant modes of social conduct' have been violated by the upwardly mobile groups, and have given way to new codes which allow for a greater variety of behavioural alternatives.

CONCLUSION

All five major approaches to the subject of changes in post-war morality would accept, to a greater or lesser extent, that the term 'permissiveness', whilst not ideal, nevertheless does describe, albeit partially, the changes they identify. Interestingly, it is only the conservative-historians who use the term 'permissiveness' to refer to changes in actual behaviour. They reference rising rates of illegitimacy, abortion, venereal disease, crime, drug abuse and so on, as indicators of the fact that *standards of behaviour* are declining. They suggest, by implication at the very least, that modern society is characterised by greater promiscuity, greater sexual licence, by altogether less controlled or constrained sexual behaviour. The liberal-historians also tend to suggest that permissiveness has allowed greater freedom for sexual (and other forms of) expression, though for feminist critics this was simply a reordered means of continuing women's oppression. Both the Marxist and the Eliasian approaches, on the other hand, although implying that there may have been great changes in sexual behaviour, fall short of actually saying so. Hall *et al.* talk of a 'changing moral climate' and point to legislative change that decriminalised certain forms of behaviour, but further than that they do not go. Wouters turns Caxton's famous quotation on its head and says 'things formerly forbidden are now allowed', but not only does he not go into detail as to what these things might be, he certainly does not suggest that 'things now allowed are actively engaged in'. For most commentators, permissiveness refers to a process of liberalisation, informalisation or differentiation in attitudes or moral rules. Rarely is any reliable evidence provided which charts changes in sexual behaviour.

As was intimated in the introduction, although there is little evidence to suggest that sexual behaviour changed greatly in the period, the feeling remained for many people at the time that this was nevertheless what was happening. Something was happening in Britain that allowed the period to be plausibly described, both at the time and later, as permissive. For many of the authors discussed above, it was changes in the rules (however defined) governing behaviour. Whatever these changes were, many who witnessed them found them worrying and unsettling. The following chapter looks at the debates over permissiveness in more detail, by examining the preoccupations of the moral entrepreneurs of the period, and in particular, Mary Whitehouse and the National Viewers' and Listeners' Association.

2 Permissiveness and moral protest
Mary Whitehouse and the National Viewers' and Listeners' Association

As has already been suggested, so pervasive has the term 'permissiveness' become that there are few, if any, commentators who are prepared to argue that the term is one that mystifies rather than elucidates. Many would argue that the idea of permissiveness has been overstated, exaggerated or misapplied, but few seem to doubt the underlying reality of this supposedly permissive Britain of the 1960s. In this chapter, then, the term 'permissiveness' is subjected to further critical scrutiny, and an attempt is made to isolate those 'factors' or characteristics that are most usually invoked by moral entrepreneurs in their discussions of the 'permissive society'. The chapter takes as its focus the work of Mary Whitehouse and the organisation with which she is most closely associated, the National Viewers' and Listeners' Association (NVALA).

THE NATIONAL VIEWERS' AND LISTENERS' ASSOCIATION

The NVALA developed out of an organisation called 'The Clean-up TV Campaign' (CUTV) launched in January 1964 by Mary Whitehouse and Norah Buckland, the wife of the Rector of Langton in Staffordshire. Both were concerned with what they saw to be 'declining standards' on television, and the problems that they felt were created or exacerbated by this 'decline'. Feeling that little was to be gained by personal protest either to the BBC or through their local MP to Parliament, they decided that the best approach was to issue a Manifesto. It is worth reproducing the Manifesto in full at this point, for many of the major planks of future NVALA 'policy' were contained in this Manifesto in embryonic form. It read:

1 We women of Britain believe in a Christian way of life.
2 We want it for our children and for our country.
3 We deplore present day attempts to belittle or destroy it, and in particular we object to the propaganda of disbelief, doubt and dirt that the BBC projects into millions of homes through the television screen.

4 Crime, violence, illegitimacy and venereal disease are steadily increasing yet the BBC employs people whose ideas and advice pander to the lowest human nature and accompany this with a stream of suggestive and erotic plays which present promiscuity, infidelity and drinking as normal and inevitable.

5 We call upon the BBC for a radical change of policy and demand programmes which build character instead of destroying it, which encourage and sustain faith in God and bring Him back to the heart of our family and national life.[1]

The campaign was launched via an article in the *Birmingham Mail* with a promise from Mrs Whitehouse to hold the initial meeting in Birmingham Town Hall. The meeting took place on 5 May 1964 and was attended by approximately 2000 people, causing *The Times* to comment:

Perhaps never before in the history of Birmingham Town Hall has such a successful meeting been sponsored by such a flimsy organisation. There are no committee members, no officers, and no hard plans for the future, except for the hope that the people at this meeting will go out and spread the word in other parts of the country.[2]

Telegrams of 'interest' and 'support' were received from the Archbishops of Canterbury and York respectively, and by the end of the year Mrs Whitehouse and Mrs Buckland were claiming to have over a quarter of a million signatures on the Manifesto. As Tracey and Morrison point out, however,[3] CUTV were soon criticised for their negative stance and consequently metamorphosed from being merely a protest group into a campaigning organisation with more reformist goals. By November 1965, the National Viewers' and Listeners' Association was being launched in London to the full glare of press publicity by James Dance, MP for Bromsgrove, by then another leading figure in the campaign. The first aim of the NVALA was to establish a Viewers' and Listeners' Council which would consist of elected representatives of the 'churches, women's organisations, magistrates, doctors, educationalists, parents, youth, social workers, police, political parties, local government and writers'.[4] The aim of this Council was putatively to 'represent the opinions, ideas and experience of the whole country to the broadcasting authorities'.[5] Where was it that Mrs Whitehouse and the NVALA actually claimed to gain support? On the one hand there have been those who have claimed that, at least in the early days, the campaign was no more than the minority group Moral Re-Armament (MRA) by a different name; on the other there is Mrs Whitehouse herself, who clearly believes that the organisation represents the 'silent majority' in the country. As to the former suggestion the position seems fairly clear. Mrs Whitehouse, at what was a troubled period in her personal life, joined the Wolverhampton Oxford Group in 1935. The Oxford Group was founded in the early years of the century by Frank Buchman, a Lutheran Minister, whose controversial evangelistic movement was based on the four principles of Absolute Honesty, Absolute Purity, Absolute Unselfishness and Absolute Love.[6] In a speech in 1938, Buchman suggested that '...nations must re-arm morally'[7] and the phrase stuck, the Oxford Group becoming known thenceforward as the Moral Re-armament movement. Tracey and Morrison (1979) in their book on Mrs Whitehouse point to several similarities of outlook between supporters of the NVALA and MRA. They argue that, for Whitehouse in particular, though after the war her formal ties with the Oxford Group diminished, her years of close association with it provided her with a very clear intellectual approach to the perceived ills of the modern world. Mrs Whitehouse herself has never sought to deny the intellectual and theological debt she owes to the Oxford Group and the MRA, but has been quick to silence those critics who have suggested the existence of more formal links between the NVALA and MRA.[8]

From its Midlands grassroots in the Clean-up TV Campaign, the NVALA has grown into an organisation with over 30,000 members,[9] and has on several occasions organised nationwide petitions which have secured a formidable number of signatures. It is the success of these petitions that Mrs Whitehouse feels are a more realistic indicator of her support, and she claims that the 31,000 or so members who pay the small annual subscription are but 'the tip of the iceberg'.[10] She estimates that the NVALA has the block support of organisations totalling up to three million people and, in defence of the NVALA's 'mandate', points to the memberships of the British Humanist Society and the National Council for Civil Liberties (now Liberty) which she quotes as standing at 2,000 and 6,000 respectively. Whatever the reality of the membership and support situation, two important points emerge from a reading of the NVALA literature and Mrs Whitehouse's autobiographical writings. Firstly, as has already been suggested, she feels that the true campaign she is involved in gives a voice to Britain's silent moral majority. Secondly, and related to this, opponents of the silent majority are seen as being a small, but fairly influential and vociferous elite.

This elite, otherwise referred to by Mrs Whitehouse as the 'humanist lobby', is left in no doubt by her that it is the influence of their humanism to which she most vociferously objects:

> It is vital to any understanding of the present state, both of public debate and personal morality, to realise the part played by what might generally

be called the 'humanist lobby'. This works, not only through the British Humanist Association, but through the various other anti-Christian pressure groups which proliferated in the 1960s....

and, she continued, 'today's militant humanists not only reject God, they are anti-Christian, from political as well as "theological" conviction'.[11] The 'humanist' pressure groups, and what she identifies as a 'secular intellectual elite', were the major protagonists for 'permissive' change in the 1960s, according to Mrs Whitehouse. These groups represent a minority opinion, she suggests, and it is up to the NVALA and groups like it to defend and reassert 'traditional' values before humanism takes a grip of society generally, rather than just at the BBC where it is viewed as already having a stranglehold. To confirm her assertion that there are radicals and revolutionaries in every corner of contemporary social life who are campaigning to overthrow the 'traditional' moral order, Mrs Whitehouse reels off a formidable list of 'folk devils'. Pride of place in this list goes to Hugh Carleton Greene, Director-General of the BBC from 1960 to 1969, who Mrs Whitehouse viewed as being almost single-handedly responsible for all the ills of the supposed 'permissive society':

> If anyone were to ask me who, above all, was responsible for the moral collapse which characterised the 1960s and 1970s, I would unhesitatingly name Sir Hugh Carleton-Greene.... He was in command of the most powerful medium ever to affect the thinking and behaviour of people – television. His determination to give the freedom of the screen to the protagonists of the new morality, excesses of violence and sex, had the most profound effect upon the values and behavioural patterns of the day.[12]

There are two important points in this quotation which will be returned to during the course of this chapter. The first is Mrs Whitehouse's emphasis on the power of television as a medium, the second the notion of the 'new morality' which was widely used in the mid-1960s and which Mrs Whitehouse focused upon in her attacks on both broadcasting and the 'South Bank' theologians. Most prominent among the 'South Bank' theologians was John Robinson, the Bishop of Southwark, whose book, *Honest to God*, divided theological opinion when it was published in the early 1960s. Robinson had argued that the Church was in a critical position in that it was becoming ever more remote from modern society and that it must therefore rethink its position. For Robinson, it was necessary to cease to talk in terms of moral absolutes and, consequently, he argued, 'nothing can of itself always be labelled as wrong'. This position, part of a wider body of thought known as 'situational ethics', was anathema to Mrs

Whitehouse and her supporters, whose world-view was constructed very much in terms of absolutes. However, the significance of the 'South Bank' theologians was not only to be seen in their effect on the Church, but also, according to Mrs Whitehouse, in their affinity with the secular intellectual elite which held sway in the 1960s:

> The significance of the support for the Southwark [sic] theologians which flooded in from left-wing humanists, will not be lost on anyone who had learned, the hard way, that these people, who reject all concept of man as a child of God both for themselves and everyone else, make common ground with soft permissives wherever they can find them – in or out of the Church.[13]

Representing the 'degenerate youth' in Mrs Whitehouse's litany of folk devils was Richard Neville, who, as one of the defendants in the *OZ* trial, represented the antithesis of all that Mrs Whitehouse wished to see in modern youth. Neville and his co-defendants James Anderson and Felix Dennis, were found guilty in 1971 of publishing an obscene article, namely *OZ* 28, otherwise known as *Schoolkids' OZ*, and were given prison sentences ranging from nine to fifteen months. The sentences, however, were suspended and reduced on appeal. For Whitehouse, Neville's avowed 'revolutionary' stance was aimed particularly at the young and innocent and was a form of 'ideological warfare' from which they needed to be protected. Mrs Whitehouse had no doubts about the damage of Neville's influence, nor the response of parents:

> But thousands of parents who had seen their children's life-style changed through the impact of the underground press were only too well aware of its significance. They knew Richard Neville not as some hard-done-by humourist but as the author of the paperback *Playpower* which became the handbook of the international drop-outs and bemused pot-smoking youngsters, persuaded to believe that society was rotten, life was too tough and the odds too heavily stacked against them – the best thing to do was to drop out and bum around.[14]

Themes that arise time and again in Mrs Whitehouse's writing are present in this passage: firstly, the power of the media to shape and influence opinion and behaviour – in this case the medium being an underground magazine; secondly, the idea that permissive changes were focused upon the young; and finally that the political intent behind the attack on traditional morals is essentially revolutionary. This particular passage ends with the sentence: 'the purpose of the underground press is "not so much to dissent as to disrupt", and its editorial policies explicitly and implicitly seek to overthrow society as we know it, and of this it makes no secret'.[15] The list of folk devils doesn't end with Greene, Robinson and Neville, however, although they represent the three crucial strands in Mrs Whitehouse's philosophical position – broadcasting, the Church and rebellious youth. Also in the list and discussed below are: Alex Comfort and Dr Martin Cole in the area of sex education, John Calder the publisher, John Trevelyan the erstwhile film censor, Roy Jenkins, Labour Home Secretary in the 1960s, as well as John Mortimer, the barrister, novelist and playwright, and what Mrs Whitehouse referred to as his 'travelling circus of expert witnesses' who were regularly in court to defend publications charged under the Obscene Publications Act. There were many others playing more minor roles. Nevertheless, this list covers a group of people whom Mrs Whitehouse and the NVALA saw as being in the frontline of the attack on established values. In each of the areas of major concern for the NVALA, there appeared to them to be influential individuals whose determination to 'push back the frontiers of permissiveness' was seen as the greatest threat to traditional Christian morality.

BROADCASTING AND THE NVALA

Mrs Whitehouse's concern with the output of the major broadcasting companies began in the early 1960s and is still going strong today almost thirty years later. It is worth paying particular attention to one of two programmes or issues that particularly disturbed Mrs Whitehouse and the NVALA for they sum up quite neatly the major ways in which broadcasting is seen by them as falling short of the standards that, they suggest, ought generally to apply. The late-night satirical shows such as *Not So Much a Programme, More a Way of Life* and *That Was the Week That Was* (TW3) were among the first to cause the NVALA concern. TW3, staffed by the likes of David Frost, William Rushton, Bernard Levin (who in later years became a critic of 'permissiveness'), and a future *bête-noir* of Mrs Whitehouse, John Mortimer, was, in its short history, massively popular and controversial. In 1963, having perhaps insulted one Prime Minister too many in the run-up to a general election, TW3 was taken off the air, although it was stoutly defended by Hugh Greene. Mrs Whitehouse viewed these programmes as having no redeeming qualities whatsoever, and it was not long before she herself became the subject of a satirical programme in her own right. Entitled *Swizzlewick*, it 'starred' a Mrs Smallgood, a Councillor Salt – the chairman of the NVALA committee was a Birmingham councillor by the name of Pepper – and Ernest the postman, Ernest being the name of Mr Whitehouse and 'Postman's Piece' the name of the house they were living in at the time. The programme marked perhaps the beginning of Mrs Whitehouse's attempts to influence the content of particular programmes. She was sent the script for one of the episodes – she has never said by whom – and was so enraged by one scene in which the councillor was to have been seen leaving a prostitute's room doing up his trousers, that she sent it straight to the Postmaster General, the Minister responsible. In the end the scene to which she had objected was cut and, directly or indirectly, Mrs Whitehouse became *persona non grata* at the BBC for eleven years.

The BBC at this time was also thought by Mrs Whitehouse to be 'theologically biased'. It was what she saw as the excessive time and attention given to the 'South Bank' theologians which she objected to most strongly, feeling that it would only be a matter of time before the Governors took action to alter the position. She wrote to the Director General, was invited to meet, and met, his Deputy, Harman Grisewood, who impressed her with his sympathy for her concerns. However, not long after, Grisewood resigned and Mrs Whitehouse later said that he was, to her mind, 'too sincere and too gentle a Christian to be at ease amongst the demolition men who frequented the BBC at the time'.[16] Little seemed in Mrs Whitehouse's eyes to change at the BBC and, in early 1964, the Corporation's Charter was renewed for a further twelve years without any of the additional 'safeguards' that Mrs Whitehouse would have liked to have seen written in. It was roughly at this time that the Clean-up TV Campaign was launched.

The 'theological bias', the humanism, the anti-establishment propaganda, the 'declining' moral standards, and the increasing use of 'foul' language, for which Mrs Whitehouse continually criticised the BBC, were almost all to be found aplenty, she felt, in one particular television programme, and the battle over this series is in many ways illustrative of the wider battle between the NVALA and the Corporation at this time. *Till Death Us Do Part*, with its intended anti-hero Alf Garnett, was one of the BBC's most popular shows in the late 1960s and early 1970s. There has been much written about the central character in the programme and Johnny Speight's intentions in creating a 'foul-mouthed bigot' such as Garnett. Speight described it as follows:

> To me there are prototypes of Alf all over the country: far too many of them in fact. And if I didn't use words like 'blast' and 'blow me' and so on, he wouldn't be a real character. And he *is* a real character. But what I set out to do was to show the idiocy of his ideas by bouncing them against other ideas, some of them perhaps equally extreme and absurd.[17]
> (emphasis in the original)

Two episodes in particular are mentioned by Mrs Whitehouse as exemplifying the series' worst qualities. The first is described by Tracey and

Morrison as the 'Virgin Birth' episode because of its controversial subject-matter. The offending section involved Alf and his wife Elsie discussing a conversation they had 'unfortunately' overheard in the pub. The conversation concerned the question of Mary's virginity and why she had had only one child. Mike, their son-in-law, then suggested that as that was two thousand years ago, 'they could have had another fifteen hundred by now' and, sensing his in-laws' disapproval, continued 'unless they're on the pill'.[18] Mrs Whitehouse wrote immediately to the Minister of Posts and Telecommunications to complain about the episode, receiving an apologetic reply from Lord Hill of the BBC.[19]

The second episode which Mrs Whitehouse says she remembers with a mixture of 'amusement and incredulity' involved a scene in which Alf and his son-in-law were in the living room reading: Mike, a football book, and Alf a book that cannot at first be seen. Alf is periodically nodding at his son-in-law and suggesting that he would be better off if he read the book Alf has in his hands. The book turns out to be Mrs Whitehouse's newly published volume, *Cleaning-up TV*. Mrs Whitehouse describes the rest of the scene as follows:

> The whole episode was built around the book and before very long, and not for the first time, the fascist implications were there again, not only as far as Alf was concerned but, by implication, involving me too. The whole country needed 'cleaning up', particularly of the 'coons', Alf ranted (can anyone imagine that happening now?). And with the usual loud-mouthed flourish he marched off to the lavatory taking my book with him. The twist to the story came when the old man was found to be a carrier of the very germs that he blamed the coloured people for bringing into the country. How else could he have contracted them but by reading my book? So what was the best thing to do with that? Burn it, of course. And the programme ended as it dropped onto the fire to a chorus from the rest of Alf's family of 'unclean, unclean'.[20]

Although many areas of British social life were attacked in *Till Death*, it was the general ridicule to which Christianity was subjected that caused Mrs Whitehouse and the NVALA most difficulty. That this was true for NVALA supporters generally and not just for their figurehead is shown by the large correspondence the programme generated within the Association.[21] As will be seen throughout this chapter, this is perhaps the central plank in the overall ideological position adopted by Mrs Whitehouse and the NVALA. The declining importance of religion in social life in general, and in particular the declining influence of Christianity on the great moral questions of the day was (and is) the spur to action that has kept the NVALA going for over twenty years. Although the campaigns in which

Mrs Whitehouse and her associates have been involved during this period may, on the surface, seem particularly disparate and eclectic, if one looks below the surface – as Tracey and Morrison have done particularly thoroughly[22] – then it is the diminishing influence of the Church in moral issues that lies at the heart of NVALA action and concern.

Apart from the issue of declining moral standards, which Mrs Whitehouse and the NVALA thought characteristic of television and the BBC in particular, from the early 1960s onward, there is another important strand in the NVALA stance with regard to the media. It is one thing to assert that things are 'not what they used to be' and that this is part of the more 'general malaise' in society. It is quite another to suggest, as they did and still do, that television in general, and Hugh Greene's BBC in particular, were also somehow partially, but nonetheless importantly, responsible for bringing about, or encouraging, the decline in standards that, they argue, characterised the 1960s and 1970s. Television, for the NVALA, is a uniquely powerful medium, and one therefore that can have devastating effects on the social fabric if it is not checked. If we consider this aspect more closely, another important strand in the Whitehouse/ NVALA 'philosophy' becomes apparent.

The BBC is seen by Mrs Whitehouse as not only reflecting the changes that were occurring in that period, but also as actively encouraging or even precipitating them. She suggested in *Cleaning-up TV*[23] that the forces pushing for 'permissive' reform were in large part the British Humanist Association, the National Secular Society, the Homosexual Law Reform Association and the Abortion Law Reform Association. That, as pressure groups, they are free to campaign openly for the changes, Mrs Whitehouse accepted. However, she felt that they had a particularly powerful and inappropriate ally in the BBC. She said at the time 'no-one has given the BBC a mandate to promote their causes. It is surely no coincidence that plays dealing with homosexuality and abortion were shown on BBC at the time when these issues were to be debated in the House of Commons and the Press'.[24] The BBC was, then, in her view, a propagandist for the various liberal and humanist causes circulating in the 1960s. Mrs Whitehouse is concerned not only that television companies are using their influence to promote political causes but, as was suggested above, that they are in many ways responsible for the 'moral decline' which she has identified. This power can be seen very clearly in her attitude towards two major events in recent years: the 1981 urban riots and the 1985 Brussels football tragedy. Mrs Whitehouse was one of the first commentators (there were many others) to suggest that the television coverage of the urban riots could have a 'copycat effect'. She criticised the showing on television of 'pictures of young black teenagers taking calculated – and cheerful – running kicks at plate-glass shop windows, coolly helping themselves to the goods inside, shoes, shirts or whatever they could lay their hands on'.[25] In response to the news coverage of the disorder, she sent telegrams to both the BBC and the ITA asking them to 'please consider whether the massive television coverage of acts of vandalism and violence is contributing to the spread of the riots'.[26] Both companies issued statements saying that there was no conclusive evidence that television could affect behaviour in the manner suggested, but Mrs Whitehouse has still claimed that the coverage in the following days had been considerably transformed, using 'stills' rather than action sequences, and long shots rather than close-ups. The use or significance of 'stills' and long shots in this context is that they tend to lessen the impact of the coverage, making it less attractive and exciting, thus diminishing, so the argument goes, the likelihood of imitation. In much the same way, she suggested that, in the aftermath of the tragedy at the Heysel Stadium in Brussels, the television companies might care to take a long hard look at themselves when seeking to account for the behaviour of the young fans at the European Cup Final:

> Of course the culprits in those terrible events must be punished. But do not let us allow their punishment to salve our consciences. No requiems should give us peace. The answer lies deep in us all and demands a whole reorientation of our values. That will perhaps take generations. But one practical contribution could be made at once by the IBA and the Governors of the BBC. Let them govern, not sit comfortably back with the occasional 'tut tut' after the event.[27]

On both these occasions, Mrs Whitehouse suggested that the declining moral standards which she feels characterise the output of both broadcasting companies are not unconnected with the violent scenes witnessed in Brixton, Toxteth and Brussels. In the case of the urban riots, it is the nature of the television coverage which is in essence inciting other young people in different parts of the country to civil disobedience, whereas in the case of football violence, the implication is that the perceived lack of moral leadership by the broadcasting corporations has led over a period of years to a general moral climate in this country which fails to provide adequate controls over the behaviour of the nation's youth. The strand of the overall Whitehouse philosophy that was referred to above, and which, perhaps, is only implicitly suggested by the two examples discussed, is the particularly vulnerable position which, she feels, young people occupy, especially with regard to the pernicious influences of the mass media.

OBSCENE PUBLICATIONS AND THE NVALA

The NVALA's concern for the welfare of children – young people would perhaps be a more accurate term, given the ages Mrs Whitehouse generally included in her statements – extends further than television to the printed picture and word. As will later become clear, Mrs Whitehouse has been involved in many campaigns in this area but there are two in particular which are of immediate relevance to this discussion. The first of these campaigns involved *OZ* magazine whose editors were prosecuted for obscenity. *OZ* 28, the *Schoolkids' Issue*, took such a name because it was largely written and edited by children, a fact that was largely ignored during the trial. Indeed, during what was the longest obscenity trial in British publishing history, great play was made of the involvement of school-children, one of the charges being that the editors:

> had conspired with certain other young persons to produce a magazine that would corrupt the morals of young children and other young persons and had intended to arouse and implant in the minds of these young people lustful and perverted desires.[28]

It was the fact that the young were the supposed 'object' of the publication that most concerned Mrs Whitehouse. Indeed, after the three defendants successfully appealed against the prison sentences she accused them of endangering British youth:

> I do not have anything personal against the three men but I think it is an unmitigated disaster for the children of our country. If they cannot be protected by the law from this kind of material then the law should be tightened up.[29]

The other related campaign in which Mrs Whitehouse was involved at this time – and more centrally than in the *OZ* case – was the prosecution brought against the publisher of a book of advice for schoolchildren called *The Little Red Schoolbook*. The book was small in format, although 208 pages long. It was divided into chapters, each of which contained advice on a separate topic such as homework, teachers, discipline, drugs, etc. The central cause for concern was the 20-page section devoted to advice on sexual matters. Although proceedings were not instituted as a result of Mrs Whitehouse's intervention, she had nevertheless brought the book to the notice of the Director of Public Prosecutions. This publication is of particular interest here because it pulls together several themes pertinent to a consideration of Mrs Whitehouse and the NVALA. When considering Mrs Whitehouse's views on the links between sexual and political revolution, the book will surface again. At this point, it is sufficient to note the focus of concern in the note she sent to the DPP:

> I would like to draw your attention to the chapter on sex. This book is now being sold freely to children of all ages and it is intended by the publishers to be read by children of eight years upwards. In my view this book would deprave and corrupt young children and I draw your attention in the sincere hope that you will find it possible to take action against the publishers.[30]

Protection of the young has ostensibly been a central and ever-present concern in Mrs Whitehouse's and the NVALA's campaigns ever since they began. The following heartfelt plea towards the end of Mrs Whitehouse's book, *Whatever Happened to Sex?*, sums up her thinking on the subject:

> Public opinion long ago condemned and outlawed the exploitation of child labour by nineteenth century industrialists. Yet, today, our society ruthlessly exploits the minds and emotions of young people – and now, may God forgive us, the bodies of children – for financial and political capital. Children are fodder, not for industry, but for ideas. They are no longer sent up chimneys, but they are pressured into alien patterns of behaviour to line the pockets of unscrupulous publishers and to further the cause of revolution by stealth. A nation's youth is its greatest asset. We are poor guardians if we do not ensure its unalterable right to childhood, to mystery, to dreams, to tenderness and to love; if we do not realise that by ceasing to provide authority we may also cease to care; if we do not conscientiously maintain the spiritual foundations without which the young cannot build anew; if we do not teach that there is a third way, neither reactionary nor libertarian, which still waits to be explored.[31]

It is clear from the last sentence in the quotation that Mrs Whitehouse does not view her position in the way some of her critics have done in the past, as reactionary or illiberal. She argues for a 'third way', and it is this 'third way' that is the subject of this chapter.

SEX EDUCATION AND THE NVALA

Another area of concern for Mrs Whitehouse, which also takes as its focus the young, is sex education. Sex education draws together much of the Whitehouse 'philosophy', for not only does it explicitly focus upon the young, but also it carries at least an implicit stance on the role and utility of the contemporary family. The issue also raises questions about love, sex, marriage, religion and morals. Sex education as a subject is important in any discussion of the work of Mrs Whitehouse, because her experiences of it as a teacher and parent, indirectly, if not directly, led her into the public domain of the politics of sexual morality.

As a teacher in the early 1960s at Madely Secondary Modern School in what is now Telford New Town, Mrs Whitehouse was Senior Mistress 'responsible for the moral welfare of the girls'. In that connection she became involved in the Headmaster's plans to invite marriage guidance counsellors to present several sex education films. She and other teachers insisted on the right to attend these lessons, and were taken aback by what they perceived to be the absence of a moral framework in what was, as it turned out, an 'entirely factual' approach to sex education. After this, the school itself took complete responsibility for sex education and, as was mooted in public debate in the late 1980s, they operated a system of 'opting in' rather than 'opting out' by which parents were asked whether they wished their children to participate.

Although Mrs Whitehouse recounts stories of the 'embarrassing' moments she experienced when discussing certain matters with her pupils, it appears from her accounts of this period that the school-based sex education programme she was involved in was, for her, a positive and satisfying experience. All this was to change, however, in the year she describes as 'extraordinary', 1963, as a result of what she took to be the effect that television was having on public debate. She describes the incident that sparked off, or at least increased, her concern about the content of contemporary television programmes, as happening at the height of the *Honest to God* debate. The girls came into school discussing the merits of a programme they had seen the previous evening, a 'religious' programme, *Meeting Point*, which had been about pre-marital sex. One of the girls had apparently rushed into class to inform her teacher, Mrs Whitehouse, that she now knew what was 'right'. This, it turned out, was 'that we shouldn't have intercourse until we're engaged'.[32] The incident is particularly revealing of Whitehouse's position, and indeed made a 'tremendous' and lasting impression on her. As far as the programme itself was concerned, she felt it was a 'classic example of the way in which the BBC, with its penchant for "South Bank" religion was allowing itself to be used as a launching platform for the "new morality"'.[33] Essentially, Mrs Whitehouse's argument was that 'traditional' Christian morals were no longer adequately presented on television, and that a new radical theological orthodoxy was in the ascendant. The result of this change was that one could no longer rely on notions of 'sinfulness' being used with regard to certain acts. Particularly important in this context for Mrs Whitehouse was the position adopted by the representatives of the Church:

My objection was not to discussion of the subject, but to the refusal of those who might be expected to be clear and able spokesmen of the Church to commit themselves to a firm position on right and wrong. The programme remains as a landmark in the creation of the 'permissive society' and a classic example of the power of television to create and change patterns of thought and behaviour.[34]

Mrs Whitehouse clearly felt that the religious spokespersons should be able to deal in terms of 'moral absolutes'. 'Right' and 'wrong' are, for her, immutables drawn from religious teaching, which are necessary as a context for sex education, and around which a previously existing consensus was being subverted by 'propagandists' for 'permissiveness'.

Mrs Whitehouse was also centrally involved in two major public campaigns which had at their heart questions of sex education and, in particular, what children should be shown or told. The first campaign centred around a sex education film entitled *Growing Up*, made by a Dr Martin Cole, of Birmingham University. The film was controversial for its explicitness. It contained a 15-second sequence of copulation, and shots of male and female masturbation. According to Mrs Whitehouse, it not only condoned, but advocated, teenage sex, and finally 'brought out into the open, in no uncertain fashion, the nature of the contemporary assault upon the young and upon the ethical structure which should support them'.[35]

Mrs Whitehouse's response is an interesting one. She wrote to the then Archbishop of Canterbury, Dr Michael Ramsay and, in her own words, issued a challenge to him. She asked him whether he would see the film and 'issue a statement about it both to encourage anxious parents and to ensure that the Church was seen to be caring about the matter'. The reason for approaching the Archbishop in such a manner was essentially to 'force his hand' as, according to Mrs Whitehouse, he had frequently seemed unwilling to become involved in public debates on questions of morals. Having complained on several occasions of the Church's reticence over taking the moral lead, on this occasion her plea was successful. The Archbishop did issue a statement condemning the film as 'diverging from Christian ideas of education'. The female teacher who took part in the film lost her job, and the film itself was never shown in schools.

The second campaign was one already touched upon, that against *The Little Red Schoolbook*. As has already been suggested, the 20-page section on sex was the subject of most of the furore. The book is quite explicit, and at no point does it describe practices as 'right' or 'wrong'. It was viewed by Mrs Whitehouse as 'another threat to the rights, the security and the character of the child'. The 'rights' she is referring to are, she would suggest, rights to 'innocence', and the 'security' of moral certainty. The book's candid discussion of sexual matters, the fact that it was aimed at children as young as eight, and the lack of a Christian moral framework – as well as its perceived 'revolutionary' nature which will be discussed later – all therefore contributed to its downfall. Mrs Whitehouse believed that sex education, and in particular, discussion of sexual issues on television was coming to be dominated by atheists and humanists, with a concomitant decrease in emphasis on the 'proper' moral context of sexual behaviour. This moral context would, for Mrs Whitehouse, stress the need for chastity, for an avoidance of pre-marital sex or 'trial marriage', an emphasis on marital fidelity, as well as, by implication perhaps, support for the view of homosexuality as 'unnatural'.

LATER CAMPAIGNS: BLASPHEMY AND HOMOSEXUALITY

In 1976, a Danish film-maker called Jens Jorgen Thorsen came to Britain with the intention of making a film, provisionally entitled *The Many Faces of Jesus*. The intended film was to be about the sex life of Christ, and supposedly was to involve both heterosexual and homosexual acts. Given the outlook of Mrs Whitehouse and the NVALA, it is not surprising that, on learning of Thorsen's intention to film in Britain, immediate action was taken. Mrs Whitehouse wrote on behalf of the NVALA to the then Home Secretary, Roy Jenkins, asking if he would declare Thorsen an 'undesirable alien', to which they received a negative reply. Opposition to the film was, however, building up more generally, with many column inches in the national press devoted to the story, and to indignant letters from outraged readers. Both Cardinal Hume and the Archbishop of Canterbury declared their intention to fight the making of the film, and the Prime Minister declared that Thorsen would be 'a most unwelcome and undesirable visitor to these shores'.[36] If this list of opponents to the film makes impressive reading, then it was soon to become even more so. In response to a letter from an NVALA member, the Queen replied expressing her concern that such an 'obnoxious' film might be made in Britain.[37] The NVALA got hold of a copy of the proposed script for the film, arranged to have it translated, and sent a copy on request to the Shadow Home Secretary, William Whitelaw. Another request was made by the NVALA that Thorsen should not be admitted to the country, and he was indeed excluded 'on the grounds that [his] exclusion [was] conducive to the public good', when he tried to enter early the following year.

At what should have been a time to reflect on a most successful campaign to unite both Church and public in defence of fundamental Christian beliefs, Mrs Whitehouse was 'rocked' by the breaking of another controversy. This one, however, was to be far more personally taxing for

Mrs Whitehouse, for the apparent consensus of opinion that surrounded her campaign against Thorsen evaporated as quickly as it had developed. In November 1976, Mrs Whitehouse first came across edition 96 of *Gay News*. It contained a poem by James Kirkup entitled 'The Love That Dares to Speak Its Name'. The title of the poem was a reference to a poem by Lord Alfred Douglas entitled 'The Love That Dare Not Speak Its Name'. Tracey and Morrison describe the poem and its general tenor as follows:

> The deletion of the negative by Kirkup matched well the new more assertively public attitude of homosexuals in the 1960s and 1970s; his means, the depiction of a homosexual relationship between a Roman centurion and the crucified body of Christ, depicted in the most physical sensual terms, was nothing if not polemical. It even raised adverse comments within the correspondence columns of *Gay News* itself.[38]

Mrs Whitehouse's response was again immediate, and she says that she thought that the poem was 'like the recrucifixion of Christ, only this time with twentieth-century weapons'.[39] She wrote straight to her solicitor, and by the end of the month had applied to a judge of the High Court for leave to institute a criminal prosecution for blasphemous libel. There are two facets of the campaign that are important for the discussion here. The first is Mrs Whitehouse's relationship with, and attitude toward, the Church, and in particular the Church leaders' response, or lack of response, to the claimed blasphemy of the poem, in contrast to the Church's response in the Thorsen case. The second is Mrs Whitehouse's attitude to homosexuality and homosexuals, which became quite a major issue during the course of the case.

The poem, and the editor of *Gay News*, Denis Lemon, were vigorously defended in public by, among others, the National Secular Society, the Rationalist Press Association, and the Defence of Literature and the Arts Society. Mrs Whitehouse, in turn, began to organise those organisations on whom she felt she could count for support. She wrote to the Archbishops of Canterbury and York, but both declined to appear as witnesses in the trial, Dr Coggan arguing that a jury were far more likely to be influenced by ordinary people testifying to the poem's blasphemous nature than by 'professional' Church leaders. Mrs Whitehouse, in her account of the campaign, argued that the real reason why they did not wish to become involved was because of the topic of the poem – homosexuality – rather than its blasphemy. The Church, then, neither publicly condemned the poem, provided explicit support for Mrs Whitehouse, nor even appeared able to produce a united front in response to the prosecution. Mrs Whitehouse consequently felt particularly isolated:

In no way could I ever have imagined that this poem could have done anything but rouse the Church to action. Now I find myself alone – that is irrelevant in terms of what happens to me, but for the idea that the Lord was homosexual, and for the perverted practices on his dead body not to be seen to be blasphemous if the case is lost – about that I am lost for words![40]

Although on several previous occasions Mrs Whitehouse had felt that either the response, or the public face that the Church presented was unsatisfactory – for example over the *Honest to God* debate – this case, with the vociferous support for *Gay News*, made her feel particularly vulnerable. At the finish, Lemon was found guilty, and received a suspended prison sentence. Mrs Whitehouse proclaimed herself very happy with the outcome, although she had no wish for Lemon to be jailed. Tracey and Morrison suggest that what she was trying to achieve in bringing the prosecution 'lay not in punishing Lemon, nor in a sense bringing back to life the blasphemy laws. Both those were necessary means towards a much more profound end, which was re-establishing the role of God within social life.'[41]

The Gay News Defence Committee organised many forms of protest, including a march and meeting in Trafalgar Square which attracted 5,000 people. Mrs Whitehouse was portrayed in many circles as being anti-homosexual. This opposition, she felt, was orchestrated by the 'homosexual/humanist/intellectual lobby'[42] – adding homosexual to the usual list – who were well organised and united in a way the Church was seen not to be. Mrs Whitehouse's attitude to homosexuals and homosexuality, though, is somewhat more complex than was perhaps allowed for at the time. She sets out her position in detail in her book *Whatever Happened To Sex?* (1977), and repeats it in full in *A Most Dangerous Woman?* (1982) in her own defence. She is also quoted at length by Tracey and Morrison (1979). What she wrote is worth repeating here:

When I say what is true – that I am not against homosexuals as people, but believe homosexual practices to be wrong, I am very conscious of the inadequacy of what probably sounds a very negative declaration. Homosexuals have as much right to be understood, to be treated with compassionate love as the rest of us. And as people they should be 'judged' no more, no less, than are those of us whose problems are perhaps less obvious but equally undesirable. Compassion without patronage, but without compromise – how to achieve it? The natural repugnance which most people feel when homosexuality and lesbianism is mentioned can result in a harshness of attitude and thinking, which is, at least, unhelpful and certainly as unChristian as the perverse practices which are condemned. But to go to the other extreme and elevate people suffering from such abnormalities into a norm for society not only threatens society but is dangerous to the individuals themselves, since it excludes them from the consideration of help and treatment. Society to its shame, once hurled that word at the homosexual. In our crazy 'value-free' society the 'shame' is now attached only to those who dare to say that homosexuality is less than 'gay'. Such an attitude is as dogmatic, doctrinal and restrictive in its own way as was the fearful silence or sniggering scorn of earlier decades.[43]

Mrs Whitehouse was accused at many points of being motivated by 'hatred' of homosexuals and, whilst the extract suggests that her attitude was not one of 'hatred' – indeed far from it – by including in her attitude to homosexuality such words as: undesirable, repugnant, perverse, suffering and abnormal, it is also easy to see how the gay community might be less than happy with the description. Mrs Whitehouse's position was, then, that homosexual behaviour was abnormal and sinful. Given that, as Tracey and Morrison point out, her stance on sin would also involve condemning a number of heterosexual practices – her position was not simply something that was specifically 'anti-homosexual'. Her attack on the poem in *Gay News* was an attempt to reassert the importance of Christianity, to re-establish the centrality of 'traditional' Christian teaching, which would provide the moral basis for a society in which homosexuality would be once again viewed by all as perverse, yet requiring of sympathy and treatment. Homosexuality, though, was, not really the target. It was the 'symbol' of a wider goal:

> Whitehouse's was not primarily an attack on homosexuals: it was in the first instance an attack on the imputation of a sexual context to Christ's death; in the second it was a confrontation with an anti-Christian and, to her, sexually-obsessed society, and it was this latter symbolic aspect to the events of the blasphemy trial which was the main point.[44]

The issue of 'homosexual practices' was to rise again in another case in which Whitehouse was a central figure. In 1980 the National Theatre staged a play entitled *The Romans in Britain*, in which there is a scene where three Roman soldiers sodomise a young Briton. The scene caused quite a stir, and although there were threats about grants being withdrawn etc., there was no talk of prosecution. Mrs Whitehouse was determined that something should be done, and arranged for a QC to visit the theatre and watch a performance. John Smyth QC reported to Mrs Whitehouse that, 'having seen the play I have no doubt whatever that a *prima facie* case exists that a criminal offence has been committed'.[45] An application was then made to the Attorney-General for permission to take action, but this was turned down. The solution to this problem was for Mrs Whitehouse personally to take a private prosecution of the play's director, Michael Bogdanov. The statute chosen for the prosecution was the Sexual Offences Act, under which it is a criminal offence to procure persons for acts of gross indecency in a public place. The hearing was held at Horseferry Road Magistrates Court where it was eventually decided that there was a case to answer, and Bogdanov was committed for trial. The trial did not last long, for once the Judge decided that public performance in the theatre was in fact covered by the Sexual Offences Act, 1967, and that Mrs Whitehouse was therefore able to bring a prosecution, the case was withdrawn. There was some confusion in court as to whether a private prosecution can be withdrawn once it has been decided that there is a case to answer. In the end, the Attorney-General issued a *nolle prosequi* and the case came to an end. Much was made in the press of the sudden climax to the case. Some argued that the case had been brought to an early end as there was little chance of the prosecution being successful, others suggesting that the case had in all but final verdict already been won.

Mrs Whitehouse suggests that, having achieved what she argues they set out to do – show that the Sexual Offences Act covered all 'public' acts of gross indecency, including simulated acts in the theatre – it would have been oppressive to have continued a private prosecution against the director of the play. This is not inconsistent with statements made by Mrs Whitehouse in previous cases. As was shown at, for example, the close of the *Gay News* case, Mrs Whitehouse suggested that she was pleased that the paper's editor, Denis Lemon, was not sent to prison for she had nothing against him personally. However, what is slightly more problematic than the end of the prosecution is why it was brought in the first place. In the previous two cases considered above, it was explicit attacks upon the Church that prompted action by Mrs Whitehouse and the NVALA, but there was no such dimension in the *Romans* case. Mrs Whitehouse explains the rationale thus:

> I have felt troubled because I am lacking in regard to 'The Romans' prosecution the same sense of identification with Jesus that I felt in the blasphemy case. That was very personal; this is not. But of course they are quite different by their very nature. Last time it was an expression of love, this time a matter of law. Which brings me to the heart of the matter – how important is it to God that the law is upheld? In that such material on stage degrades not only those who play but those who watch – it is important. I need to see this action as one step – even if we lose it will

perhaps serve to show the nation how far it has fallen, that it no longer is concerned that such things happen in its midst.[46]

For Mrs Whitehouse the case was but one step in the attempt to preserve our 'national morality' and our 'culture'. Many cases documented in the following chapters on obscenity, in which Mrs Whitehouse was involved, be it either centrally or peripherally, may, quite unlike the *Gay News* or Thorsen cases, have no direct or obvious link with Christianity. Both those cases involved blasphemies, Mrs Whitehouse felt, and therefore there was no question in her mind that she would become involved. To understand her involvement in the cases where there is no such link, it is to her explanation of her involvement in the *Romans* case to which one must turn. Each of these campaigns must be viewed, as she says, 'as one step' towards the protection of traditional values and morals, and the re-establishment of a society in which those values are paramount.

CHRISTIANITY AND POLITICS

There are a number of connections between elements in the Whitehouse/ NVALA philosophy and aspects of the relationship between law and morality described by Lord Devlin in *The Enforcement of Morals*.[47] In both, it is assumed that the criminal law can and should be used to protect or to reinforce moral principles. In both, it is argued that the basis of moral principles in this has been, is and should be, Christianity. A third connection between the two is the importance attached to the notion of a 'shared morality'.

Lord Devlin argued in *The Enforcement of Morals* that a shared morality is necessary for the continued existence of society, an assumption also central to Parsonian sociology. This is the manner in which he justifies legal intervention. For if a shared morality is necessary in this sense, then anything which threatens it also threatens society, and the law may therefore be used to protect it. Hart, in criticising Devlin's position, suggested that his conception of morality was like that of a 'seamless web' where attacks on one part were seen as threatening the life of the whole. A closer look at the Whitehouse/NVALA stance on the 'politics of morality' makes visible a somewhat similar position. Turning once more to the campaign surrounding *The Little Red Schoolbook*, this point should become clear.

Mrs Whitehouse, as has been shown, drew the attention of the DPP to *The Little Red Schoolbook* (*LRSB*) as soon as it was published in Britain, arguing that it was a 'threat to the rights, the security and the character of the child'. For Mrs Whitehouse and her supporters, publications such as this were dangerous not only because of their sexual content, but because of their political stance. Mrs Whitehouse, for example, says she received a phone call at the time of the case from an evangelist who was travelling in Denmark. The evangelist had managed to obtain an affidavit from one of the three Danes responsible for the publication of *LRSB*, but who had since become a Christian, stating that 'Mao money' had financed the publication of the book in Denmark.[48] Ross McWhirter, a supporter of the NVALA and a campaigner in his own right, wrote to the *Guardian*, and made the point even more clearly. He said 'the real issue is, in my submission, that the book is not only obscene, but also seditious'.[49]

The link between what are referred to as 'sexual anarchists' (for example, David Tribe of the National Secular Society) and 'political anarchists' (for example, the publishers of the *LRSB*) is one that is frequently made in Mrs Whitehouse's writings. Her concern is not a narrow one of how sexual matters should be treated and presented, but how one is to construct and preserve a society in which the dominant values are Judaeo-Christian. The campaign against the *LRSB* illustrates this well:

> It is part of our thesis that sexual and political revolution go hand in hand and that indeed the first is prerequisite of the second. That *The Little Red Schoolbook* was a revolutionary primer there can be no question.[50]

Morality is attacked for political reasons, she argues, and the political beliefs at the core of the attack are fundamentally anti-Christian. Political and sexual revolution is a recurrent theme in Mrs Whitehouse's books and articles. Whilst she frequently attacks Marxism and Communism, it is not simple political opposition, but rather an attack on what she sees as the effects of the spread of Marxism for Christianity, for 'it is of no mean significance that the secular/humanist/Marxist philosophy makes the destruction of Christianity one of its main priorities. It understands its importance in relation to character and morale, to the standard of values and behaviour.'[51] Not only does Mrs Whitehouse believe that Christianity is under threat from political revolution, but also that it is the last line of defence against such revolution. The 'permissive revolution' was, for Mrs Whitehouse, in many ways a political revolution. In her terms, there was a plot by – whatever one might wish to call them – Marxists, Communists, Humanists, Libertarians, etc. to transform society. This revolutionary change would be achieved most simply by attacking moral standards and promoting sexual revolution. Whitehouse considered moral order to be synonymous with Christian moral principles, and therefore any attack on the former was perceived as being an attack on the latter. The full-scale attack which she believed to be taking place was therefore seen as a fundamental and all-encompassing attack upon Christianity.

There were, of course, many very clear signs that organised religion was feeling the effects of rapid social change, and this served to reinforce the general philosophical position adopted by people such as Mary Whitehouse. Max Caulfield, in his biography of Mrs Whitehouse, sums up the argument in one sentence, saying 'as to the purpose of all this frenzy – it was easy to explain that the forces of revolution, unable to achieve their objectives at the ballot box or, because of the existence of the nuclear bomb, by full-scale war, were endeavouring to encourage moral decay'.[52] How does Mrs Whitehouse make the connection between sexual and political revolution? She has, she suggests, ample evidence from history. One example that she uses is Nazi Germany:

> Both before, and when, the Nazis took over Poland they flooded the bookstalls of that country with pornography. This is a fact. Why did they do so? Because they believed – and we had better believe it also – that if they could make individuals conscious only of the need for personal gratification, they would have neither desire nor energy to combine and work for the downfall of the enemy. The Nazis' scheme was the deliberate use of pornography as the means of social castration.[53]

Having established both the 'purpose' of revolution, and the existence of what appears to be 'revolutionary change', the final task is to find the revolutionaries. A number of people who have been singled out by Mrs Whitehouse as playing particularly crucial roles in the process of supposedly 'permissive change' have already been mentioned. Perhaps one person in that list, however, stands out, as representing in the early 1970s almost all that Mrs Whitehouse was fighting against. Richard Neville, one of the editors of *OZ*, was referred to frequently by Mrs Whitehouse, as a revolutionary. She has made much of statements made by Neville, and has quoted him as saying that 'the weapons of revolution are obscenity, blasphemy and drugs'[54] and as further saying during the *OZ* trial that the whole point of pornography was to promote promiscuity.[55] In the passage quoted from *Whatever Happened to Sex?* when Richard Neville was discussed above (p.21), Mrs Whitehouse described his book Playpower as 'the handbook of the international drop-outs', the purpose of the underground as 'not so much to dissent as to disrupt' and the implicit and explicit goal contained in *OZ* editorial policies as the overthrow of society. Whether or not the likes of Richard Neville were accurately described in this manner by Mrs Whitehouse and other members of what Neville and his associates perceived to be the 'establishment', or whether they could genuinely be described in Cohen's (1988) terms as 'folk devils', 'persons emerging to become defined as a threat to societal values and interests', it is clear that, for Mrs Whitehouse, they represented a grave threat to all that she held dear. As has been suggested, it was particularly the perceived threat to the importance of organised religion that they represented which galvanized Mrs Whitehouse and others into action.

In the course of this discussion it is Christianity, and the Christian basis of 'moral values' which have emerged as the key to understanding Mrs Whitehouse's and the NVALA's response to the cultural, social and political transformations occurring in post-war Britain. Included in this overview have been the campaigns against the Thorsen film and James Kirkup's poem in *Gay News*, where blasphemy was the central explicit issue; Mrs Whitehouse's criticism of television, in particular the BBC's supposed bias toward 'South Bank' theology, and *Till Death Us Do Part*'s irreverence towards Christianity; the perceived lack of support for the NVALA from Church leaders. It has also been suggested that there were many signs available to Mrs Whitehouse that, in her terms, all was not well within the Church, and that this reinforced her view that the established order was under threat, and that urgent action was necessary.

THE NEW MORALITY

Perhaps the most symbolically significant event in the general area of religion and morals in the early 1960s – if not the whole period under discussion – was the publication of John Robinson's *Honest to God* in 1963. The 'radical theology' contained in the book formed the basis of the movement called 'situational ethics' which proposed that 'our moral decisions must be guided by the actual relationships between the persons concerned at a particular time in a particular situation, and compassion for persons overrides all law. The only intrinsic evil is lack of love.'[56] For Mrs Whitehouse, the publication of *Honest to God*, although it was only one – albeit significant – event, was a key moment in the emergence of what both she and John Robinson described as 'the new morality'. Mrs Whitehouse felt that this 'new morality' was given far too much publicity and even support by the BBC, particularly at the expense of the proponents and supporters of 'traditional Christian ethics'. She identifies a 'golden age' of broadcasting, which was essentially contemporaneous with the 'Reithian' era at the BBC, where some sort of Christian moral absolutism held sway. With the continued rise of secular attitudes, it became increasingly apparent to the Church – or certain sections of it – that it was, or was in danger of, becoming ever more marginal or peripheral to contemporary social concerns. There were basically two major responses: firstly by those who tried, in a manner similar to Mrs Whitehouse, to re-establish the importance of the Church through a critique of contemporary social forms. That is, Mrs Whitehouse and the traditionalists within the Church were extremely

critical of what they perceived to be the 'character' of modern society, and
their solution was largely backward-looking, dominated by the desire for
the retrieval of a 'bygone golden age' where traditional religious teachings
and the Church generally were a more central part of the social fabric. The
second response was more forward-looking and concentrated on presenting
the Church in a manner that would be more acceptable to, more relevant to,
and essentially more 'in-tune' with contemporary social concerns. These
more 'radical' theologians formed the basis of the intellectual group that
was identified with the 'new morality'.

For Mrs Whitehouse, this radical theology constituted a new moral
orthodoxy, and one which, in an inaccurate paraphrasing of John
Robinson's argument, it was believed that 'God is Dead'. Here Mrs
Whitehouse spells out the message:

> One would imagine that it is a long, long way from the Church to Soho.
> But most certainly the road to the latter, with its decadence and exploi-
> tation, has been made a great deal smoother, shorter and more popular
> by the compromise and self-interest of the clerics and assorted fellow
> travellers of the so-called 'new morality' school. The permissive society
> did not begin with the publication of Dr John Robinson's *Honest To
> God*, but this certainly smote the ramparts of the established Church
> which, until that point, had been seen – mostly with approval – as the
> defender of the faith and of public and private morality.[57]

According to Mrs Whitehouse, there was a time not so long ago when the
Church was, and was seen to be, the defender of both public and private
morality. Thanks to, among others, John Robinson and the radical theologians, however, the way has been paved for humanist concerns to become
more widely accepted and for the established Church to lose its importance
in the areas of both public and private morality. This is also the essence of
Mrs Whitehouse's campaigns. Her long-term goal is the re-establishment
of a society in which the Church once more occupies this central role. The
1960s seemed to her, and her supporters, to be a watershed in the history of
Christianity. For Mrs Whitehouse it seemed that the Church was under a
concerted attack and that, if it was not vigorously defended, then there
would be nothing to prevent 'the tide of permissiveness' or the advance of
the 'new morality'. Publications in the 1960s, such as *Honest to God* and
Toward a Quaker View of Sex, represented for her the encroachment or
infiltration of a new moral orthodoxy into the Church itself. As has been
suggested, the existence, seemingly side by side, of two distinct moral
codes – a traditional Christian position and the 'new morality' – and the
public 'battle' between the two, as new ideas came into conflict with old,
gave the impression to many that the Church could no longer present a

united front. For those like Mrs Whitehouse, who believed in the importance of moral absolutes and moral certainty, this was a crucial period. The
Church appeared no longer to be the guiding force that she believed it once
had been, and felt it ought still to be. Her aim has been to return British
society to that former 'golden age'.

OTHER MORAL ENTREPRENEURS

The National Viewers' and Listeners' Association is by no means the only
'moral entrepreneurial' group of this sort, although it is one of the most
long-standing, and it has, through Mary Whitehouse, generally achieved a
higher profile than many of the others. During the period under discussion
there have been a considerable number of such pressure groups – for
example, the Nationwide Festival of Light; the Order of Christian Unity;
the Responsible Society; the Society for the Protection of the Unborn Child,
LIFE, as well as a host of other, smaller groups – most of which actually
originated in this period.

The Nationwide Festival of Light (NFoL) developed largely as a result
of the work of one person, Peter Hill, an evangelical Christian who, on
returning to this country after several years abroad, was shocked to find
explicit sexual material on open sale. He believed that there should be some
form of demonstration against such displays and set about organising the
'march for righteousness'. This was to be a 'one-off' event and was not
conceived of as the beginning of a moral protest movement or group. The
Festival of Light rally – the name had been thought up by Malcolm
Muggeridge – took place in Trafalgar Square in September 1971, and
attracted between 25,000–30,000 people. The success of the one-off rally
prolonged the life of the movement and although it kept its basically
evangelical outlook for a couple of years, Roy Wallis suggests that the likes
of Peter Hill began to be replaced by a leadership that was 'more directly
concerned with the civic–political aspects of moral reform, rather than with
evangelism.'[58] With the changing outlook of its leadership, the NFoL's
early concentration upon opposing pornography broadened out into a
general opposition to the modern permissive society. As with the NVALA,
it was a return to what was perceived as a now lost age of Christian
orthodoxy that was being sought:

> Literature distributed at the rally and the speeches from the platform
> stressed respect for the Ten Commandments, deplored the loss of a firm
> traditional moral stand by national leaders, and called for a return to
> Christian moral standards, buttressed by firm legal controls and
> sanctions.[59]

The Nationwide Festival of Light is still in existence, although it has by now even outgrown its original name. In 1983 it became known as CARE (Christian Action Research and Education). The name change was necessary, it was argued, because the original name referred to a single event that had taken place over a decade previously, that it gave the wrong image, and didn't properly describe the work being done by the organisation. The stated aims of the organisation continue to be those originally associated with the NFoL, namely: 'the advancement and propagation of the Christian Gospel in particular as it bears on or effects national or individual morality and ethics'.[60]

Another organisation whose concerns and objectives have changed and broadened during this period is the Order of Christian Unity (OCU). Founded in the 1950s to encourage ecumenicalism,[61] by the early 1970s the OCU had become a campaigning moral protest group, opposing abortion, liberal divorce laws, and seeking the 'advancement of Christian values' in education and broadcasting.

The Responsible Society is the one organisation working in this general field that is not explicitly Christian in outlook. Indeed, in proclaiming its independence, the Responsible Society argues that it is not affiliated to any political party, pressure group or religious body. Whilst it does not have the theological aims of the NVALA, the NFoL/CARE or the OCU, it still appears to have developed in response or opposition to many of the same social trends highlighted by those other groups. The Responsible Society was formed in 1971 by a group of people 'concerned about the damage being done to human dignity, welfare and happiness by the misuse of new social freedoms'.[62] One of their original sponsors was Pamela Hansford Johnson. 'Sexual irresponsibility' is the Society's major concern and their aim is to encourage responsible sexual behaviour through education. Such behaviour is seen as taking place within 'the basic unit of society', the family, 'which is founded on marriage'.[63] In a pamphlet entitled 'Saying NO isn't always easy ...!', the message is that 'casual sex' should not be confused with sexual liberation:

> Real freedom comes from being true to your real beliefs. Saying 'no' isn't negative – 'no' to 'having sex' is saying 'yes' to a real caring relationship for the future. Sex is only really fulfilling when it's part of the total commitment of marriage.[64]

Responsible behaviour, they suggest – and this is another point of contact between their views and those of the NVALA, the NFoL, etc. – is also firmly heterosexual. They accuse the gay community of propagandising and leading the young to believe that, if they're actively heterosexual, then they must be repressing their homosexuality. 'Don't be fooled', they warn,

'It's rarely a biological condition. It's more a matter of conditioning. You don't have to be gay.'[65]

What, if anything, connects these groups? They all arose, or at least underwent significant transformations, in the period generally described as the 'permissive age'. They are all oppositional in character. Although they vary either in their particular concerns or in the foci of their campaigns – even the Responsible Society, which states that it does not take part in demonstrations and public protests, campaigns through its literature – it was 'permissiveness' or their particular interpretation or conception of permissiveness that was the galvanizing force behind their development. The central concern for all these groups is with what they perceive to be declining moral standards.

THE EMERGENCE OF MORAL CAMPAIGNS

It is not immediately obvious why moral campaigns should have developed in post-war Britain. Why should organisations such as the NFoL, the NVALA and others have developed when they did? A number of authors, whose work will be considered below, have attempted explanations largely in terms of social class. It is suggested that support for such organisations is drawn disproportionately from the middle class, and in particular those sections of the middle class that feel most at threat from the structural changes taking place in contemporary British society. Other authors have suggested that it has been the process of secularisation which has been most central in giving rise to moral protest groups. The final attempts at explanation have been in terms of 'cultural defence' and see moral protest groups arising in response to broader cultural changes, as opposed to changes in class structure or the role of religion.

Examinations of the development of protest groups such as the NVALA invariably begin with the work of Howard Becker and his notion of 'moral entrepreneurship'.[66] Moral entrepreneurs engage in the process of establishing moral rules by attempting to define certain actions or forms of behaviour as deviant. As such, the term has been seen as being a particularly appropriate description for the endeavours of organisations involved in 'moral protest'. Perhaps the most widely quoted and influential study of 'moral entrepreneurship' is Joseph Gusfield's study of the American Temperance Movement.[67] Building on Weber's conception of 'status' and the way in which such social honour is differentially distributed between social groups, Gusfield notes that, at times of (rapid) social change, certain groups may experience an increase or loss of social honour. During periods of change such as this, what he refers to as 'status movements' may emerge which attempt, through symbolic rather than instrumental means, to increase or simply maintain the prestige or honour of a particular social group. Using this approach, moral reform movements are viewed as a form of status politics. By seeking support for a set of values or beliefs, the social honour of the group(s) that adhere to them is *symbolically* affirmed. Gusfield does not suggest, however, that all moral reform movements are identical in approach and he distinguishes between two basic types. The first he refers to as 'assimilative', the second as 'coercive'.

The first, as is implied by its name, is sympathetic and persuasive, attempting to 'convert the deviant' to the dominant way of thinking and behaving. The coercive approach to moral reform, however, seeks either to change the law, or at least, to invoke legal sanctions in its attempt to reaffirm the status attached to a particular social group or class. The assimilative approach, Gusfield suggests, is associated with groups that are largely secure, where the values and opinions they hold either are, or are perceived to be, supported by the majority of the population. Coercive reform is associated with groups that feel threatened, with groups that feel their social superiority is being challenged or diminished.

In his study of the Women's Christian Temperance Union (WCTU), Gusfield argued that the movement shifted from assimilative to coercive reform as the old middle class lost ground to upwardly mobile immigrant groups and the new middle classes. As such, temperance became a significant symbolic difference between the old and the new:

> The establishment of Prohibition laws was a battle in the struggle for status between two divergent styles of life.... A function of Temperance activities was to enhance the symbolic properties of liquor and abstinence as marks of status.[68]

The important word here is symbolic. According to the argument, it was the passing of the law that was important to the reformers, not how effectively it was enforced afterwards. The values and beliefs of the reformers were enshrined in the law; 'it was *their law* that the drinkers had to avoid.'[69] As Gusfield argued:

> Status issues function as vehicles through which a non-economic group has deference conferred upon it or degradation conferred upon it. Victory in issues of status is the symbolic conferral of respect upon the norms of the victor and disrespect upon the norms of the vanquished.[70]

A certain similarity may be noted here between Gusfield's interpretation of the aims of the WCTU and Mrs Whitehouse's explanation for some of her own actions. Of all the campaigns Mrs Whitehouse has been involved in, one of the most contentious was the private prosecution of Michael Bogdanov over *The Romans in Britain*. What was particularly contentious was the way in which the prosecution was eventually withdrawn. Although she was accused of backing down, Mrs Whitehouse firmly suggested that she had achieved what she set out to do, i.e. to show that certain acts could be defined as indecent within the parameters of the law as it stood. There can be little doubt that this was in essence for Mrs Whitehouse a symbolic or political victory. The intention behind Mrs Whitehouse's actions was not that Bogdanov should be punished, but that the values and beliefs espoused by the NVALA should be seen to be supported, to be successfully and, above all, publicly defended from attack.

Suggesting, however, that the notion of 'symbolic politics' as used by Gusfield may be pertinent in some respects for an analysis of the campaigns of the NVALA and comparable groups, is not to argue that the full-blown theory of status politics used to explain the rise of the WCTU in the United States can be simply and completely applied to the 'moral crusades' of the so-called 'permissive era' in Britain. Although other American sociologists such as Zurcher and Kirkpatrick have (not uncritically) applied Gusfield's theory to contemporary anti-pornography movements, the most recent attempts at explaining the rise of groups such as the NVALA and the NFoL have been very critical of the theory of status defence.[71]

Wallis originally explained the rise of the NVALA in terms very similar to those used by Gusfield. He has, however, in his more recent writings on this subject, repudiated this earlier position. Wallis is critical of Gusfield for failing to provide evidence of motivation in his study of WCTU participants in the movement. Whilst, on the surface, Gusfield's argument may seem a plausible one, Wallis argues that 'there are clearly other grounds for moral indignation than resentment at lost status'.[72] He suggests that Gusfield fails to provide evidence of such motivation in the accounts of movement participants. Indeed, Wallis argues that these would in fact be most unlikely. Wallis further throws doubt on Gusfield's claim that he had in fact identified a status group. Much of the evidence, indeed, suggests that a substantial section of support for the WCTU came from the working class, and that it was not homogenously white, Anglo-Saxon, Protestant, old middle class as Gusfield claims. Far from identifying a 'status group', Wallis argues that in fact the WCTU were in fact a 'cultural group'. Their crusade was to preserve a particular style of life, or culture, from increasing erosion in American society. This he refers to as 'cultural defence'. Although Wallis is extremely critical of Gusfield's theory of 'status defence', his own notion of 'cultural defence' is linked to Gusfield's through Weber's conception of 'status groups'. Thus, whilst Wallis and Gusfield disagree over the likely causes of resentment, both appear to be identifying 'status groups' as central to moral campaigns. Wallis' identification of 'style of life' as the crucial component of moral entrepreneurial groups is also a characteristic of 'status groups' as identified by Weber. Such 'status groups', he suggests, engage in 'cultural defence', which he describes as follows:

> There is no reason to believe that an increasing disparity between the standards of morality and behaviour which one has grown up to believe were true and right and those displayed and legitimated in the surrounding society can not of itself provide the ground for commitment to a movement of moral reform.[73]

One fundamental question remains, however. That is, why is it that some people rather than others who experience the type of disparity described above become committed to a movement for moral reform? The hypothesis put forward by Gusfield, that it is those people who have experienced status erosion who become committed, remains at least *a priori* plausible. This is not to say that Wallis' notion of 'cultural defence' loses any value it may have. Rather, it is to say that Gusfield's theory may continue to have explanatory power, particularly with regard to the initial motivation of participants in such a movement, and that where Wallis' work is important is in pointing to the cultural concerns that may also underpin the rise of specific moral entrepreneurial groups.

The earlier part of the chapter sought to describe in some detail the major concerns articulated by Mrs Whitehouse and the NVALA, the most basic of which, it was suggested, revolved around the perceived declining centrality of organised religion in British social life. The NVALA's long-term goal has been the re-establishment of a society in which the Church once more occupies a central role. This basic argument tallies with the general thesis put forward by Tracey and Morrison in their study of Mrs Whitehouse and the NVALA. Those authors suggest:

> What is clear is that for [Whitehouse] and others like her, there is a determination to restore a Christian culture to Britain, and in that battle the greater availability of sexually explicit cultural forms, the easier access to abortion and divorce, the legitimation of homosexuality between consenting adults and so on are developments which must at all costs not only be stemmed but at some ill-defined date in the future actually reversed. It is a crusade to recapture Jerusalem, nothing short of a call for a new theocracy.[74]

What Tracey and Morrison argue, although they do not use terminology derived from Gusfield or Wallis, is that the discrete campaigns engaged in by Mrs Whitehouse and the NVALA were important symbolic battles in a larger cultural 'war'. It is a movement of 'cultural fundamentalism'[75] dedicated to the reassertion of 'traditional' values in the face of massive cultural change[76] and, in particular, the process of secularisation. There is ample evidence on which to argue, following Wallis and others, that the NVALA's campaigns should, in the first instance, be viewed as shot through with 'cultural fundamentalism'. The same almost certainly applies to the NFoL, the OCU and even to the Responsible Society although their focus is a secularised version of the NVALA's. The concern of these groups has grown in response to a perceived widening of the gap between cherished moral values and actual day-to-day behaviour. Their general aim has been to recreate a perceived 'golden age', to secure a return to a status quo ante, where, they believe, divorce rates were low, children respectful of adult authority and, most importantly, where religion was the binding force, the 'social glue' which provided moral authority. Whilst Wallis' notion of 'cultural defence' has been utilised here in addition to, rather than in place of, Gusfield's notion of 'status defence' in accounting for the activities of the NVALA, Wallis' explanation is perhaps not as comprehensive as it might be. That is, we are provided with only a partial picture of the cultural position that the NVALA are defending. Whilst the major focus in their campaigns may have been the declining centrality of the Church, the other major reformist concern is explicitly with the family and, by implication at least, with women and youth. The major 'victim' of permissiveness according to Mrs Whitehouse has been 'the child'. Indeed, the major underlying concern in debates over pornography, homosexuality, abortion, the age of consent, divorce and drugs during the period under consideration here has been the welfare of children. By association, therefore, there is a direct link, according to the ideology of groups such as the NVALA, with the role of the mother, and the strength of the family.

As was noted in Chapter one, Stuart Hall has argued that the key interpellated subjects of new legislation in the 1960s were women. It can further be argued that the principal objects, or targets, of the new legislation were not only women, but also children. The cultural position being defended by the NVALA consisted of a society governed by a religious moral consensus and also, crucially, built on the back of the traditional nuclear family. The debate over the family, its constitution and its role, forms a second major focus of organisations such as the NVALA, the NFoL and the Responsible Society. Indeed, Simon Watney suggests that this 'concern' underpins the current so-called 'panic' over AIDS:

> We are not, in fact, living through a distinct coherent and progressing moral panic about AIDS. Rather, we are witnessing the latest variation in the spectacle of the defensive ideological rearguard action which has been mounted on behalf of 'the family' for more than a century.[77]

As the Bergers (1984) point out, the 'family has become a problem' in contemporary society. This has not consisted simply of middle-class reformers defining the working-class family as problematic, for which there is a long tradition. The ideological net has widened so that the idea of 'the family' as a given and immutable social unit is no longer accepted, rather, the family is generally problematised. It is the resolution of this problem that groups such as the NVALA seek. Their symbolic political struggle is in defence of a cultural order in which there exist strong moral rules to provide solutions to the problems of the appropriate constituents and roles of the family.

Many of the commentators on the 'permissive era', discussed in Chapter one, have suggested that it was a period characterised by radical changes in both behaviour and the rules that govern behaviour. Such commentators have, however, singularly failed to provide evidence to support the first argument, that there were radical changes in behaviour. And they have too readily assumed that legislative changes, such as the Obscene Publications Act, 1959, the Sexual Offences Act, 1967, the Abortion Act, 1967 and others, are sufficient evidence in support of the second, that the rules governing behaviour changed. The lasting impression of these accounts is that everyone agrees that there was a 'permissive age', or a process of change that can be described as 'permissive', but that no-one can actually agree what constituted 'permissiveness'.

The overview presented here suggests that many things happening in the period were seen as being representative of significant social changes. These changes were of particular symbolic importance for moral entrepreneurial groups, and brought into sharp relief what appeared to be the declining importance of certain social arrangements concerning the family, and certain moral ideals and values affecting the social significance of Christianity. Most moral entrepreneurial groups contend that a (partial) sexual revolution has taken place, though little evidence of radical changes in sexual behaviour is forthcoming – other than evidence of a circumstantial kind. However, legislative change is generally treated by both moral entrepreneurs and other social commentators as being an accurate and reliable index of general changes in 'standards' or the rules governing behaviour. The moral protest groups, by and large, have adopted what Gusfield has termed a 'coercive' approach to moral reform. Several of the legislative changes during or around the 1960s are viewed by them as being 'permissive' and as therefore sanctioning many of the forms of behaviour to which they object. Their response has been to aim for legislative repeal or reform. The chapters which follow look more closely at some of the relevant legislative changes that took place during this period, and the background and responses to these reforms.

3 The Wolfenden Report and legislative change

The decade after the end of the Second World War saw a substantial increase in the number of prosecutions for offences such as 'gross indecency', importuning and indecent assault. Indeed, the size of the increases, together with the publication of the *Kinsey Report* in 1948 (which suggested that homosexual behaviour was more widespread than had been commonly thought) and the media-highlighted prosecution of Lord Montagu of Beaulieu on an indecency charge in 1954, culminated in what may reasonably be described as a 'moral panic' over homosexuality.

Although it was later denied any truth by Wolfenden, it has been suggested that the immediate post-war period witnessed a 'witch-hunt' or 'purge' of homosexuals.[1] It has been claimed that the 'purge' occurred at the point at which Sir Theobald Mathew, a devout Catholic, was appointed as Director of Public Prosecutions in 1944. Mathew believed that the war was responsible for an upward trend in homosexual behaviour and, together with Herbert Morrison, a policeman's son, Labour right-winger and Home Secretary in the Attlee Government, sought to put an end to it.[2] According to Hyde, the 'purge' only really took off after the Burgess/Maclean scandal in 1951 when the two diplomats fled to the Soviet Union.[3] The clampdown was continued by the appointments of Sir John Nott-Boyer as Commissioner of the Metropolitan Police – his stated aim was to 'rip the cover off all London's filth spots'[4] – and a new Home Secretary, Sir David Maxwell-Fyfe, whose attitude toward homosexuals was that they were, in general, 'exhibitionists and proselytisers and a danger to others, especially the young. So long as I hold the office of Home Secretary, I shall give no countenance to the view that they should not be prevented from being such a danger.'[5] The threat to the 'young' mentioned here by the then Home Secretary was probably the fear most frequently expressed by those who later resisted legislative change in this area. The possible corruption of youth was to be a powerful motif in future campaigns.

In 1953–4, the prosecutions of Lord Montagu, Peter Wildeblood, Robert Croft-Cooke and Michael Pitt-Rivers focused the nation's attention on this campaign. Their trials, the sentences imposed on them and the police methods that had been used, caused a public outcry and put the government under great pressure. The increase in the number of prosecutions did not result, however, in a feeling of sympathy for homosexuals, but rather the feeling, as John Wolfenden expressed it, that 'nobody had any idea how much of it there was ... but there was an impression that it was increasing; and there was a feeling that if it was then it ought to be curbed'.[6]

Pressure on the government to intervene had come as early as 1952 with the publication of the Church of England Moral Welfare Council's Report entitled *The Problem of Homosexuality*,[7] which advocated reform of the law. The Report distinguished between homosexuality as a 'condition' and homosexual behaviour, and, although it advocated the removal of the latter from the criminal law, it remained firm in its condemnation of homosexuality. Not long after its publication, the Montagu trial took place at Winchester Assizes, and the twelve-month prison sentences that he, Wildeblood and Pitt-Rivers received added fuel to the reformist fire:

> Regardless of the guilt or innocence of the defendants, of their social status, and of the humanity of the law relating to homosexuality, the Winchester trial provides, by itself, ample reason for an inquiry into the present methods of the Director of Public Prosecutions and the Police. It also makes abundantly clear the need for a permanent committee ... to review and as occasion demands to recommend reforms in the whole of our criminal law and procedure.[8]

Although the *New Statesman* suggested that it was possible abuses of the law that required assessment, much of the pressure for change, as has been suggested, came from those who viewed with concern what appeared to be the increasing visibility of homosexuality.

As with the area of homosexual conduct, the origin of public concern about prostitution lay, not in some liberal or permissive attitude of tolerance, but in a 'moral panic' over what was believed to be the increasing visibility of a form of deviant behaviour, this time over the increasing visibility of prostitutes and prostitution. John Wolfenden described the feeling well:

> ...there was increasing public concern at what was regarded as the growing shamelessness of prostitutes, in the streets of London and some other big cities. Granted that prostitution was not itself an offence against the law, soliciting was, and it was becoming more open and more persistent. Besides breaking the law they were, by flaunting themselves

and pestering passers-by, causing an intolerable degree of embarrassment and giving visitors a deplorable impression of London's immorality.[9]

Wolfenden also hints at the other motives behind the widespread public indignation. Firstly, the Festival of Britain in 1951 and the Coronation in 1953 had focused the eyes of the world on Britain's streets, and the number of tourists over here in those years gradually gave rise to concern over the embarrassment caused by prostitution. In particular, it was feared that London was becoming known as the 'vice capital of the World'. Secondly, as Smart points out,[10] later in the 1950s prostitution came to be linked with fears about immigration, not only, she suggests, because prostitutes were often linked with pimps who were, for example, Maltese, West Indian or Italian, but because it was also believed, for instance by the Wolfenden Committee and many in Parliament, that the ranks of prostitutes were being swollen by large numbers of immigrant women.

In April 1954, the government announced that it was proposing to appoint a Departmental Committee to examine and report on the law on homosexual offences and the 'parallel' problem of the law relating to prostitution. Sir John Wolfenden, the then vice-chancellor of Reading University, was chosen to be its Chairman, a job which he was to hold for the three years that the Committee took to produce its Report. The terms of reference of the Committee were that they were to consider, firstly, the law and practice relating to homosexual offences and the treatment of persons convicted of such offences by the Courts; and secondly, 'the law and practice relating to offences against the criminal law in connection with prostitution and solicitation for immoral purposes'.[11] It is important to note here that its terms of reference precluded any consideration of the moral basis of either of the two areas to be investigated. All that the Wolfenden Committee was empowered to do was to consider the usefulness of applying the criminal law to these specific offences.

Unlike its recommendations on homosexual conduct, the section of the report that dealt with prostitution was largely uncontroversial. The Committee recognised that the greatest public concern had arisen as a consequence of the 'presence and the visible and obvious presence of prostitutes in considerable numbers in the public streets of some parts of London and of a few provincial towns'.[12] The major plank of what has been termed the 'Wolfenden philosophy' was a distinction between 'public' and 'private' behaviour. Private behaviour was viewed by the Committee as the personal and private responsibilty of the individual, and the law, it was argued, should only concern itself with those activities which constituted offences against 'public order and decency'. Along with this distinction between 'public' and 'private', the Wolfenden Committee also distinguished between 'crime' and 'sin', making it clear that it was only concerned with the former. (However, there can be little doubt that the Committee considered homosexual relations to be sinful). Despite the differences in the content of, and the public reaction to, the two halves of the Report, it had, as has been suggested, an underlying philosophy which informed the proposals in both areas. As John Wolfenden pointed out:

> ...the two halves of our recommendations were governed by the same logic. We had argued, to put it very briefly, that since one of the law's concerns was the preservation of public order and decency, steps ought to be taken to remove the affront to public order and decency which was presented by the obtrusive presence of large numbers of prostitutes openly soliciting on the streets. At the same time we argued that private morality or immorality was a private affair and therefore that 'there must remain a realm of private morality or immorality which is ... not the law's business'. It followed, or so it seemed to us, that while steps should be taken to clear the streets of soliciting prositutes, the behaviour of consenting male adults in private was their affair and not the laws'.[13]

On these grounds the Wolfenden Committee decided that the abolition of prostitution was not something that it ought to recommend, or that if it did, could have any chance of success. It therefore asserted what it considered to be the position at which the public/private distinction should be fixed, a position which would allow prostitution to be effectively a private matter as long as it was not conducted on the streets. The logical extension of this was, of course, increased commodification of prostitution, such as the increased use of advertising, but the Committee felt that the establishment of call-girl systems, for example, was a fair price to pay to free the major cities from what was visibly 'offensive or injurious'. The Committee's recommendations on prostitution were acted upon with far more haste than those concerning homosexual conduct. Indeed the Street Offences Bill was in Parliament not much more than a year after the Report had been published. In debate, the Home Secretary reiterated Wolfenden's general position over the legal position of prostitution:

> ...it is not the object of the Bill to make prostitution illegal, or to provide a cure for prostitution. The object of the Bill is to help to clear the streets, and, for this purpose, to make it possible to charge prostitutes who ply their trade in the streets and to stiffen the penalties against them.[14]

The first major recommendation in the Bill was that the requirement to establish that the conduct of the prostitute caused annoyance to inhabitants, residents or passers-by should be removed. This increased the ease with which the police could prosecute prostitutes, as they no longer required the assistance of an 'offended' member of the public, despite the fact that it was the supposed 'public nuisance' of street prostitution that had given rise to the need for legislation.

The second section of the Bill enacted other parts of the Wolfenden proposals by increasing the penalties liable for offences under the new law, such as loitering, soliciting, keeping or managing a brothel, or living on the earnings of prostitution, etc. The Bill, although subject to some criticism in Parliament, had a relatively quiet passage, and became law less than two years after the publication of the Wolfenden Report.

The Act provided no definition of a 'public place', but it refers to any place to which the public have access, irrespective of whether or not they have a legal right to go there, even when there are particular and restricted rules of entry. It would only become a private place if the entry was restricted to a specific class of persons only, although even this is unclear. As will be seen in Chapter four, those who, like Frederick Shaw, try to by-pass the law by publishing a directory or 'contact magazine', could be guilty of publishing an obscene article, living off the earnings of prostitution, and conspiring to corrupt public morals. Other pieces of legislation such as the Vagrancy Act 1898 and the Licensing Act 1964 have been used to tighten up what could be seen as loop-holes in the law. The ownership of massage parlours and saunas is also no protection against charges of, for example, living off the earnings of prostitution.[15]

By using the dichotomy between 'public' and 'private', the Wolfenden Committee was able to propose an extended series of controls over prostitutes, particularly over those who were highly visible, although the law – the Street Offences Act 1959 – in practice has also been extended to other less visible sectors of prostitution. Essentially the Wolfenden recommendations and their legislative enactment were a public denouncement of prostitution and an affirmation of the importance of 'normal' sexual relationships (monogamous and within the family). To use Greenwood and Young's terminology,[16] it was the 'ghettoisation' of one class of women, a reiteration of the division between 'normal' and 'deviant'[17] and the embodiment of this division in an Act of Parliament. This is seen, for instance, in the denial to prostitutes of 'normal' family relations through the existence and increased harshness of the offence of living on the earnings of prostitution, which effectively stops them from living with a partner.

Smart makes the point that prostitutes became the focus of a moral panic in the 1950s, in spite of the growing liberation of female sexuality.[18] She could, however, have taken this point one step further, for, given that the central organising theme of the Sexual Offences Act was the re-establishment, albeit in a modified form, of male control over one area of female sexuality and thereby indirectly over female sexuality as a whole, it would seem highly likely that the choice of prostitutes as 'folk devils' occurred in large part in response to this growing liberation. Prostitutes, that is to say, therefore became the focus of a moral panic in the 1950s, at least partially *because* of the growing liberation of female sexuality. The legislative response reasserted the fundamentals of the status quo: the relatively dominant position of men, the need for monogamous sexual relationships and the primacy of the family.

The Wolfenden Committee's 'utilitarianism', i.e. its declared aim of non-intervention where no public harm was caused, must be judged in the light of its recommendations, as must its supposed 'liberality'. Its major recommendation, and certainly the one for which it is most often remembered, was 'that homosexual behaviour between consenting adults in private be no longer a criminal offence'.[19] It is important, however, not to read into this recommendation more than was intended for, as will become clear, it was never the intention of either the Wolfenden Committee or those who were eventually successful in their campaign to incorporate the majority of its proposals in the criminal law, to remove the stigma from homosexuality. The Report states that the 'limited' modification to the law that it proposed 'should not be interpreted as an indication that the law can be indifferent to other forms of homosexual behaviour, or as a general licence to adult homosexuals to behave as they please'.[20]

In this extract, some indication is given of the 'limited' nature of the reform being proposed. There is a reference, firstly, to 'other forms of homosexual behaviour', and secondly, to the fact that the proposed process of decriminalisation should only apply to adults. For this purpose, 'adulthood' was fixed at 21. This was despite the fact that probably the most influential piece of evidence they received during the three years they sat, the Church of England Moral Welfare Council's (CEMWC) updated report, *Sexual Offenders and Social Punishment*, recommended a universal age of consent of 17. The CEMWC's suggestion of 17, as opposed to 16 as the age of consent then was for heterosexual relations, was made on the basis that the higher age would provide 'better protection of youth'.[21] As was suggested above, the young were consistently represented as being in need of protection. At one point in the Report, the Wolfenden Committee argued that it was illogical to presume that boys needed greater protection from 'would-be seducers' than do girls.[22] Nevertheless, it went on to argue that a higher age of consent was necessary to protect the young from 'attentions and pressures of an undesirable kind'.[23] The Committee was explicit about what it considered these pressures to be, saying that they had 'encountered several cases in which young men have been induced by means of gifts or money or hospitality to indulge in homosexual behaviour with older men'.[24] The Committee were particularly concerned about the possible corruption of the young. That is, although they generally rejected the idea that people might be 'converted' to homosexuality through seduction, they suggested that some might be tempted into other corrupt activities:

> ...a boy or youth who is induced by means of gifts whether in money or in kind to participate in homosexual behaviour as a source of easy money or as a means of enjoying material comforts or other pleasures beyond those which he could expect by decent behaviour, and we have encountered cases where this has happened. Indeed, it is our opinion that this source of corruption is a more likely consequence than the possible conversion of the victim to a condition of homosexuality.[25]

As was suggested earlier, the arguments put forward both by reformers and their opponents were closely tied to what they considered to be the especially 'sensitive' position of the 'young' in modern Britain. Indeed the Committee even extended this logic to a position whereby they felt themselves able to justify the decriminalisation of adult homosexual behaviour in private as a form of protection for the young:

> With the law as it is there may be some men who would prefer an adult partner, but who at present turn their attention to boys because they consider that this course is less likely to lay them open to prosecution or to blackmail than if they sought other adults as their partners. If the law were changed in the way we suggest it is at least possible that such men would prefer to seek relations with older persons which would not render them liable to prosecution.[26]

The Report, as well as recommending that homosexual relations between adults in private should no longer be an offence, and that the age of consent should be 21, also sought to increase substantially the maximum penalties in respect of certain offences. The only dissenting voice in the Committee over its central recommendations with regard to homosexuality was that of James Adair who, in his minority report, argued that the implementation of the major recommendation would lead to a weakening of the criminal law. This was firmly denied by the Committee, both before and after publication, who argued that to urge a change in the law was not necessarily to approve or endorse homosexual behaviour. To an extent, Mr Adair's fears were reflected by some of the national press after the Report's publication. The *Mail*, *Express* and *Sunday Times* were worried about its effect on moral standards, but the majority of the national press were most favourable, particularly the *Daily Mirror* which exclaimed, 'Don't be shocked by this Report. It's the Truth, It's the Answer. It's Life.'[27] The balanced and reasonable manner in which the Report was written and presented, produced on the whole the same characteristics in the media coverage of the proposals it contained. Indeed, it is undoubtedly the Wolfenden Committee who were responsible for the generally high level of debate concerning reform of the law in this area in the following eight or nine years.

The months after the initial furore over the Report's publication were fairly quiet, particularly as far as the possibilities of legislation on the matter were concerned. The subject returned to the public eye, however, with the formation by two Cambridge graduates of the Homosexual Law Reform Society, a pressure group whose aim was to see the Wolfenden proposals enacted. The Reverend Andrew Hallidie Smith and A.E. Dyson then went about the task of enlisting support for the organisation, a process which was successful, as can be seen from the thirty-three signatories (including Lord Attlee, the Bishops of Birmingham and Exeter, Isaiah Berlin, Julian Huxley, Bertrand Russell) to the letter that appeared in *The Times* in March 1958.[28]

The first appearance of the Report in Parliament was in November 1958, when the Home Secretary, R.A. Butler, moved the motion that 'this House takes note of the Report of the Committee on Homosexual Offences and Prostitution'.[29] Butler, far from pressing for early reform of the law, was at pains to dispel the fears of those who felt that the recommendations of the Report would lead to a sudden increase in homosexuality, or to its condonation:

> An impression has undoubtedly gained ground – which I do not think is fair to the Wolfenden Committee – that the Committee desired to legalise homosexual conduct. This gives a sort of impression that it wished to make it easier. In fact what the members of the Committee wished to do was to alter the law, not expressly to encourage or legalise such practices, but to remove them, like adultery and other sins, from the realm of the law.[30]

What has since been called the 'Wolfenden strategy' is made explicit here. It consisted of an alteration of the relationship between law and morality that allowed the Committee to recommend a partial decriminalisation of homosexuality, rather than a defence of homosexuality itself. The essence of the change was the removal of sin from the ambit of the law. Butler nevertheless felt the public would still misunderstand the intentions of the proposed legislative change, and argued that they would be deeply outraged by what they perceived, however mistakenly, to be the approval by Parliament of homosexual conduct, which was still regarded as a great social evil. Therefore, despite the fact that a little over a year had passed since the Report had been received, he suggested that the interval between publication and the debate was not a matter for regret.[31] Even before the debate took place, *The Times* was able to sum up the situation accurately:

> Parliament debates the Wolfenden Report today. It is a foregone conclusion that the homosexual laws will not be reformed yet. It is equally a foregone conclusion that reform must come eventually. For the majority of well-informed people are now clearly convinced that these laws are unjust and obsolete in a society which refuses to punish lesbian practices, prostitution, adultery, fornication or private drunkenness.[32]

There were those in Parliament who felt that things had already gone too far, despite the Home Secretary's reassurances that it was too soon for legislation. James Dance, the MP for Bromsgrove and future Chairman of Mary Whitehouse's 'Clean-up TV Campaign', had the following to say:

> There are far too many people looking into the mind of the murderer and not at the agony of mind of the relations of the murdered person. There are far too many people looking into the minds of the Teddy cosh-boys and not into the minds of the old ladies who have been coshed. In exactly the same way, too many people are looking into the mind of the homosexual rather than considering the repugnance that is caused to millions of decent people all over the country ... I feel that it was the condoning of these offences which led to the fall [sic] of Nazi Germany. Yes that is perfectly true. I believe that here at home if these offences are allowed to continue unchecked our moral standards will be lowered.[33]

Although it is difficult to assess its importance, on the eve of the second reading debate a letter appeared in *The Times*, signed by eight peers, including Lord Devlin. It is worth quoting in full:

> Sir – In 1957, the Wolfenden Committee recommended, after three years study of evidence, that homosexual behaviour between consenting adults in private should no longer be a criminal offence. This proposal has been endorsed by the British Council of Churches, the Church Assembly, and the Moral Welfare Council of the Church of England, a Roman Catholic Advisory Committee, appointed by the late Cardinal Griffin, the Methodist Church, and leading spokesmen of many other leading Christian denominations, as well as by prominent humanists. It has received the support of the Howard League for Penal Reform and the Institute for the Study and Treatment of Delinquency, and also of other experts in Criminology, including several judges, as well as of very many doctors, psychiatrists and social workers.
>
> The great majority of national daily and weekly newspapers have strongly and consistently advocated the reform. In February of this year

a resolution calling for its enactment was passed by the Liberal Party Council, and it has also been supported by many individuals and groups in both the Labour and Conservative parties.

Seven years ago a distinguished list of signatories wrote in your columns that the existing law clearly no longer represented either Christian or liberal opinion in this country, and that its continued enforcement would do more harm than good to the community as a whole.

We hope that in response to the Motion calling attention to the Wolfenden Committee's recommendations which Lord Arran is to move in the House of Lords on May 12, Her Majesty's Government will now recognise the necessity for this reform and will introduce legislation.[34]

The letter was signed by the Bishops of Birmingham, Bristol, Exeter, London and St Albans, as well as by Lords Brain, Devlin and Robbins.

Having received its second reading, the Bill went to Committee where many amendments were tabled, such as the raising or lowering of the age of consent, but few were accepted. Baroness Wootton tabled an amendment that, had it been accepted, would have made it no longer an offence 'to procure or conspire to commit a homosexual act which by virtue of this Act is not itself an offence'. The question arose after the *Ladies' Directory* case in which Frederick Shaw was convicted of 'conspiring to corrupt public morals', and in which one of the Appeal Judges, Lord Simons, had stated that 'there remains in the courts a residual power to conserve not only the safety, but also the moral welfare of the State'. Baroness Wootton's fears were in fact well grounded for six years later *IT* were convicted of 'conspiracy' when they published a list of 'contact' advertisements for homosexuals.

A private member, Humphrey Berkeley MP, picked up Arran's Bill after its successful third reading and introduced it in the Commons. The Bill looked like being reasonably successful despite a reported last-ditch effort by the Bill's Conservative opponents. According to the *Observer* on 6 February 1966, it was revealed at a meeting of the Conservative backbench 1922 Committee that a 'private and anonymous circular' had been distributed with the warning that it should be destroyed immediately after reading. It simply appealed 'to all Conservatives to stand up and be counted against Humphrey Berkeley's Bill in favour of homosexuals'.

At its second reading in the Commons, the Bill passed by 164 votes to 107 and, just as its progress seemed assured, a General Election was called and Parliament dissolved. When Parliament sat again, the government announced that there would not be a ballot for Private Members' Bills in the first session, and therefore there was no possibility of homosexual law reform, a decision which prompted the Earl of Arran to reintroduce his

Sexual Offences Bill into the House of Lords to keep up the pressure. Just as he did this, the government had a change of heart and decided that there would after all be a Private Members' ballot. Arran announced that he would prefer a Bill of this nature to be introduced in the Commons, but that he would keep his Bill going in the Lords until an MP could be found to sponsor an equivalent measure in the other House. Arran's Bill again went through the Lords without too much trouble but, by this time, a sponsor had been found, and Leo Abse introduced the Sexual Offences Bill in the Commons in July 1966, although its second reading was delayed until 19 December. By this time, all the arguments had been well rehearsed in both Houses. The reformers consistently stressed the need to remember that, whilst the liberalising tendencies of the proposals were making all the headlines, a set of controls was also included which was an essential part of the package. The dominant message that was being provided for the public was that the law reform being proposed was essentially 'permissive' in character. The restrictions that were also part of the reform, however, were by and large ignored by the media. Abse, in his speech during the second reading, spelled out to the House what these controls involved. Firstly, he pointed out that the Wolfenden Committee had recognised in its Report that, for the preservation of discipline and for the protection of those of subordinate rank, the services might wish to retain section 6 of the Army Act which provides for the punishment of those guilty of 'disgraceful conduct of an indecent or unnatural kind'. Under the Bill introduced by Abse, these controls were not only maintained but extended, so that, in addition to the Army Act, section 66, it would be possible to take proceedings under section 64, with reference to 'officers who behave in a scandalous manner'; or under section 69 of the Air Force Act, with reference to air force discipline.

Secondly, in accordance with the Wolfenden recommendations Clause 2 of the Bill set a penalty of five years imprisonment for the offence of buggery committed by a man over 21 with a consenting youth over 16. The maximum penalty for gross indecency committed by a man over 21 with someone aged under 21 would be increased from two to five years, as would be the penalty for the offence of attempting to procure or procuring a man under 21 to commit an act of gross indecency. The penalty for an act of buggery against a boy was life imprisonment. There was no doubt in Abse's mind who these controls were designed to protect:

> I believe that those provisions make it abundantly clear that the penalties that will be visited upon those who attempt to corrupt youth will be stern and relentless. No-one except those who are wilfully blind to the nature of our proceedings can possibly spell out of the Bill any condonation

whatever of homosexual conduct which can affect young people in their formative years.[35]

There are distinct parallels here between the statements made by those such as Leo Abse who were in favour of homosexual law reform, and the position adopted by those who opposed 'permissive' reform of all kinds. For both groups, the key subjects were 'youth'. It was the young who needed to be protected, and this realisation could be, and was, used both to justify limited reform and to resist it. The reformist position was reiterated in debate by Dr David Owen:

> Let us deal with the suggestion that it would be psychologically damaging to the country to show that the House condones homosexuality. If that feeling comes out from the debate it will be the direct result of misreporting, because no Hon. Member whatever viewpoint he or she put forward, has condoned homosexual behaviour. The Bill lays down very clearly that under certain circumstances the House is increasing the penalties, that it is trying to stamp out corruption of youth and minors, which is possibly the most important element in the Bill.[36]

What the proposed Bill actually did, in fact, was to give the representatives of the law far greater scope for intervention in the conduct of homosexuals than in the case of other sexual activities. For, as Giles Playfair rightly pointed out, when children under 16 are thought to be the victim of indecent assault, they would not, as could homosexuals under these proposals, be also treated as the culprits. He argued that the purpose of the age of consent included in the Wolfenden proposals was 'not only to deter the old from corrupting the young, but to deter the young from allowing themselves to be corrupted and, furthermore, from misbehaving with each other'.[37]

After around twelve years of what had been almost continuous debate, the recommendations of the Wolfenden Committee were about to reach their legislative conclusion. Lord Arran, who had been instrumental in the success of Abse's Bill by his efforts in the Lords, was given the final word in that House. As one might expect, given the two-sided nature of the debate and the legislation that grew out of it, his closing speech was not the singularly 'permissive' one some might have expected:

> I ask those who have, as it were, been in bondage, and for whom the prison doors are now opening to show their thanks by comporting themselves quietly and with dignity. This is no occasion for jubilation, certainly not celebration.
>
> Any form of ostentatious behaviour, any form of public flaunting, would be utterly disgraceful and make the sponsors of the Bill regret what they have done.

Homosexuals must remember, while there may be nothing bad in being a homosexual, there is certainly nothing good.[38]

The Bill went on to receive its third reading in the Commons, and received the Royal Assent on 27 July 1967. Writing about the passage of the Bill through Parliament, Nigel Warner suggests[39] that the net result of the fact that Abse's Bill merely amended earlier legislation prohibiting homosexual behaviour, rather than repealing it, is that such behaviour remains unlawful, except for the circumstances included in the new Act, and he quotes Norman St John Stevas' recognition of this fact. Stevas said that the Act 'would create no recognised status for homosexuality. It would remain contrary to public policy. Homosexual relations would give rise to neither rights nor duties'.[40] It is this 'position' that homosexuals find themselves in in modern Britain that requires further consideration. As has already been suggested, and will be discussed in detail in Chapter five, the Sexual Offences Act was put under the microscope during the *IT* case in the early 1970s.

IT was one of several 'underground' magazines which found themselves in court in this period. Knuller Ltd, the publishers of the magazine, had offended sensibilities by printing on an inside page, under a column headed 'Males', a series of 'gay contact' advertisements. The publishers were convicted on charges of 'conspiring to corrupt public morals' and 'conspiring to outrage public decency'. They appealed on several grounds, but particularly that 'an agreement by two or more persons to insert advertisements in a magazine for the purpose of homosexual acts taking place between consenting adult males in private did not constitute an offence'. The Court of Appeal dismissed the appeals, but granted leave to appeal to the House of Lords on the grounds that points of law of general public importance were involved. In rejecting that appeal, Lord Reid stated:

There is a material difference between merely exempting certain conduct from criminal penalties and making it lawful in the full sense. Prostitution and gaming afford examples of this difference. So we must examine the provisions of the Sexual Offences Act 1967 to see just how far it altered the law. It enacts, subject to limitation, that a homosexual act in private shall not be an offence, but it goes no further than that ... I find nothing in the Act to indicate that Parliament thought or intended to lay down that indulgence in these practices is not corrupting.[41]

Lord Reid summarised the situation quite succinctly. In employing essentially utilitarian criteria, the Wolfenden Committee gave rise to legislation which decriminalised certain forms of homosexual conduct. Neither the Committee nor the sponsors of the subsequent legislation suggested that this should imply greater tolerance of, or a lessening of the stigma attached to, homosexuality. Although both of these may have been indirect or possibly unintended consequences of the legislative change, homosexuality was still open to interpretation in law as immoral and corrupting.

The Sexual Offences Act of 1967 was also limited in its geographical scope, for it was not until 1980, and the passage of the Criminal Justice Bill of that year, that the law was altered in Scotland in this regard. Indeed, an attempt at reform had been tried in 1977 and failed. It was not until the European Court of Human Rights ruled in 1981 that the law in Northern Ireland was in breach of its convention that the process of reform started there, bringing change that was fifteen years behind England and Wales, and twenty-five years after the publication of the Wolfenden Report. Homosexuals are still discriminated against in many areas, such as over the custody of children, in employment, in education, by the police, and in the media.[42] Despite the fact that the Criminal Law Revision Committee and the Policy Advisory Committee have recently considered the question of homosexuality, there appears to be little possibility of change in the conditions of lawful homosexual conduct. The position in the armed forces has been reiterated in Parliament. The Police Federation has made it clear that any proposals to reduce the age of consent would be vigorously resisted. Much of the concern expressed prior to the passing of the 1967 Act centred around the supposed vulnerability of children, and this has made the possibility of a lowering of the age of consent a remote one. Linked to this have been a series of vigorous campaigns against paedophile organisations, including the use of the conspiracy laws.

Finally, there is also the question of the policing of the offences defined by the Act. Between 1967 and 1977, the recorded incidence of the offence of indecency between males approximately doubled, and the number prosecuted, trebled.[43] Although the number of recorded offences in that decade was not as high as it had been in the 1950s it is nevertheless an important trend. It is possible that this increase may have been, on the one hand, indicative of a greater frequency of homosexual activity 'in public' and, hence, of a degree of 'permissiveness'. On the other hand, it may have been indicative of the increased regulation that went along with this. Walmsley points out that most of the increase involved the conviction of persons aged over 21 whose partners in the offence were also aged 21 or over (the offence generally occurring, or at least being detected, in public conveniences). It appears therefore that whilst 'private' homosexual conduct may have been decriminalised, the 'public' margins came to be increasingly policed.

Walmsley looks at several possible explanations and concludes that the change is largely due to the Act itself, firstly in the simple sense that the passing of the 1967 Act brought to an end a trial period of uncertainty for the police by making quite clear that, although in the future homosexual acts in private between consenting adults were to be legal, such acts in 'public' as defined by the Act were not. This provided the police with a firm indication of where their duty lay. More importantly, perhaps, Walmsley argues that the 1967 Act, because it introduced summary trial for the offence of indecency between males, made it easier for the police to bring prosecutions, for when there are no minors involved, the Director of Public Prosecution's consent is unnecessary. This makes the processing of such cases, where the magistrates court is involved, a particularly quick affair, indeed, less trouble for all those involved, including possibly the offenders.

The important point for present purposes, however, is that, in this and other ways, the Sexual Offences Act is not a piece of legislation which can be simply and easily catagorised as 'permissive'. Those who advocated reform argued consistently that it ought not to be interpreted as a permissive move for two reasons. Firstly, homosexual conduct, although no longer subjected to criminal penalties, except when it occurred in clearly defined *public* circumstances, would continue to be viewed as morally reprehensible; and secondly, the move did not imply a relaxation of control over homosexual behaviour or was not intended by its main supporters to imply such a relaxation of control. What was hoped would occur was a shifting of responsibilities from 'external' control to 'self-control'. This was the essence of Lord Arran's final speech in the Lords debate on the Sexual Offences Bill, when he pleaded for homosexuals to 'comport themselves quietly and with dignity.... Any form of ostentatious behaviour, any form of public flaunting would be utterly disgraceful.'[44] This was explicitly recognised by the Wolfenden Committee:

> Unless a deliberate attempt is to be made by society, acting through the agency of the law, to equate the sphere of crime with that of sin, there must remain a realm a sphere of private morality and immorality which is, in brief and crude terms, not the law's business. To say this is not to condone or encourage private immorality. On the contrary, to emphasise the personal and private nature of moral or immoral conduct is to emphasise the personal and private responsibility of the individual for his own actions, and this is a responsibility which a mature agent can properly be expected to carry for himself without the threat of punishment from the law.[45]

The debates in parliament, and the legislation which they preceded, had a 'dual' nature or character. On the one hand, as far as the criminal law was concerned, they removed one set of controls entirely, whilst on the other hand, a new and sometimes increased set of controls was introduced to deal with those forms of homosexual conduct which were still considered to be 'public' and criminal. This 'double taxonomy' took the form that it did partly as a result of a generalised concern over the perceived vulnerability of the young. As such, much of the debate over homosexuality was intimately bound up with the wider argument that has already been identified over the role and significance of the modern 'nuclear' or 'bourgeois' family. It was the defence of this social unit that set many of the boundaries to the debates and limited the eventual legislative reform. The view that this was a central organising feature of the Wolfenden Report is reinforced by the Committee's approach, in its proposals on prostitution, to what it saw to be 'legitimate' avenues for female sexuality.

It was the phrase, 'in private', that was the critical one in the change to the law recommended by the Wolfenden Committee, and it is the distinction between public and private that also effectively separates the two major camps in all the morality debates in this period. The Wolfenden Committee, in distinguishing between public and private behaviour, also drew a distinction between 'crime' and 'sin', and concluded that 'as a general proposition it will be universally accepted that the law is not concerned with private morals or ethical sanctions',[46] and further, 'it is not the duty of the law to concern itself with immorality as such...it should confine itself to those activities which offend against public order and decency and expose the ordinary citizen to what is offensive or injurious'.[47] In this way, the Committee was able, quite consistently, to propose what, on the one hand appeared to be a relaxation of the law in the area of homosexuality, whilst on the other hand it recommended stronger sanctions in the area of prostitution. What appeared to be a more liberal approach towards homosexual relations could be adopted because of the essentially 'private' and 'invisible' nature of the behaviour, whereas a seemingly more punitive line was adopted in relation to soliciting because of its 'public' and 'visible' character. The importance of the distinction between 'public' and 'private' can be made somewhat clearer by considering an important jurisprudential debate that took place largely in response to the deliberations of the Wolfenden Committee.

In 1958 Lord Devlin, a practising Judge, was invited to deliver the British Academy's second Maccabean Lecture in Jurisprudence. The lecture he gave and the responses it provoked form perhaps the most widely read debate in jurisprudence in Britain in the period since the Second World War. His lecture took as its starting point the distinction drawn by the Wolfenden Committee between public and private behaviour, and what it thus considered to be the proper role of the criminal law in these areas. The questions provoked by the Wolfenden approach were not new ones (John Stuart Mill and James Fitzjames Stephens had both discussed such issues)[48] but they were particularly topical at this point, for questions of law and morality were at the forefront of public consciousness at this time because of, for example, the Wildeblood/Pitt-Rivers case. The positions outlined by Lord Devlin in the lecture referred to above, and the reply by his major critic H.L.A. Hart, in his book *Law, Liberty and Morality*[49] can be used as models of the relationship between the criminal law and contemporary moral rules or mores.

Devlin suggests that, at first, he read the Wolfenden Report's formulation of the functions of the criminal law with 'complete approval'. However, on reflection and after further study, he was persuaded that he was, in fact, wrong. His lecture was an outline of his reasons for believing that he was wrong. He opened by stating that he felt 'that a complete separation of crime from sin would not be good for the moral law and might be disastrous for the criminal'.[50] Is there a jurisprudential justification that can be advanced for such a feeling, he asked, and if so, how should the relationship between the criminal law and the moral law be stated? In approaching these questions, he first argues that the criminal law has always been concerned with morals, or moral principles, and that these moral principles are, in this country, inextricably tied to religion – 'the moral standards generally accepted in western civilisation being those belonging to Christianity'.[51] He uses the attitude of the criminal law towards consent as an example of what he believes to be the necessary connection between criminal and moral law. Under the criminal law, he argues, a victim cannot, except in a limited number of quite specific circumstances, consent to the commission of an offence against themselves. So, for example, the consent of the victim is no defence to a charge of murder or, in the case of an assault, 'that the victim thought his or her punishment well deserved and submitted to it'.[52] This illustrates that the law does not exist simply for the protection of individuals, for if it did one would be able to refuse its help if one did not want it. There is a parallel here between Devlin's argument and that used by Durkheim in *The Division of Labour in Society*. The law, Devlin argues, exists in order in some way to protect society:

> There is only one explanation of what has hitherto been accepted as the basis of the criminal law and that is that there are certain standards of behaviour or moral principles which society requires to be observed, and the breach of them is an offence not merely against the person who is injured but against society as a whole.[53]

There are therefore, Devlin suggests, many matters of private morality which are brought within the ambit of the criminal law, for if everything that was not designed to preserve order and decency or to protect citizens were removed from the criminal law, several crimes would cease to be just that, e.g. euthanasia, suicide, attempted suicide, abortion, incest between brother and sister, etc.

Having set out his stall, Lord Devlin goes on to ask himself three questions, the answers to which, he suggests, will provide the evidence to back up his earlier assertion. His questions are:

1 Has society the right to pass judgement at all on matters of morals? Ought there, in other words, to be a public morality, or are morals always a matter for private judgement?
2 If society has the right to pass judgement, has it also the right to use the weapon of the law to enforce it?
3 If so, ought it to use that weapon in all cases or only in some; and if only in some, on what principle should it distinguish?

Devlin answers question one positively in two ways. Firstly, he points to the recommendations contained in the Wolfenden Report and argues that if society were not able to pronounce homosexuality morally wrong, then there would be no basis for a law which aims to protect youth from 'corruption', or for punishing men who live off the earnings of a homosexual prostitute. Secondly, he suggests, an a priori argument may also be advanced: 'What makes a society of any sort is a community of ideas, not only political ideas, but ideas about the way its members should behave and govern their lives; these latter ideas are its morals.'[54] If then, as Devlin contends, all societies have a moral structure, on what basis should society use the weapon of the law to enforce its moral rules? The answer to the first question determines how the second should be answered, he argues, for if a recognised morality is crucial to the continued existence of society (and this is clearly what he *is* arguing), then just as it would use the law to safeguard any other essential part of its structure, so 'society has a prima facie right to legislate against immorality as such'.[55]

Finally, and in answer to the third question, Devlin is critical of the apparent necessity, according to Wolfenden, for special circumstances to exist in order to justify the intervention of the law. For Wolfenden, these special circumstances were defined as the 'provision of sufficient safeguards against exploitation and corruption of others who are especially vulnerable because they are young, weak in body or mind, inexperienced or in a state of special physical, official or economic dependence'.[56] Devlin's argument is that 'exploitation' and 'corruption' are such nebulous terms that almost any field of morality could be defined in a way to allow at least the theoretical intervention of the law. It is therefore not possible to set a theoretical limit to society's power to use law to enforce moral rules, i.e. it is not possible to define an area of morality into which the criminal law may not under any circumstances intervene. Then, in perhaps the most crucial passage in his lecture, Devlin argues:

> Society is entitled by means of its laws to protect itself from dangers, whether from within or without. Here again I think that the political parallel is legitimate. The law of treason is directed against aiding the King's enemies and against sedition from within. The justification for this is that established Government is necessary for the existence of society and therefore its safety against violent overthrow must be secured. *But an established morality is as necessary as good Government to the welfare of society.* Societies disintegrate from within more frequently than they are broken up by external pressures. There is disintegration when no common morality is observed, and history shows that the loosening of moral bonds is often the first stage of disintegration, so that society is justified in taking the same steps to preserve its moral code as it does to preserve its Government and other essential institutions.[57] (my emphasis)

The suppression of vice is therefore, Lord Devlin argues, just as important as the suppression of subversive activities, and just as it is impossible to point to an area of morality which should not be subject to the law, so there is no area of morality which can be described as 'private'. This brings us to his third and final question, which is, should the law be used in all or some cases, and if only the latter, on what basis does one make the decision about where and when to intervene? Before answering his final interrogatory, Devlin asks a further question. How are we to discover society's moral rules? How are those concerned with the law to ascertain society's moral judgements? In answer, he uses the idea of the 'right-minded man', the 'reasonable man' or 'the man on the Clapham omnibus':

> For my purpose I should like to call him the man in the jury box, for the moral judgement of society must be something about which any twelve men or women drawn at random might after discussion be expected to be unanimous.[58]

This type of definition (i.e. one that implicitly assumes that there are general positions which average or ordinary people occupy and agree upon) is similar to that utilised by many moral entrepreneurial groups in their attempts at redefining, for example, obscenity. The assumption – which is also contained in Devlin's quasi-functionalist explanation of the role and ubiquity of a moral structure for any given society, that there is a basic consensus surrounding questions of morality – is something that was then, and is still now, widely held by those in particular who want to repeal or reform what they perceive to have been the 'permissive' legislative changes of the 1960s.

Society has the right, according to Devlin, to protect itself from immoral acts, and these acts are immoral if, by definition, every 'right-minded' person could be assumed to consider them so. In direct criticism of Wolfenden, he argues that one cannot make a simple distinction between public and private morality. The courts have to try to strike a balance between the two.

Devlin completes his lecture by returning to a question he had briefly considered at the beginning, and one which is central here; that of the relationship between the Church and the moral order. Devlin felt that the relationship was a straightforward and uncomplicated one: there was, he believed, little difference between Christian morals and 'those which every right-minded member of society is expected to hold'. Although, with study, one could no doubt detect gaps, nevertheless, 'for the purpose of the limited entry which the law makes into the field of morals, there is no practical difference'. And importantly he concluded:

> It seems to me therefore that the free-thinker and the non-Christian can accept, without offence to his convictions, the fact that Christian morals are the basis of the criminal law and that he can recognize, also without taking offence, that without the support of the Churches the moral order, which has its origin in and takes its strength from, Christian beliefs, would collapse.[59]

This again, of course, has direct parallels with the general position adopted by groups such as the NVALA and the NFoL.

H.L.A. Hart's *Law, Liberty and Morality*, like Devlin's work before it, was inspired by the debates fostered by the publication of the Wolfenden Report. The central question addressed by Hart is: 'is the fact that certain conduct is by common standards immoral sufficient to justify making that conduct punishable by law? Is it morally permissible to enforce morality as such?'[60] Essentially, Hart follows John Stuart Mill in answering 'no', and suggests, as Mill did, that power can only be used over someone against their will in order to prevent harm to others. On the other hand, he points out that Devlin had in fact answered the question in the affirmative, and had justified this response by suggesting that, just as society can take steps to preserve itself against acts of treason, then so it may protect itself from attacks on established morality, for this too can threaten society's existence. As has been noted, the debate between Hart and Devlin was in part stimulated by the publication of the Wolfenden Report, and Hart begins by noting the striking similarity between J.S. Mill's argument outlined above and the position adopted by the Wolfenden Committee in s.13 of their Report:

> [The] function of [the criminal law], as we see it, is to preserve public order and decency, to protect the citizen from what is offensive and injurious and to provide sufficient safeguards against exploitation or corruption of others, particularly those who are specially vulnerable because they are young, weak in body or mind or inexperienced...[61]

As suggested above, one of the central planks in Lord Devlin's argument that the law does not simply exist to protect the individual, but also to protect society, was the fact that in all but a few cases the victim may not consent to the commission of an offence against themselves. This is challenged by Hart who suggests that, far from simply being an example of the law enforcing a moral principle – for example the sanctity of human life – it may on the other hand 'perfectly well be explained as a piece of paternalism, designed to protect individuals against themselves'.[62]

This, as should by now be clear, is a crucial distinction in this argument, for it underpins (along with the public/private distinction utilised by Wolfenden) many of the conflicts and disagreements over morality and the 'proper' role of the criminal law during this post-war period. The adoption by Hart of a position which accepts the possible paternalistic role of the criminal law requires a 'certain modification of the laissez-faire principles propounded by John Stuart Mill'. In so doing, Hart argues, it is not necessary to abandon the position that resists the use of the criminal law to enforce morality. One merely has to allow that harming others may itself be resisted by invoking the sanction of the criminal law. This is the basis of the distinction between 'paternalism' and what Hart calls 'legal moralism', for:

> It is too often assumed that if a law is not designed to protect one man from another its only rationale can be that it is designed to punish moral wickedness, or in Lord Devlin's words 'to enforce a moral principle'. Thus it is often argued that statutes punishing cruelty to animals can only be explained in that way. But it is certainly intelligible, both as an account of the original motives inspiring such legislation and as the specification of an aim widely held to be worth pursuing, to say that the law is here concerned with the *suffering*, albeit only of animals, rather than with the immorality of torturing them.[63]

Hart then moves on to consider Devlin's assertion that attacks upon, or threats to, the established morality of a society, are also attacks upon, and threaten the continued existence of, that society. He questions the validity of such a statement and argues that, in Devlin's formulation, it was intended to be a statement of empirical fact, or more likely an a priori assumption.

Devlin, he suggests, provides no evidence with which to support the statement, and further no reputable historian has argued that deviation from
sexual morality could be seen, like an act of treason, as threatening
society's existence.

Hart accuses Devlin of moving from

> the acceptable proposition that *some* shared morality is essential to the
> existence of any society, to the unacceptable proposition that a society is
> identical with its morality, as that is at any given moment of its history,
> so that a change in its morality is tantamount to the destruction of a
> society.[64]

Devlin has, however, been defended against such a charge by several
commentators, and one of these, Basil Mitchell, argues that it would be
fairer to suggest that Devlin's position is that there are no types of immorality which are not in some way capable of threatening society, and which
could therefore be considered to be 'outside' the scope of the law:

> So the argument would appear to be this. We do not know just how much
> cohesion is necessary for a society to exist, but we know that some
> cohesion is necessary. Some degree of shared morality is essential to this
> minimum of cohesion, and any weakening of moral belief may reduce it
> below this minimum; hence we cannot bind ourselves not to use the law
> to safeguard existing moral beliefs, no matter how peripheral they may
> appear to be.[65]

Nonetheless, Hart is highly critical of Devlin's identification of society
with its shared morality and he further accuses Devlin of conceiving of
morality as a 'seamless web', so that those who deviate from one part of it
are almost bound to deviate from the whole. Although there is little or no
evidence to support the contention that those who deviate from shared
sexual morality are likely to be 'deviant' in other ways as well, it was
argued in Chapter two that it is precisely this quality that Mrs Whitehouse
felt she had detected in young 'revolutionaries' such as Richard Neville.
The importance of this part of the debate is that it illuminates one crucially
important difference between, on this occasion, Devlin and Hart: that is, the
disagreement over whether or not it is possible for there to be areas of
behaviour which, whilst they might be considered to be 'immoral', could
also be considered to be 'private'. Clearly, Devlin does not believe this to
be possible, whereas Hart insists that it must be.

4 Obscenity and the law
The permissive years?

The all-permissive, the 'swinging society': under its Big-Top, the whole garish circus of the new freedom, freedom to revel, through all kinds of mass-media, in violence, in pornography, in sado-masochism. The walls of the police storerooms are almost bulging outwards with the pressure of tons and tons of dirty books – the ones still within the scope of the law. But there are plenty outside its scope, so we do not seem to be worrying about that just yet.[1]

Both this and the following chapter document the changes that took place in the construction and implementation of the laws of obscenity in Britain during the period which is now colloquially referred to as the 'permissive age'. The term 'permissiveness' is, as has been shown, generally taken to refer to a relaxation in standards of behaviour, or morals, and for most commentators it is taken by implication to involve a lowering in the quality of life. With reference to questions of obscenity and censorship, a change in a 'permissive' direction implies less censorship and, therefore, more obscenity. Mrs Mary Whitehouse exemplified this view when she said 'whatever may have been the intention of the Home Secretary of the time, Roy Jenkins [sic], it is now a legal fact that his Obscene Publications Acts of 1959 and 1964 opened the floodgates to obscenity'.[2] Although the Home Secretary at the time of the passage of the 1959 Act was actually R.A. Butler, Mrs Whitehouse's point is nevertheless clear. The essence of her idea is that legal changes have been in one direction only, i.e. a permissive direction.

It is confidently asserted by many commentators on the post-war period, that the Obscene Publications Act, 1959 heralded a new era in British attitudes to censorship and, in particular, towards obscenity. The first question that must be asked is, what were the reasons for the introduction of such legislation? Who was behind its successful passage through Parliament and who and what was it designed to protect? This, of course, leads on to the main question; namely that, if the new legislation did indeed signify a new era and set of mores, can it be adequately described as 'permissive'?

Most accounts of the development of legislation to deal with obscenity generally begin with the case of Sir Charles Sedley[3]. In 1663, after a night's revelry, he blasphemed in public (in Covent Garden) having stripped naked and urinated in the street. This action eventually gave birth to the charges of obscenity and conspiracy to corrupt public morals. In years to come, prosecutions for pornography were fairly common, but it was not until 1857 under the direction of the Lord Chief Justice, Lord Campbell, that Obscene Publications legislation was enacted. Under this Act, magistrates were empowered to order the destruction of 'suspicious' books. Because this legislation had been designed simply to give powers of destruction, and not the power to implement criminal proceedings, it contained no definition of obscenity. However, it was only eleven years before one was created, and incredibly it has changed very little in the hundred years or so since. In a case in 1868[4], the then Lord Chief Justice, Sir Alexander Cockburn, made the following comment:

> I think the test of obscenity is this, whether the tendency of the matter charged as obscenity is to *deprave and corrupt* those whose minds are open to such immoral influences, and into whose hands a publication of this sort may fall.[5] (my emphasis)

The new definition armed the Victorians with a weapon powerful enough to suppress any publication to which they took offence, including a previously uncontentious pamphlet on birth control entitled *The Fruits of Philosophy*, and published in the 1870s by James Bradlaugh and Annie Besant, the novels of Emile Zola,[6] and Havelock Ellis' acclaimed study of homosexuality, *Sexual Inversion*.[7] It is, however, the twentieth-century prosecutions for obscenity that are best remembered, and the authors they involved were often just as distinguished. In 1915, Lawrence's *The Rainbow* was not even defended by its publishers, McOwen and Co., because of the pressure that was placed upon them. Eventually, it was ordered to be destroyed. Probably the best remembered case of the period, however, was Radclyffe Hall's *The Well of Loneliness*, which was also successfully prosecuted. In the intervening years, many books received the attention of the censors. Indeed, even the second volume of the *Kinsey Report*, published in 1948, came close to a destruction order, and the 1950s saw several events that were eventually to lead to a change in the obscenity laws in 1959.

In 1953, the International Criminal Police Commission held a meeting in Oslo on the subject of 'obscene and licentious publications', which concluded that the increase in the number of sex offences since the war could have links with the reading of pornography, and the British police, together with the then Home Secretary, Sir David Maxwell-Fyfe and the Director of Public Prosecutions, Sir Theobald Mathew, responded with an 'anti-vice' drive that was directed not only at pornography but, as has already been mentioned, also at homosexuality and prostitution. With respect to 'obscenity', the drive was directed mainly at 'cheap pornographic novels'. In most of the prosecutions, the booksellers made very little fuss. However, in one case in 1954[8] the shopkeeper produced a number of books that had been published by major companies and, in defence of his own stock, questioned their right to free circulation. The Judge ruled that this type of comparison was not permissible, and despite this ruling, and the fact that it was upheld by the Court of Appeal, the Lord Chief Justice suggested that the matter should be investigated, and the DPP duly complied. This led to five prosecutions for obscenity in 1954 and brought into the dock, not some seedy back-street publishers, but some of Britain's biggest and most reputable publishing houses. The first of these cases to be contested[9] involved Martin Secker & Warburg Ltd (as well as the Camelot Press Ltd and Frederick John Warburg) for publishing Stanley Kauffman's novel, *The Philanderer*. The trial took place in late June to early July and was held at the Central Criminal Court. During the case, it was decided that the defence could not call evidence in which *The Philanderer* was compared to other books, and would not have been able to have recourse to lawyers, critics, authors, etc. to testify to the merits of the book.[10] Mr Mervyn Griffith-Jones, appearing for the prosecution, had, it seems, already made up his mind. Referring to the book, he said:

> If that hasn't got a tendency to deprave and corrupt people whose minds are open to such immoral influences, what on earth has? ... Members of the jury, if you searched every beastly little back-street bookshop in the world you wouldn't find more typical pornography.... It will be a sorry day if you should find that this book and others of similar type are fit to be published at large....[11]

The case was tried by Mr Justice Stable, who showed his sympathy towards the publisher, Mr Frederick Warburg, by allowing him to sit with his solicitor in the well of the court, rather than remain in the dock. His summing-up in the case received great praise at the time, and it is worth repeating much of it here, as it stands in contrast to many of the statements made by judges and magistrates on obscenity at that time and since:

> Remember the charge is a charge that the tendency of the book is to corrupt and deprave. The charge is not that the tendency of the book is

either to shock or to disgust. That is not a criminal offence. Then you say: 'Well, corrupt or deprave whom?' and again the test: those whose minds are open to such immoral influences and into whose hands a publication of this sort may fall. What exactly does that mean? Are we to take our literary standards as being the level of something that is suitable for a 14-year-old girl? Or do we go even further back than that, and are we to be reduced to the sort of books that one reads as a child in the nursery? The answer to that is; of course not. A mass of literature, great literature from many angles is wholly unsuitable for reading by the adolescent, but that does not mean that the publisher is guilty of a criminal offence for making those works available to the general public.

...The book that you have to consider is, as you know, in the form of a novel, and I venture to suggest for your consideration the question: what are the functions of the novels when people write a story of some past age?

I am talking about the contemporay novelist. By 'the contemporary novelist' I mean the novelist who writes about his contemporaries, who holds up a mirror to the society of his own day, and the value of the novel is not merely to entertain...; it stands as a record or a picture of the society when it was written. Those of us who enjoy the great Victorian novelists get such understanding as we have of that great age from chroniclers, such as Thackeray, Dickens, Trollope and many others.... The only real guidance we get about how people thought and behaved over the ages is in their contemporary literature.

It is equally important that we should have an understanding of how life is lived and how the human mind is working in those parts of the world which, although not separated from us in point of time, are separated from us in point of space. At a time like today, when ideas and creeds and processes of thought seem to some extent, to be in the melting pot this is more than ever necessary.... This is an American novel written by an American, published originally in New York and purporting to depict the lives of people living today in New York, to portray their speech and their attitude in general towards this particular aspect of life. If we are going to read novels about how things go on in New York it would not be much assistance would it, if contrary to the fact, we were led to suppose that in New York no unmarried woman of teenage children has disabused her mind of the idea that babies are brought by storks or are sometimes found in cabbage plots or under gooseberry bushes?

You may think that this is a very crude work; but that it is not, perhaps, altogether an exaggerated picture of the approach that is being made in America towards this great problem of sex. You may think that if this does reflect the approach on that side of the Atlantic towards this great question, it is just as well that we should know it and that we must not close our eyes or our minds to the truth because it might conceivably corrupt or deprave any somewhat puerile young mind.[12]

Mr Justice Stable's summing-up received favourable 'reviews' from almost all quarters. Not altogether surprisingly, the defendants were found not guilty, and in an article in the *New Statesman*[13] a couple of months later, Mr Frederick Warburg suggested that the determining factor had, in fact, been Mr Justice Stable's 'summing-up'. The importance of this part of the proceedings was reinforced in the next prosecution for obscenity: the trial of Hutchinson for publishing Vivian Connell's *September in Quinze*, which, although it took place only three months later, bore no relation at all to the Secker and Warburg prosecution. The defence used the summing-up from the previous trial as part of their argument, yet reports of the trial suggest that the summing-up by the Recorder, Sir Gerald Dodson, was a point for point contradiction of the views put forward by Mr Justice Stable. He said, for example:

A book which would not influence the mind of an Archbishop might influence the minds of a callow youth or a girl just budding into woman-hood. Sex is a thing, members of the jury, which you may think has to be protected and even sanctified, as indeed it is by the marriage service, and not dragged in the mud.... I should have thought any reader, how-ever inexperienced, would have been repelled by a book of this sort, which is repugnant to every decent emotion which ever concerned man or woman.[14]

It was not altogether a shock for Hutchinson, after this, that they were found guilty and consequently fined £500. Passing sentence, the Recorder said:

It is a very comforting thought that juries from time to time take a very solid stand against this sort of thing and realise how important it is for the youth of this country to be protected and that the fountain of our national blood should not be polluted at its source.[15]

Of the five publishers to be prosecuted at this time, the only ones who pleaded guilty were Werner Laurie Ltd in respect of Margot Bland's novel *Julia*, and in a further case, that against Heinemann for the publication of a book entitled *The Image and the Search* by Walter Baxter, the jury were unable to come to a decision.[16] The book described the amorous adventures of a nymphomaniac. It had received very varied responses from critics since its publication in 1953, although seemingly it was only the *Sunday Express* which felt strongly enough about it to demand its withdrawal.[17]

The first trial began at the Old Bailey in October 1954, and by the end of the second trial in late November, the jury still could not agree on a verdict. Mr Griffith-Jones, appearing for the prosecution, announced that the DPP did not intend to proceed with the case, and the defendants were discharged. At roughly the same time as these trials were taking place, Arthur Barker Ltd were being prosecuted for publishing Charles McGraw's *The Man in Control*. An uneventful trial ended with a verdict of 'not guilty', bringing to an end what had been an eventful year as far as allegedly 'obscene' publications were concerned. However, as has been suggested, the machinations in the five cases had far wider implications for the general question of censorship than would have been suspected at the time. The trials led to a vociferous public debate much of which was conducted through the letter columns of *The Times*.

First reaction to the events of 1954 came in the form of a prolonged correspondence in *The Times*, started by Graham Greene.[18] In his letter, he condemned the prosecutions and warned of the dangers of attacking writers' freedoms. A second correspondence began on 28 October 1954 and was entitled 'Freedom of the Pen'.[19] The first letter expressed grave concern over the prosecutions for alleged obscene libels, and it went on:

> It would be disastrous to English Literature if authors had to write under the shadow of the Old Bailey if they failed to produce works suitable for the teenager, and if publishers were forced to reject books which, however serious in intent and however lit by genius, contained passages which might be blue-pencilled by a police sergeant or a common informer.

It was signed by seven eminent literary figures[20] and referred explicitly to the value of the summing-up provided earlier in the year by Mr Justice Stable. The debate occupied much space in the press at the time. Indeed, the scale of the coverage is a good indication of the widespread interest that was aroused.[21] Possibly the most significant reaction to the activities of 1954 was the formation in November of that year of a Committee of the Society of Authors, which was organised to investigate the existing state of the law on obscenity and to make recommendations as to how it might be reformed.[22]

The results of the Committee's deliberations were made known in early February 1955, and their report included a Bill drafted by Norman St John Stevas which contained an extended definition of obscenity, covering 'publications that unduly exploit horror, cruelty or violence whether pictorially or otherwise'.[23] They brought in as a central question, the 'intent' of the accused in publishing the article and also wished to introduce the opportunity for the courts to assess the literary, artistic or other merits of the work, as well as to allow evidence to be called concerning the type of audience the publication was most likely to be directed at. It would, under the Bill, also be declared that obscene libel should not be punishable under common law.[24]

The proposals, it may be said, received very wide support from the press, favourable leading articles appearing in *The Times*, the *Sunday Times*, and the *Economist* amongst others.[25] The reason that the definition of obscenity had been extended to include matters exploiting horror, cruelty or violence was in response to a growing 'moral panic' concerning the importation from America of children's magazines, known as 'horror comics', which, among other things, were described as no more than purveyors of 'sadism' and blamed for the rise in juvenile delinquency.[26] Such was the concern in Parliament that legislation was introduced almost immediately to deal with the matter. Given the problems that had been encountered in administering the law in prosecutions for obscenity in 1954, the Society of Authors felt that this was an opportunity to reform the laws of obscenity as a whole. The government, however, persisted with the narrower legislation, arguing that its very narrowness would make it more effective. Roy Jenkins made his feelings clear in the debate over the Bill's second reading, arguing that he thought it 'a thoroughly bad Bill that will do more harm than good.... I think it is a great pity that when a Bill of this kind has been introduced, the opportunity has not been taken to deal with the much wider problem of the law relating to obscenity in literature generally'.[27] Michael Foot, speaking in the same debate, described the atmosphere in the country as one of suppression, and compared the DPP's attitude to that of a former Home Secretary, Joynson-Hicks, in the 1920s. Nigel Nicolson, a publisher and MP, also voiced concern, but from a different angle:

> I have an obvious interest in this debate. I do not want to be imprisoned, to have my premises invaded or my property confiscated, and I can only avoid those penalties, if I know more precisely than this Bill tells me what I may publish and what I may not.[28]

In an attempt to force the issue, Roy Jenkins introduced under the 10-minute rule a draft Bill for the wider reform of the law, and it was given an unopposed first reading, but there its life ended. The committee stage of the Children and Young Persons (Harmful Publications) Bill began ten days later, and although many amendments were moved, the Bill emerged virtually unscathed after five days.[29] The terms of the Bill applied to:

> any book, magazine or any other like work which consists wholly or mainly of stories told in pictures (with or without the addition of written matter), being stories portraying:-

(a) the commission of crimes; or

(b) acts of violence or cruelty; or

(c) incidents of a horrible or repulsive nature;

in such a way that the work as a whole would tend to corrupt a child or young person into whose hands it might fall.[30]

There are certain parallels that may be drawn between the campaign which gave rise to this piece of legislation and other moral campaigns. As was suggested earlier, the most useful concept for understanding the work of moral entrepreneurs is a slightly revised version of Wallis' concept of 'cultural defence'. According to Martin Barker[31] the British horror comics campaign originally surfaced as part of a general anti-American backlash by the Communist Party, but was later appropriated and narrowed by a number of other interest groups. The comics became an outlet or scapegoat for a more general threat to what were seen as traditional British values. Barker quotes one of the campaigners thus:

> We wanted to get back to some sort of English tranquillity. It was a very romantic notion, of countryside, Merrie England, Elgar's music.... And anything that was American was material and brash and vulgar, and that included their comics and motorcars.[32]

Thus, just as the NVALA campaigns of the 1960s and 1970s were under-pinned by a desire to recover a lost 'golden age', so the earlier horror comics campaign appears to have tapped similar feelings. At the centre of both the horror comics campaign and the NVALA concerns was 'the child'. This idealised child is innocent and uncorrupted, but vulnerable to attack by any number of modern phenomena which place their innocence at risk. Although, in this campaign, the focus was horror comics, both its literature and rhetoric are not dissimilar to those surrounding campaigns against a range of books, plays and films in the last twenty-five years, as well as to two specific campaigns against child pornography in the late 1970s and 'video nasties' in the early 1980s. What, in essence, is at stake for the moral reformers is a particular conception of the family and, by implication at least, also a particular conception of 'the child', as well as of the roles of men and women – and especially that of woman as 'mother'. In this conception, the family is neither single-parent nor lesbian or gay, but nuclear and firmly heterosexual. It is the symbolic defence of a society based on such an institutional arrangement that is the basis of the bulk of such moral campaigns.

Finally, it is worth considering the Children and Young Persons (Harmful Publications) Act 1955 as a piece of legislation in relation to the jurisprudential debates outlined earlier. The Act is in many respects utilitarian in character. The preamble to the Act, for example, says that its purpose is 'to prevent the dissemination of certain pictorial publications *harmful* to children and young persons' (my emphasis). Generally, the Bill's sponsors in Parliament did not seek to justify the censorship of horror comics in terms of some intrinsic quality that they possessed, e.g. that they were perhaps 'evil' or 'sinful', but in terms of the *harm* that they might do. Some even argued in terms of possible increases in juvenile delinquency that the spread of comics might result in. There was, however, nothing permissive about the legislation. Its single aim was the censorship of a certain genre of pictorial publication that had hitherto been freely published. It also resurrected the 'deprave and corrupt' definition of obscenity that reformers such as the Society of Authors had been campaigning to replace. The passing of this Bill heralded the end of the 'panic' over horror comics and there has never, in fact, been a prosecution under the Act. Was it, then, entirely successful, or was it as *The Times* labelled it at the time, 'The Wrong Measure'?[33] Given that the comics did not disappear overnight, it would seem that the latter was closer to the mark.

The Society of Authors continued to press for reforms of the law of obscenity and, later on in 1955, Roy Jenkins reintroduced the Bill under the Ballot System. He was, however, too far down in the Ballot to make any impact, and the Bill again failed, only to reappear in the next session under the wing of Viscount Lambton, who had been similarly successful in the Ballot. The government's attitude to the Bill was that, as a piece of legislation, it would be unworkable, and so, under pressure, referred it to a Select Committee.[34] The Committee took evidence from the Society of Authors, the Public Morality Council, the British Federation of Master Printers and two authors, T.S. Eliot and E.M. Forster, as well as from the usual official channels (Home Secretary, DPP, Customs and Excise, Chief Police Officers). In fact, so much evidence, and therefore time, was taken, that the Committee failed to complete its enquiries by the end of the session. In the next session, the work of the Committee continued and they reported early in 1958.

In his evidence to the Committee, the Home Secretary outlined the official position: 'it is the accepted function of government to suppress pornography'[35] and indeed, this position was to play a significant part in the formulation of the report. The recommendations were divided into two parts, the first designed to bring greater certainty to the law of obscene publications, and the second to strengthen the powers for the suppression of pornography. In fact, from the beginning, the Committee had had impressed upon them the existence of a 'considerable and lucrative' pornography trade in Britain, and they resolved that the control of this should be one of their main objectives.

In their recommendations, the Committee made it clear that provision should be made for the defence of literary or artistic merit, and that the explanation of the law contained in R. v Secker should be used to define the class of persons liable to be depraved and corrupted. The recommendations also gave the relevant authorities increased powers to search, seize and, if necessary, destroy potentially obscene material, with the proviso that any proceeding being initiated should have the prior consent of the DPP. In defining the test of obscenity as 'whether the matter tends to deprave and corrupt', the Committee were explicitly rejecting the Society of Authors' suggested extension to refer to matters 'unduly exploiting horror, cruelty or violence'.

As has already been observed, the Report of the Select Committee was based upon two lines of attack: firstly, it was intended to make the law on obscene publications clearer and more exact, and secondly, to clamp down on the hard-core pornography trade. This came out clearly in the minutes of evidence in an 'exchange' between Roy Jenkins and senior police officers.[36] Mr Jenkins pointed out the problems arising from the prosecution of what he called 'borderline cases' – i.e. cases where an article's supposed obscenity was in some doubt – whilst the hard-core pornography trade, whose obscene nature was in no doubt, continued unabated. He therefore asked:

Supposing that it were possible to get more effective means of proceeding against the really filthy stuff, would it be a matter of comparative indifference to the police what happened to the borderline stuff? Complete indifference.
Even if the position in getting prosecutions was made rather more difficult?
Completely.[37]

This view, namely that one could distinguish between pornography and literature and apply different rules to each, pervades the whole of the Report. What must be noted, therefore, is that it would be quite inappropriate to describe the measures as either 'permissive' or 'restrictive'. The Report clearly embodied two wholly different attitudes to the written word, printed picture or photograph. On the one hand, it was argued, and there was much support for the argument at the time, that 'good' or 'worthwhile' literature was being submerged under a wave of moral indignation, whilst on the other hand, purveyors of hard-core pornography, which was unjustifiably obscene, were able to continue their trade without fear of retribution. Although these two views obviously had widespread support – for instance, Roy Jenkins, the champion of the author's cause at the time, was quite adamantly in favour of the suppression of pornography – and were later to become embodied in one piece of legislation, the 1959 Obscene Publications Act, they cannot be placed under a simplistic concept like 'permissiveness'.

That an intention to regulate as well as to licence permission was the subject of the recommendations may be seen in the debate that took place in Parliament on 16 December 1958. Mr Peter Rawlinson had the following to say:

> There is overshadowing this debate the knowledge and appreciation of the vast quantities of pornographic matter, which has been referred to already by my Right Hon. Friend, which are displayed and sold and which are rightly the subject of continuous police action. Anyone who has been concerned with cases involving these books of sheer pornography would realise the great duty that rests upon the law to ensure that this filth is stamped out as quickly and efficiently as possible.[38]

Viscount Lambton, a member of the Select Committee and a supporter of the push to reform the law relating to obscene publications, summed up the debate succinctly:

> I think that the real cause of this trouble and of this wave of morality is that the publication of a vast amount of genuinely obscene literature goes on throughout the length and breadth of the country, and is in no way abated. In other words, while genuine literature suffers, obscenity itself comes to very little harm.[39]

The Bill received fairly strong opposition from the government, and the whole process of trying to reform the obscenity laws was referred to by Sir Alan Herbert as being like a game of snakes and ladders.[40] Having been to Select Committee, the Bill was due to go into Standing Committee. However, during the following weeks when the Bill's name was called, Conservative backbenchers exercised their right to stop its progress by crying 'Object!' Sir Alan Herbert, by then with almost five years as Chairman of the Society of Authors' Committee on the obscenity laws under his belt, responded by announcing in a fit of pique that, if the government were not careful, he would stand as an independent candidate at the forthcoming by-election at East Harrow. Seemingly, however, the threat was enough:

> But I was 68, I did not really for my own sake want to go back to the Commons, and I had no desire to damage the Conservatives. So, privately, I let them know that if the obstruction to the Bill was ended I would withdraw from the by-election.... It worked.... When Parliament met again after the Christmas recess no Hon. Member cried 'Object!'

and the Bill at last received a Second Reading 'on the nod', without a word.[41]

There was still some wrangling to be done over amendments, but at last, some changes were to be made. The Obscene Publications Act became law on 29 August 1959.

In discussing the unfolding of the obscene publications debate, it has been suggested that there were dual tendencies in public feeling towards literature and the law at this time. Before discussing the new machinery itself, this previous view may be reinforced with a further thought from Sir Alan Herbert, who is here discussing the passage of the Bill through Parliament after its second reading:

> Thereafter the Law Officers of the Crown more or less took the Bill over – for the worse we thought. They were not so much interested as we were in protecting the genuine 'respectable author': they were hotfoot after the 'straight' pornographer (the Soho style) and we were not highly excited about that. So it was an uneasy collaboration.... The Bill – a Bill – became law in the summer of 1959. The sad thing was that after all this effort we were not wildly keen about it.[42]

One must be careful not to underestimate the strength of the anti-pornography lobby in the formulation of the final Act. There is a tendency for the new aspects of the law (those designed to protect genuine literature) to be emphasised simply because they were an innovation, yet, as Sir Alan Herbert points out, the new law was by no means ideal as far as those involved in the Society of Authors' Committee were concerned. Indeed, they felt they had conceded rather a lot.

The concessions 'Roy Jenkins *et al.*' had to make to those whose primary aim was the restriction of the pornography trade led eventually to a two-headed piece of legislation. The preamble to the Act encapsulates its dual purpose, suggesting that it will both 'provide for the protection of literature, and ... strengthen the law concerning pornography'.

The new legislation included a definition of obscenity that was primarily based upon Chief Justice Cockburn's ruling in the Hicklin case.[43] Section 1 – (1) contains the full statutory definition:

> For the purposes of this Act an article shall be deemed to be obscene if its effect or (where the article comprises two or more distinct items) effect of any one of its items is, if taken as a whole, such as to tend to deprave and corrupt persons who are likely, having regard to all relevant circumstances, to read, see or hear the matter contained or embodied in it.

The definition introduced the idea of 'a target audience'[44] whereby the circumstances under which the material was seized would have to be considered, e.g. both the location of a shop or cinema and the potential custom would have to be taken into account. As far as 'Jenkins *et al.*' were concerned, the value of this point is, as was pointed out by Justice Stable, that of not making our literary standards conform to 'the level of something that is suitable for the decently brought up young female aged 14'.[45]

The main push for reform of the law had been by people such as Roy Jenkins and the Society of Authors whose wish it was to protect 'worthwhile' literature from being branded as pornography. The way they felt this could be achieved was by admitting evidence from experts as to the merits of particular articles. However, rather than including this in section 1 with the definition of obscenity, it was included as a completely separate section of the Act, section 4, which reads as follows:

> 4. – (1) A person shall not be convicted of an offence against section 2 of this Act, and an order for forfeiture shall not be made under the foregoing section, if it is proved that publication of the article in question is justified as being for the public good on the ground that it is in the interests of science, literature, art or learning, or of other objects of general concern.

As will become clear in due course, the fact that this defence was not open to those prosecuted under section 3 was to be a source of controversy. This, then, was what Jenkins *et al.* had been battling for. Yet not even this was gained without giving up certain other provisions that they felt were necessary. During the report stage, in order to succeed with the 'defence of public good', they had to relinquish the provision which would have required the DPP to be responsible for all cases brought under the Act.[46] Norman St John Stevas emphasised what he saw as the importance of the DPP's involvement:

> Uniformity in administering the law is ensured by making all proceedings subject to the consent of the DPP. At present the police are bound to consult the Director before they bring criminal proceedings but they are not obliged to listen to his advice. Furthermore, there is no obligation to even consult him when the 1857 proceedure is used. Private persons are free to bring prosecutions and in the past this power has been abused.... The Bill[47] ensures that such abuses shall not occur in the future.[48]

This, then, was the 1959 Obscene Publications Act, not perhaps what some had envisaged, but rather a product of five years' sparring between groups with almost diametrically opposed interests. Mrs Whitehouse, however, was in no doubt as to the purpose of the Act, saying that it 'set out – it really did – to punish anyone who publishes an obscene article whether for gain or not'.[49] Indeed, many proposals put forward by the Select Committee for strengthening the powers of the police were accepted. Evidence of sale was not necessary. The power to search premises, vehicles, books, records to do with the business was permitted, and the power to order seizure and destruction was retained. This led A.P. Herbert to comment that, even though the five-year fight he had been engaged in had not been in vain and even though the Act contained many improvements, it was still fundamentally at fault.[50] The question now to be considered is, how did the new legislation work in practice?

THE OBSCENE PUBLICATIONS ACT 1959 IN PRACTICE

Of all the books that have been prosecuted for obscenity or similar offences in Britain, the one that has gained the most notoriety is D.H. Lawrence's *Lady Chatterley's Lover*. Indeed, Pamela Hansford Johnson has suggested that it was 'the event which more than any other had outwardly heralded the approach of the sexually permissive society'.[51] Without doubt, one of the main reasons for this is that it was the first work prosecuted under the new legislation, i.e. it was the first work that could have been published, even if it had been found to be obscene, if it could have been shown that its publication was for the public good under section 4 of the 1959 Act, a clause which Mrs Whitehouse has described as having both 'breached the dyke' and 'opened the floodgates to obscenity'.[52]

Lady Chatterley's Lover itself had a fairly notorious history. It was first published from Florence in 1928, but was confiscated by both the American and British customs very quickly. Pirated editions were rife and expurgated editions poor. The occasional copies that were brought before the courts were always found to be obscene. Even an expurgated version was brought to trial in 1953. The introduction of the new Act encouraged Penguin Books to attempt to publish the book in its unexpurgated form. They informed the police and the DPP of their intention, and postponed general publication until after the issue had been settled. On 19 August 1960, a summons was applied for on behalf of the DPP under the 1959 Act.[53] The company (for it was only Penguin Books that were to be prosecuted, not its individual directors as well, as is often the case) elected for trial by jury. The decision to prosecute was by no means unanimously accepted as a wise one. The *Guardian* felt that: 'there should be no great difficulty in showing that an important work by a major English novelist is a work of literature which ought to be published in the public interest'.[54]

The *Daily Telegraph*, under the heading 'A Strange Choice', and with great foresight, was more concerned with the effects of the prosecution:

Many people who have never heard of it, and who would never have dreamed of reading it, will learn of its possibilities and will be attracted to it for the worst possible reasons. That they will be disappointed and probably disgusted if they pursue their researches so far as to actually read the book is beside the point. Surely the police would be better employed in what a previous Commissioner described as their main task in this field: 'dealing with the very large quantity of absolutely filthy pictorial and written publications which no sane person could defend as having any artistic or literary merit, whatsoever'. However repugnant, *Lady Chatterley's Lover* does not fall into this class.[55]

The *News Chronicle* summed up what seemed to be the general air arguing that it was best to 'let Lady Chatterley lie among the other paperbacks as a minor work of pornography'.[56] Roy Jenkins, the sponsor of the 1959 Act, was also less than happy about the decision to prosecute. He suggested that discussions had taken place in which it had been decided that new legislation should be introduced that gave the police stronger powers to deal with the real pornography trade, whilst giving security to works of literary merit.

The trial began on 20 October 1960, at the Central Criminal Court before Mr Justice Byrne. Penguin Books were charged under section 2 of the Obscene Publications Act, 1959, with publishing an obscene article, to which they pleaded 'not guilty'. Appearing for the prosecution were Mr Griffith-Jones and Mr Morton, and for the defence Gerald Gardiner QC and Mr Hutchinson and Mr Du Cann. Mr Griffith-Jones opened for the prosecution. His main lines of argument were that there were twelve or thirteen explicit descriptions of sexual intercourse in the book which varied only in their time and location, and that the emphasis was always on pleasure:

The curtain is never drawn. One follows them not only into the bedroom, but into the bed, and one remains with them there ... the only variations, in effect between all 13 occasions are the time and locus in quo, the place where it happened.... The emphasis is always on the pleasure, the satisfaction and the sensuality of the episode.[57]

Sex, he suggested, was dragged in at every conceivable opportunity. Moreover, the plot was not much more than padding between these episodes. His final bone of contention was the frequency of four-letter words and 'bawdy conversation' to be found in the text:

Even a description of the girl's father, a Royal Academician, has to introduce a description of his legs and loins; and members of the jury ... not only that type of background, but words, no doubt they will be said to be good old Anglo-Saxon four-letter words, and no doubt they are – appear again and again.... The word 'fuck' or 'fucking' occurs no less than 30 times, 'cunt' 14 times, 'balls' 13 times; 'shit' and 'arse' 6 times apiece ... 'cock' 4 times, 'piss' 3 times and so on. Members of the jury it is against that background ... that you have to view those passages.[58]

After this, Mr Gardiner made his opening speech for the defence. He explained the law, saying that the book must be seen as a whole, and for it to be declared obscene, its overall tendency must be to deprave and corrupt those who are likely to read it. Central to the defence case was the assertion that Lawrence was a strong supporter of marriage. It is interesting that, at what is supposed to have been the dawn of the 'permissive age', this sort of justification should have been used. Speaking to the jury, Gardiner said:

You will observe that he [Lawrence] is clearly a very strong supporter of marriage – I mean except in those cases where marriage is obviously perfectly hopeless and for which the law allows divorce. It is quite plain, in my submission, from the whole of this book that the author is pointing out that promiscuity yields no satisfaction to anyone and that the only right relationship is one between two people in love which is intended to be a permanent one.[59]

As has been argued above, many of the debates surrounding permissiveness were centrally focused on the family. Perceived moral decline was seen as hitting at this, the supposed heart, of British society. Thus the prosecution case (and much of the response by the defence) was built around notions of infidelity, adultery and the sanctity of marriage. Bernard Levin even goes as far as to argue that, after a particularly torrid time cross-examining one of the defence witnesses, Mr Griffith-Jones actually gave up attempting to show that the book was obscene, and the trial ceased 'to be a trial of Penguin Books for publishing an obscene work, or even of D.H. Lawrence for writing one. It became instead a case against Constance Chatterley for adultery, and the jury was invited to condemn her for it.'[60] Mr Griffith-Jones attacked the book on these terms, and effectively 'set the agenda' for the trial. That he was able to do so tells us much about the period in which the trial took place.

The defence case rested largely on section 4 of the 1959 Act, and in all, they called 35 witnesses, although this was apparently only half the number that were available. Those who were called included: the Bishop of Woolwich, Richard Hoggart, E.M. Forster, Roy Jenkins MP, Raymond

Williams, Norman St John Stevas and C. Day Lewis.[61] The object of the defence seemed to be to show the standing of Lawrence as an author and his intentions in writing the novel. The prosecution called into question these intentions, suggesting instead that promiscuity and adultery were put on a pedestal by the author. By no means all the witnesses were cross-examined by the prosecution. Nor did the latter produce any witnesses of their own. There was some discussion in the media over the role of counsel, particularly over the part that personal prejudice might play in the final outcome. Bernard Levin wrote the following criticism of Mervyn Griffith-Jones:

> He felt deeply moved, not by the lawyer's indignation assumed for the sake of his brief, but by a perfectly genuine revulsion from what he regarded as an obscene book with no redeeming qualities. This feeling of his – and it is clear that the Judge, with equal sincerity, shared it – stemmed not from wilfulness, but from an inability to see in the book what others of all levels of education could see.[62]

Despite the righteous indignation of Mr Mervyn Griffith-Jones and Mr Justice Byrne the jury, after retiring for three hours, appeared to conclude that wives and servants should not be prevented from reading such a book and returned a verdict of 'not guilty'. Although the trial was over, the debate was not. Press response was generally one of polite approval, although *The Times* seemed less sure that the verdict was the correct one:

> Now that this novel can go into the hands of ... every man, woman, adolescent and child with a jury's blessing, is it possible to be sure it will have no harmful effect on morals? ... Yesterday's verdict is a challenge to society to resist the changes in its manners and conduct that may flow from it. It should not be taken as an invitation to succumb.[63]

The fact that the Bishop of Woolwich had given evidence in the trial to the effect that the book stressed 'the real value and integrity of personal relations' also caused a stir. The Archbishop of Canterbury said the Bishop was 'mistaken to think that he could take part in this trial without becoming a stumbling-block and a cause of offence to many Christians'.[64]

This was still not the end. Many libraries and bookshops decided not to stock or sell the book,[65] and two newspapers, the *Guardian* and the *Observer*, were both censured by the Press Council for printing a four-letter word that had been used in the trial. The overall effect was one of huge publicity for the book, enabling Penguin to sell over four million copies.

Not content with the verdict, Mr Ray Mawby, Conservative MP for Totnes, put down an amendment to the Queen's Speech regretting that the legislative programme contained no proposal to repeal the 1959 Act, 'which has had such dire consequences'[66] and sought to introduce a Private Member's Bill. The verdict was also hotly disputed in the House of Lords, with Lord Teviot and the Earl of Craven criticising, and Lord Hailsham defending.

The old adage, 'you can't please everyone all of the time', certainly applies to the verdict in this case. Responses to it, as has been shown, ranged from the cautiously critical *Times* editorial and the overtly hostile Ray Mawby MP, to those like A.P. Herbert who felt that the verdict was a fine illustration of the intentions of the legislation, the protetion of literature. There are those, however, like Roy Jenkins, who do not fit into either of these categories, in that he felt that the whole prosecution should never have arisen and was breaking an agreement between himself and the Commissioner of Police on the workings of the Act.[67] Mrs Whitehouse on the other hand felt that the result had established 'a major bridgehead for pornographers'.[68] No doubt one of the people who would have fallen within Mrs Whitehouse's definition of a 'pornographer' was Frederick Shaw who was on trial at roughly the same time as *Lady Chatterley*. The result of his case is a good illustration of the complexity of the changes that were taking place.

In 1960, a 28-page booklet was published, most of which contained advertisements for prostitutes, including their addresses and telephone numbers as well as an indication of the types of services they provided. The publisher, Frederick Shaw, openly admitted that the purpose of the booklet was to assist prostitutes to go about their trade since they were no longer permitted to solicit in the street as a result of the Street Offences Act, 1959. The idea of a prostitutes' *Who's Who* was in no sense a new one. The *Ladies' Directory* was described by Robertson as 'a pallid imitation of the *Exact description of the most celebrated Ladies of Pleasure*, published in the eighteenth century'.[69] Nor were these types of advertisement unforeseen. In fact, the Wolfenden Report had argued that prostitutes would ply their trade by advertising in newsagents' windows and the like, and that this was an acceptable price to pay for removing the problem from the streets.[70] Nor had Shaw attempted to hide the purpose of his magazine. He had, in the previous October, taken a copy of it to Scotland Yard and to the Director of Public Prosecutions, asking if it was all right for him to publish. He was told that they were unable to advise him.[71]

In August 1960, he was committed for trial at the Central Criminal Court, charged with:

1 conspiracy to corrupt public morals, in that he conspired with the advertisers and other persons by means of the *Ladies' Directory*, and the advertisements, to debauch and corrupt the morals of youth, and other subjects of the Queen;

2 living on the earnings of prostitution, contrary to section 30 of the Sexual Offences Act, 1956, and;

3 publishing an obscene article contrary to section 2 of the Obscene Publications Act, 1959.

During the trial, prostitutes said that they had paid from 2 to 25 guineas for advertisements and that the latter were an exceptionally good way of bringing clients in.[72] In defence, Mr Anthony Babington said that Shaw 'took a chance. He believed he was keeping inside the law, albeit very narrowly.' He also said that Shaw had decided to discontinue the directory, had sacked his staff, and broken up the photographic blocks.[73]

The jury were out for 90 minutes, but eventually found Shaw guilty on all three counts. Judge Maxwell Turner said to Shaw that:

To indulge in perversions of the type advertised in your directory is a serious matter which of necessity has grave public consequences. It may be, I know not, that you did not realise how grave. But it is clear these directories encouraged both prostitutes and the practices advertised. You were clearly enriching yourself at the expense of public morals.[74]

Shaw was sent to prison for 9 months, but he appealed on the grounds that there was no such offence in common law as the conspiracy that was alleged and that the conspiracy charge was barred by section 2(4) of the Obscene Publications Act, 1959. He also argued that he had not received any of the prostitutes' earnings, simply the profits from the sales of the magazine.[75] Although no reasons were given for its decision, the Court dismissed the appeal, but leave to appeal to the House of Lords was granted on the counts of conspiracy and living on the earnings of prostitution, though not on publishing an obscene article.[76] Again in the Lords it was argued that new offences relating to public morals could not be created by the courts. In the House of Lords, Viscount Simonds stood firm:

I entertain no doubt that there remains in the courts a residual power to enforce the supreme and fundamental purpose of the law, to conserve not only the safety and order, but also the moral welfare of the state, and that it is their duty to guard it against attacks which may be the more insidious because they are novel and unprepared for.... It matters little what label is given to the offending act.... To one of your Lordships it may appear an affront to public decency, to another it will seem a corruption of public morals. Yet others may deem it a public mischief. I now assert that there is a *residual power*, where no statute has yet intervened to supersede the common law, to superintend those offences which are prejudicial to the public welfare.[77] (my emphasis)

This is a particularly important judgement. Within this excerpt from the House of Lords judgement there are a number of phrases, e.g. 'conserve ... safety and order, but also the moral welfare of the state', 'superintend those offences which are prejudicial to the public welfare', which appear to reflect the role of the law as set out by Lord Devlin. There is in this judgement and, perhaps more importantly in the charges brought in the case, no mention of specific harms to individuals, but rather a general threat to the nation's morals. The reason that the courts must have this residual power to enforce morals, it was argued, is so that there will remain a method of dealing with all the 'ways in which the wickedness of men may disrupt society'.[78] The implications of this are not a great deal removed from what Hart described as Devlin's 'disintegration thesis'.

From a legal point of view, the judgement was contentious. One of the judges, Lord Reid, dissented, and in doing so commented 'where Parliament fears to tread, it is not for the courts to rush in'.[79] The major problem with the law of conspiracy is that it is uncertain. That is, one cannot be certain that one is breaking such a law until one is found guilty of having done so. This was certainly the case for Shaw who had attempted to get some advice on the legality of his operation, failed, and was later convicted. When conspiracy law reform was considered by the Law Commission in the early 1970s, it was recommended that all conspiracies to commit acts that were unlawful or immoral, but not criminal, should be abolished. Conspiracy to corrupt public morals is a particularly tricky area for it is based on the assumption that there exists a basic moral consensus in society, just as in Devlin's view of the role of the criminal law in relation to morals. Robertson goes on to suggest:

> ...this assumed moral consensus is further assumed by the conspiracy law to be so vulnerable that a single publication is capable of jeopardising it. It is not illegal to take advantage of a prostitute's services, but to facilitate this, to help short-cut the sordid and sometimes dangerous process of tramping Soho by publishing a prostitute's telephone number, is a serious crime.[80]

As far as the question of the implementation of the law is concerned, particularly in the light of the supposedly 'permissive' social and moral context in which this took place, one is forced to ask why the newly passed Obscene Publications Act 1959 was not used? O'Higgins suggests that 'the answer is probably that it [was] done in order to deprive the accused of the defence to which they would, under the Obscene Publications Act, [have been] entitled'.[81] This was not the only occasion on which the charge 'conspiracy to corrupt public morals' was used, and this general argument is one that will be returned to below.

The debate that ensued in the media and elsewhere following the Shaw case did not centre around the question of Shaw's conviction, but rather on the nature of the case itself. The *Economist* suggested:

The decision in the House of Lords in the case of the *Ladies' Directory* has disturbing implications. No sympathy need be wasted on the convicted Mr Shaw – either on the pseudo-liberal argument that this enterprising scoundrel provided a dubious public service ... or on the irrelevant historical ground that there is a long if unrespectable tradition behind this publication.[82]

Rather the concern was with the novel interpretation of the law that had been used in the case, and with how it would affect serious authors:

An essential principle of English criminal law is that crimes should be closely and narrowly defined. A conspiracy to corrupt public morals is so loosely phrased that it virtually gives the Judges 'carte blanche' to punish whatever at a particular time happens to arouse their moral indignation. If the criminal law is to be just, it is necessary that it be known and certain. Their Lordships have exposed a vast field in which it will be obscure and arbitrary.[83]

The decision provoked widespread and often angry criticism.[84] The criticisms of the law aroused by the Shaw case were compounded by the way in which the next case of importance was brought. Both, in fact, became talking points in the debates over the 1964 Act and the ways in which prosecuting authorities and members of the public were able to utilise certain sections of the law to their advantage.

The next major obscenity trial was the prosecution of John Cleland's *Fanny Hill*, first published in 1749 (although it has been suggested that there were earlier editions).[85] Cleland wrote the book whilst in debtor's prison and used this as an excuse for his work when summoned to appear before the Privy Council, it being, he said, 'the necessity of my present low abject position, that of a writer for bread'[86] and he sold the copyright to a London bookseller for 20 guineas. Hyde suggests that many attempts were made to suppress the book during its long history, and yet it was 215 years before legal proceedings took place. Late in 1963, the police seized copies of the book in London and Manchester, and on 7 November successfully applied 'for process' on the instructions of the Director of Public Prosecutions at Bow Street magistrates' court.[87] This was effectively an injunction against the book pending the outcome of legal proceedings. Consequently, a summons was served on Mr Ralph Gold, a director of G. Gold and Sons, in respect of 171 copies of a paperback edition of the book published by Mayflower Books Ltd at 3s 6d, and seized by the police in

November 1963 from The Magic Shop, Tottenham Court Road. The summons issued under section 3 of the Obscene Publications Act, 1959, called on the booksellers 'to show cause why the articles or any of them should not be forfeited'.

The publishers attempted to persuade the Director of Public Prosecutions to proceed against them, under section 2 of the 1959 Act, as publishers rather than as retailers, which would thus allow them a trial by jury, rather than before a single magistrate. This was refused on the seemingly disingenuous grounds that:

... your clients have acted throughout with a proper sense of responsibility, and took immediate steps on being informed that search warrants were issued to stop any sales to the public, that it was decided that the prosecution would be oppressive in the circumstances.[88]

Mervyn Griffith-Jones once again appeared for the prosecution. He appeared in many of the obscenity trials in the period, as well as the trial of Stephen Ward after the Profumo Affair. Eton and Cambridge educated, a judge later in his career, he was described by the journalist, Ludovic Kennedy, as 'a good-looking man in a chiselled square sort of way. Square is a word that suits him. He is so ultra orthodox that some aspects of modern life seem to have escaped him altogether.'[89] Unlike the *Chatterley* case, however, he was on this occasion successful, the Magistrate, Sir Robert Blundell, taking only two minutes to decide on his verdict.

Rather than the verdict being subject to specific criticism, it was the procedure by which it was reached that came under fire. The decision to prosecute under section 3 rather than under section 2 was widely criticised on the grounds that it denied the defendant the right to a trial by jury. It was felt that in a case involving a decision on the balance between 'obscenity' and 'public good' 'the unanimous view of twelve ordinary citizens is to be preferred to the decision of a single judge or magistrate'.[90] Furthermore, forfeiture under section 3 is also inconclusive in that it only applies to such copies of a book as are actually seized. Perhaps the most influential critic of the proceedings was Roy Jenkins who had been a principal driving force behind the 1959 Obscene Publications Act, and who now suggested that a simple decision by the Director of Public Prosecutions or the Attorney-General (to prosecute under section 2) would have allowed for a continuous trial in suitable surroundings. However, the result was 'an unsatisfactory trial, in an inappropriate court, with an inconclusive verdict'.[91]

The only way to resolve this problem in the future was, he said, for the Attorney-General to announce that, whenever the defence of literary merit was to be raised, he would allow a trial by judge and jury. In fact, during a debate on the Obscene Publications Bill 1964, Roy Jenkins moved an amendment encapsulating this very idea. An assurance to this end was given by the Solicitor-General, Sir Peter Rawlinson, on behalf of the Attorney-General, and the amendment was promptly withdrawn. Robertson suggests that both sides of the House understood the assurance to mean that the right to a trial by jury was ensured,[92] and confidence was expressed 'that any Government of the day will honour it'.[93] However, it would seem that the assurance has in later years not been honoured.[94] Mr Jenkins was himself criticised in the press for failing to foresee the obvious. R.A. Cline writing in the *Spectator*, suggested that it was not an 'abuse of power' that was being witnessed, simply the workings of poor legislation, for 'if a statute gives a choice to a prosecution, the prosecution has a duty to choose the procedure most likely to succeed'.[95] The *Sunday Times* pointed out that the Director of Public Prosecutions could have ignored the Obscene Publications Act altogether by invoking the common law offence of conspiracy to corrupt public morals as had been used in the Shaw case.[96] Although this option was not taken up, it would seem that the preference for section 3 of the 1959 Act involved the same type of strategy as recourse to the common law.[97]

There were those who defended the prosecution, though, and defended it vigorously. Peregrine Worsthorne argued that the *Fanny Hill* prosecution (and other similar cases) was important because the Church was a declining moral force in modern Britain which therefore placed greater responsibility for the nation's moral welfare on the state:

> That is why such cases as the *Fanny Hill* prosecution are so important, too important perhaps to be left to juries who may be unduly influenced by the dazzlingly superficial comments of the literary mandarins. For it is the decisions taken in cases such as this that now reflect society's attitude to sex much more effectively than do the rulings of Convocation or the precepts of the pulpit.[98]

He backs up this argument with two further comments on then contemporary morality:

> I cannot see how authorisation of the cheap circulation of such a book could fail to mark a profoundly different attitude to sex than has hitherto been regarded as compatible with the kind of society which Western civilization has evolved.[99]

and:

> ... it would surely be odd for a society pledged to monogamous marriage to allow any citizen with a few shillings in his pocket to buy *Fanny Hill*.[100]

Worsthorne's argument here is similar to the now famous statement made by Griffith-Jones in the *Lady Chatterley's Lover* case where he asked the jury if it was the sort of book they would like their wives or servants to read. The implication of Worsthorne's statement is that those who might afford hardback copies of the book would be less likely to be depraved and corrupted by reading it than the ordinary citizen.

Although the new legislation had only been in force for just over four years, some of the legal decisions that had been made in that time had given rise to concern over the workings of the 1959 Act. The strains between the mix of regulatory and liberal positions and views that eventually became embodied in that legislation were, seemingly, a root cause of the practical problems involved in enforcing the law in this area. Indeed, in introducing the debate over the 1964 Bill, the Under-Secretary of State for the Home Office suggested that this was one of the main reasons that the government was introducing new provisions:

> Deriving as it did from a series of compromises and in a number of cases from the introduction of amendments drafted with different, even conflicting purposes in the minds of the Hon. Members who put them forward it is not surprising that the Act has shown some imperfections in practice.[101]

There were, however, considerable disagreements during the debate over just what these imperfections were. Sir Cyril Black seemed to think that the Act was, firstly, not strong enough to deal with the widespread evil of pornography, and secondly, that the defence of public good was also having deleterious effects by letting pornography pass as serious literature:

> I hope that in Committee there will be an opportunity for a full consideration of Section 4 of the 1959 Act. I hope that the Section will either be repealed, or, if a case can be made out for it not being repealed 'in toto', that it will, at any rate, be amended to remove some of the evil that it has done.[102]

Mr Niall MacDermot, in his speech, suggested in fact that the problem with the Act was to all intents and purposes the other way around.

> The responsible book trade has been very distressed recently by the nature of the proceedings in the case of *Fanny Hill*. I do not think that anyone contemplated when the 1959 Act was going through the House, that a test case for a work with serious literary pretensions would arise by way of forfeiture proceedings.[103]

Many MPs noted that they had been completely unaware that obscene publications were giving rise to any concern at all in Parliament until the government introduced the Bill.

Looking at the Bill itself, there can be no doubt as to the intentions of the legislation. It was not to further the protection afforded to 'serious literature' but, rather, to increase powers to suppress 'pornography'. The preamble makes this quite clear, describing it as an 'Act to strengthen the law for preventing the publication for gain of obscene matter and the publication of things intended for the production of obscene matter'.

Thus, in the middle of the period that is usually referred to as the 'permissive age', a Bill backed by the government of the day was passed which was designed to strengthen, not relax, the law with regard to the censorship of written or pictorial material. The Bill became law without any due fuss or publicity, and it would seem from a reading of the debates that the question of obscenity was not at the forefront of the public imagination at the time:

> Anyone would gather from the introduction of the Bill that pornography was really a vastly important subject and that it was a major social evil. We have only to look around us for a moment to see that it is not. There are a great many other things which are far more important. One obvious thing is the gang warfare between Mods and Rockers at seaside resorts. It would surely be far better for the Mods and Rockers, and for the community at large if instead of breaking up Clacton and places like that, they all stay at home and read a little light pornography.[104]

In the intervening period, there had been two minor but still newsworthy trials, one in Sheffield and one in Blackburn. The trial in Sheffield was of Alexander Trocchi's *Cain's Book*, published by John Calder. The book was seized along with a considerable number of others in a police raid on a bookshop. After a short trial, the book was declared obscene under section 3 of the 1959 Act and all copies in the area were confiscated and destroyed. The verdict is of no great significance, but the target is. John Sutherland argues:

> It marked a new phase of obscenity-hunting in which the primary target would not be the work's text (for instance its incidence of four-letter words) but the *lifestyle* it advocated, or that was associated with its author or even its readership. If it was risking obscenity to be a junkie and a beat (the lifestyle associated with *Cain's Book*), it was soon going to be similarly risky to be a hippy.[105]

The second trial centred around a pamphlet called *The Golden Convulvulus* and described as an 'anthology of eroticism'. Two hundred copies were run off by David Cunliffe, the publisher of a small-time poetry magazine, *Poetmeat*. The pamphlet was intercepted by the GPO, and charges were brought under the Post Office Act, 1953 and the Obscene Publications Acts.

Proceedings were held in Blackburn and, after a four day trial, the jury returned a verdict of not guilty of obscenity, but guilty of sending an indecent article through the post. Cunliffe was fined £50. Referring to the *Golden Convulvulus* trial, Ray Gosling asked why

> the DPP took charge and prosecuted. Why? Was he worried about the growth of little magazines? Did he think this case, miles from London, away from the literary limelight would give him a chance to prove a point; make a legal precedent?[106]

Sutherland suggested that the answer to all these questions was 'yes'. Just as with the *Cain's Book* case, it was not the verdict but other aspects of the case that, he argued, were historically most important. If the attack on *Cain's Book* was the beginning of specific attacks on lifestyle, then that on *The Golden Convulvulus* was the first action against the 'underground' and the lifestyle associated with it.

As has been noted, most prosecutions for 'obscenity' come about after a police raid on a bookshop. The next major prosecution, however, that of *Last Exit to Brooklyn*, took a rather different path. Calder and Boyars published the book on 24 January 1966, and, as is usual, issued pre-publication copies, one of which was sent to the Director of Public Prosecutions whose reply to Calder and Boyars was described in the Appeal Court as 'inconclusive', and, in which he said 'if you find – as I am afraid you will – that this is a most unhelpful letter, it is not because I wish to be unhelpful but because I get no help from the Acts'.[107] Sir Charles Taylor, Conservative MP for Eastbourne, was, however, more direct. He brought the publication of the book to the notice of Parliament. He described the book as 'filthy and disgusting', and went on to say that 'it is too frightful for words and, for that reason, I will not quote from it tonight, for I would not wish to embarrass the people in the galleries, or anyone else'.[108] After this, Sir Elwyn Jones, the Attorney-General, referred the book to the Director of Public Prosecutions, who advised against instituting proceedings. Not to be put off, however, the Conservative MP, Sir Cyril Black, inquired about the possibility of private proceedings against the book. He received a positive response and, on Thursday 28 July, he applied at Bow Street Magistrate's Court for a summons under the Obscene Publications Act for seizure of *Last Exit to Brooklyn*. On 4 August, Sir Robert Blundell issued a search warrant for seizure of the book from any shop in the Bow Street area. The police, however, were unable to find a copy and Sir Cyril turned his attention to the area in which the publishers' offices were situated. He successfully applied for a search warrant from Great Marlborough Magistrates Court and copies of the book were promptly seized. On 12 September, Marion Boyars was served with a summons to appear at that Court on 27 October 'to show cause why the said articles or any of them seized should not be forfeited by virtue of the Obscene Publications Act of 1959, Section 3'.

There were, at the hearing, expert witnesses for the defence,[109] and unprecedentedly, for the prosecution.[110] The choice of, and stands taken by, some of the witnesses seemed to confuse many people who attended the hearing, for two of the prosecution witnesses in the *Last Exit* case had been defence witnesses in the *Fanny Hill* case, and two defence witnesses for *Last Exit* testified that they felt *Fanny Hill* was pornographic.[111] On 10 December, Mr Leo Gradwell, the magistrate, ordered the forfeiture and destruction of the book. However, because the case had been brought under section 3 of the Obscene Publications Act, the decision was only binding in the district in which the Court was situated. The publishers, therefore, informed the DPP that they were going to continue to publish the book, and the Director then reversed his original decision not to prosecute and decided to institute criminal proceedings (section 2), entitling the defendants to a trial by jury and a defence under section 4.

The case began at the Old Bailey on 13 November 1967. By this time, the costs of defending the book were mounting up, which forced Marion Boyars and John Calder to appeal for public help, leading indirectly to the formation of the 'Defence of Literature and the Arts Society' out of the Free Art Legal Fund. Its aim was simply the defence of *Last Exit* but it continued to exist long after that particular case and supported many similar causes.

The jury were sent out on the first afternoon to read the book. John Calder, writing in the *New Statesman*,[112] estimated that a good reader might get through the book in four hours, but that the average serious reader would need six or seven. When the judge called the jury back two hours later to ask how long they would need, some claimed to have already finished, whilst one commented, 'you'd need an interpreter to read this'.[113] The publisher was a little worried that the book would not receive a fair hearing, and wrote to *The Times* on the subject:

> In the new climate in which publisher and writers now find themselves, where highly complex literary concepts will be argued out in criminal courts, it is essential that the framers of the Obscene Publications Act should bring in a new provision that enables juries to be selected from those who have at least A-levels in their education and who can show to the satisfaction of the court that they are capable of reading and understanding the book they have to judge.[114]

The trial came to an end on 23 November with a verdict of 'guilty'.

Despite all the added costs, Calder and Boyars decided to appeal. They based their case on eleven points of law, and as it was to turn out, two of them were enough to ensure success. Firstly, the defence case in the original trial had been based on the argument that the horrific and frightening scenes that were portrayed in the book would, rather than encourage or incite people to commit those acts, have precisely the opposite effect, i.e. one of aversion. The judge's failure to put this defence to the jury, as well as the lack of guidance in his summing-up over the defence contained in section 4 of the 1959 Act, were the reasons that the verdict was overturned.

As has already been mentioned, one of the most contentious aspects of the case was the confusing way in which it was brought, and such were the problems caused that the government decided to put to an end the public's right to bring prosecution in this way. They did so via section 25 of the Criminal Justice Act 1967 which states:

> A Justice of the Peace shall not issue a warrant under Section 3(1) of the Obscene Publications Act 1959 (search for and seizure of obscene articles) except on an information laid by or on behalf of the Director of Public Prosecutions or by a constable.

Last Exit was, then, in the end, able to circulate freely. So was this another victory for permissiveness? If so, it was only, as Mary Whitehouse points out, a victory by default:

> the Court of Appeal did not find, as has been so often suggested, that *Last Exit* was not obscene, neither did it find as defence witnesses had claimed that its publication was 'for the public good'. It decided, in fact that the Old Bailey Judge, Judge Rodgers, who had heard the case, had not properly directed the jury, and so the appeal was upheld. This was the last word, legally, on a squalidly obscene, non-literary book.[115]

After the *Last Exit* case, pressure for reform of the law restarted, coming from a somewhat unexpected source. In June 1968, Lord Goodman, the then Chairman of the Arts Council of Great Britain, convened a conference whose task was to consider the 1959 and 1964 Acts. Twenty-two organisations and well over one hundred individuals were invited, of whom ninety, representing between them twenty-one organisations, finally attended. The conference resolved:

> ... that a Working Party be set up to investigate the working of the Obscene Publications Acts of 1959 and 1964, and other relevant Acts, with special reference to literature, drama and the visual arts, and to consider such changes including the repeal of any such Acts as in their opinion shall be expedient and to report back to this Conference with such recommendations as they deem necessary.[116]

The Working Party was chaired by John Montgomery and, in all, consisted of nineteen members.[117] Because the whole venture had come about through pressure from the National Council for Civil Liberties, it is not surprising that the Working Party had a fairly 'liberal' hue. Indeed, two of the members (John Calder and Frederick Warburg) had previously been on the receiving end of prosecutions for obscenity, one, John Mortimer QC, was to act as defence counsel in several cases, and others had acted as witnesses for the defence to testify as to the merits of certain publications against which obscenity charges had been brought. When the Working Party first met, they divided into two committees and arranged for various individuals and organisations to submit evidence. However, in doing so, it would seem they failed, in the eyes of some, to invite a sufficiently broad range of groups to represent public opinion and thus caused others to stay away. Mrs Whitehouse suggested that, although she had at first accepted the invitation to attend, she later changed her mind when she received details of the conference and of those who would be attending and realised that it was, in her words, likely to be 'loaded':

> It was interesting to see that the BBC was invited, but not the ITA; the National Council for Civil Liberties but not the police; the Albany Trust but not the BMA, who I understand were not invited to give evidence either. There was no representation of women's organizations, the Church – though the Rev. David Shepherd gave evidence to the Working Party – of magistrates, and very little of the teaching profession.[118]

The Report based itself upon a critique of the obscenity laws as they stood, pointing out the vagaries of the legislation and the lack of uniformity in its implementation. It pointed out that the existing laws constituted a threat to the freedoms of the private individual, and yet failed to provide any serious benefit for the public. They suggested that the problems encountered with the law stemmed from the inherent subjectivity of a concept like obscenity, and that, because of this, any plans to formulate a definition were doomed from the start. The Report therefore recommended that the Obscene Publications Acts of both 1959 and 1964 should be repealed on a trial basis for not less than five years, and not even then unless Parliament should decide otherwise. It also recommended that the Theatres Acts, 1968, should be brought into line with these recommendations. The Report went on:

> It [the Working Party] also recommends that certain other relevant Acts should be amended or repealed. Many of these have been or could be used as a basis for indirect censorship and contain words such as 'indecent' and 'profane' which are no more capable of definition than 'obscene' but which may be used to circumvent any need to establish harmful consequences.[119]

We recognise, however, that it is reasonable to protect individuals who may be affronted by offensive displays or behaviour in public places. There are various Acts dealing with this, for which we would substitute a single section so that there should be no overlapping.

We would not seek to interfere with the existing arrangements under which the British Board of Film Censors classifies films into various categories. Television is not in practice affected by the Obscenity Acts, and we are content that the BBC and ITA should be left to conduct their programmes on their own responsibility, with such regard as they see fit to pay to ascertainable public opinion.[120]

To this end, the Working Party set out a draft Bill in the appendices to the Report. As can be seen, the Society of Authors adopted (in contrast to the Longford group and the Society of Conservative Lawyers which followed) an essentially utilitarian approach to the role of law. The standard test of obscenity and any alternatives that the Committee thought possible were rejected on two basic grounds, both of which distinguish this approach from one which might be followed by those influenced by Lord Devlin. On the one hand, it was argued that the Obscene Publications Act 1959 'was unable to overcome the hard basic fact that no two people can be counted upon to agree what is or what is not obscene'.[121] They decisively rejected, therefore, any notion of a commonly held set of moral values or an implied moral consensus. On the other hand, the committee argued that

> it is not for the state to prohibit private citizens from choosing what they may or may not enjoy in literature or art unless there were in-controvertible evidence that the result would be injurious to society. There is no such evidence.[122]

This argument is derived from the earlier point. For if it is not to be argued that there is a commonly accepted set of moral rules in society, then it is not possible for society to be equated with its morality. Thus an article which is potentially offensive to some cannot be argued to be injurious to all. Obscenity becomes something which is merely in the eye of the beholder, and thus all that is necessary is legal protection against enforced encounters with such obscene articles. The Report stated:

> We recognize, however, that it is reasonable to protect individuals who may be affronted by offensive displays or behaviour in public places. There are various Acts dealing with this and we would substitute a single section so that there should be no overlapping.[123]

By the time it was published, the 1960s were drawing to a close and, for some, the implementation of the Working Party's Report would have been the final straw in what they considered to be the decade of 'permissiveness'. Responses to the Report were, on the whole, unfavourable. Mrs Whitehouse, in response to letters to *The Times* and the *Guardian*[124] from John Calder, Benn Levy and Jean Straker pointing out what they considered to be the importance of the Report, publicly condemned its findings as biased. Of the national newspapers, only the *Guardian* saw its way to favour parts of the Report, in suggesting as Marx had done, 'that true censorship ... is criticism'.[125] The others were of almost one accord, the *Daily Telegraph* saying:

> One of the really astounding things about the small group of essentially metropolitan people who have set themselves up to be our guides in matters of taste in art, is their parochialism. The Report of the Arts Council demonstrated that the party should have worked – and thought – rather harder.[126]

Two days later, the *Daily Telegraph*, using an argument more generally associated with Pamela Hansford Johnson, reinforced its previous position by suggesting:

> The Moors murderers read de Sade. They also committed the Moors murders. No link between these two facts, Mr Mortimer may cry: the Moors murderers were like that anyway and would have done what they did, even if their favourite reading had been *Silas Marner* or *The Pilgrim's Progress*. How can Mr Mortimer and his like be so sure? And what crimes will be on their consciences if they are wrong?[127]

The Times also came down on this side, feeling that public opinion was not ready for such a change:

> There will probably never be a truly satisfactory law on obscenity. Its application will always depend to some extent upon subjective judgement, and therefore upon prevailing fashions of thought. The British public still value their own sexual privacy, and do not want it to be invaded by pornographers or exhibitionists. Madison Avenue sex is odious enough as it is, without allowing the commercial vendor of exhibitions unlimited freedom.[128]

This notion of 'it's not a very good law, but it's the best we've got', was reiterated in *The People* (despite the fact that in the very same article,[129] they referred to Mrs Whitehouse as an 'interfering, intolerant busybody') in a way only such newspapers can: '[t]he law in this case may be a bit of an ass. But the animal serves a good purpose'.[130]

The Report also had a rather rough ride during its debate in Parliament. From the Conservative side of the House, criticism came first and foremost from Sir Gerald Nabarro, a staunch supporter of 'traditional values' and an anti-pornography campaigner who described the Report as 'revolting'[131] and went on, 'it is a further slide in the disgusting mire of permissiveness, squalor and pornographic filth of recent years'.[132] Not only did he argue in the House against the Report, but he also campaigned in the country and managed to get a motion rejecting the proposals onto the books in the Commons.[133] However, if he expected much opposition in Parliament, particularly from the government, then he had seemingly misjudged the situation. Roy Jenkins (who, given his involvement in the development of the original supposedly liberal obscenity laws, might have been expected to be favourable to the Arts Council's proposals) had left the Home Office to be replaced by James Callaghan, who, as the *Sunday Times* reported,[134] 'had no intention of becoming known as the Pornographer Royal'. In his speech in the Commons during the debate over the proposals, Mr Callaghan used the same line of argument as the one used by *The Times*:

> I shall study the Working Party report with care but my present view is that although there may be defects in the existing law, I shall need a great deal of convincing that repeal of the obscenity laws would be preferable, and I can see no prospect of the time being made available for this purpose.[135]

There can be no doubt that, whatever changes had taken place during the previous decade, the response to the proposals of the Arts Council Working Party on the obscenity law was a thorough victory for those concerned with maintaining the status quo. It was, moreover, to a certain extent the prelude to what Mary Whitehouse has referred to as a 'backlash'[136].

This brings the 1960s to a conclusion. What had occurred in relation to the law of obscenity and its implementation were a series of changes that were not uniformly in one direction, i.e. simply permissive. Indeed, the changes embodied in the main pieces of legislation of the period, the Obscene Publications Acts of 1959 and 1964, had dual tendencies, or what Hall (1979) refers to as a 'double taxonomy', on the one hand liberalising controls over literature, whilst at the same time extending the powers to control the pornography trade. Although, as has been shown, the most famous obscenity trial of them all ended in a victory for the 'libertarians', it would be overly simplistic to present this as merely a turning point in the implementation of obscenity laws. The written word was still by no means safe as the *Ladies' Directory* and *Fanny Hill* found to their cost. Furthermore, the early years of the 1970s saw a concerted attack upon the underground press and, as Sutherland (1982) argues, the lifestyle (including perceived moral values, or lack of them) that went with it.

5 Obscenity and the law
Backlash?

If Mrs Whitehouse is to be believed, the 1970s marked the return of controls to stem the tide of permissiveness that had allegedly gushed forward without check during the 1960s. This chapter examines the usage of the obscenity laws, and the debates over censorship, in the early years of the 1970s when that 'backlash' was supposed to have occurred. Much of the period was dominated by the crusade against pornography masterminded by the other famous moral entrepreneur of the time, Lord Longford.

Despite holding a number of public offices as well as having a successful career in the private sector, Longford's public 'notoriety' began around 1970 when he went to see the play *Oh Calcutta!* Before that, he says,[1] he gave debates on obscenity a wide berth. He was so shocked by *Oh Calcutta!*, however, that he left half-way through and, in April 1971, initiated a debate on pornography in the House of Lords. The issue of pornography, which was to dominate the next few years of his life, appeared to push his other interests and accomplishments into the background for some time. So much so that, at one time, he became known as 'Lord Porn'.

He has for many (along with Mrs Whitehouse) been the leader of the fight against 'permissiveness', against what was seen as a relaxation in the standards of sexual morality. In a newspaper interview in 1972, he explained his point of view. Replying to the question 'did he think that by comparison with other historical periods, we live in a permissive society today?', he answered:

> When people talk about the permissive society, they are usually talking about sex. But if you take a slightly wider view of the permissive society, which is that it does include a more humane attitude to people who go wrong, well, then I would favour it.... But if you just mean a society that is more indulgent in matters of sex, then I am entirely against it.[2]

Why, then, was he entirely against it?

> I start from a Christian point of view, which is that sex outside marriage
> is wrong ... on the whole public opinion today is still opposed to people
> who break the ordinary Christian laws of sex.[3]

Longford's general position starts from a point similar to that taken up by
the NVALA, the NFoL and others. He favours monogamous heterosexual
relationships, placing great emphasis on the importance of marriage. All
other forms of sexual relationship – male homosexuality and lesbianism,
and sex outside marriage – are seen as sinful. There is, he argues, a set of
rules ('Christian laws') which may be applied to all sexual conduct, irrespective of the context. By defining what is legitimate in this way, Lord
Longford became engaged in what Watney has referred to as the 'ideological rearguard in defence of the family',[4] and he was thus linked to the
campaigns of other moral entrepreneurial groups. Armed with this view of
sexual relations and having been shocked by a play, almost overnight he
became the 'Anti-Pornographer Royal'.[5]

Longford initiated a debate on pornography in the House of Lords on 21
April 1971. Within a month, he had not only decided to form a private
commission to enquire into the problem, but had even assembled over
forty-five people keen to help. Those invited by Longford to join were a
mixed crew, varying from the Archbishop of York to the entertainer and
female impersonator, Danny La Rue (the latter didn't accept). Of those who
made the final line-up, half may be found in the 1972 edition of *Who's Who*,
and this excludes those such as the pop star, Cliff Richard, and the disc-
jockey, Jimmy Savile. The commission included six Lords, two Knights,
one Baroness, one Archbishop, three Bishops, three professors, two QCs
and one Canon! Other well-knowns included Kingsley Amis and David
Holbrook, the novelists, Malcolm Muggeridge, the broadcaster and
Peregrine Worsthorne, the journalist. The commission's terms of reference
were 'to see what means of tackling the problem of pornography would
command general support'. From the beginning, Longford received criticism for inviting people who would be sympathetic to his views on the
subject rather than a cross-section representing all the different positions.
In presumably seeking to pre-empt these types of criticism, in the introduction to the *Report*, Lord Longford inadvertently fuelled the fire:

> We were anxious to provide, and have in fact provided, maximum
> freedom of discussion. The only commitment involved would appear to
> be a recognition that pornography does indeed represent a problem and
> one which is worth looking into seriously.... It would not be true to
> assume that all those who took part in our Inquiry agreed with my House

of Lords propositions that pornography was a manifest evil, *though anyone who thought I was completely on the wrong tack would hardly have agreed to serve under my chairmanship.*[6] (my emphasis)

Having organised a private commission to investigate 'the problem of pornography', and having received considerable sponsorship for the 'crusade', Lord Longford had to get cracking on the investigation proper. The debate surrounding pornography (then and now) revolved around the question of whether one can demonstrate a link, or a correlation, between the level of indulgence in, or consumption of, pornography, and the number of criminal offences committed that are sexually related. Methodologically, this is always going to be very tricky, if not nigh on impossible, and was therefore bound to be a bone of contention. As was his usual way, Longford met it head on with the suggestion of a visit to what was regarded at the time as the 'classic example': Denmark:

> It was obvious from the first that some of us would have to visit Denmark. The Arts Council Working Party and other libertarians had made such play with the alleged decline of sex offences in Denmark since the obscenity law was liberalised. There was only one way to counter the propaganda – to go and see for ourselves. Through the good offices of the Danish Embassy in London a series of discussions were arranged with among others government officials, leaders of the police, and the sociologist, Professor Kutchinsky, whose researches were being widely quoted by the libertarian school. Visits were also arranged to pornographic films and (with some difficulty – the Danish Government did not want to be involved) to so-called live-shows.[7]

Not everyone felt it was such a good idea. Gyles Brandreth, one of the team, described it as a 'travelling circus', and Dennis Hackett called it: 'Lord Longford's asinine tour, with his well-motivated voyeurs'.[8]

Longford took five others with him, one of whom, the above mentioned Gyles Brandreth, had several disagreements with Longford during the trip. The trip to Denmark received massive publicity. Much time was spent talking with officials, political, legal and academic, but it was the Longford party's tour of the nightspots that made the news. In their evenings in Denmark, they split up into groups and went to bookshops, film shows and 'live' shows. Lord Longford, much to the amusement of the press and to the chagrin of the proprietors, walked out of two shows. He describes both scenes in the following manner:

> There are occasions in life when there are no hesitations about actions at the time and none afterwards. This was such a one. I was moving out of the room before anyone quite knew I was going. A small plump man,

some form of manager no doubt, expostulated with restraining hands misunderstanding my grievance. 'But you haven't seen any intercourse yet – I assure you it's coming', he moaned plaintively. I was too upset to show him a reasonable civility.[9]

and secondly

Now the lady was on my neighbour's lap, caressing him indescribably, amidst mounting response from the audience. The cameras were all too obviously getting ready for her next move. But my next move was still more obvious to me. At the moment as seen through the eyes of one of the many newspapers that depicted the scene, I was sitting there like a stage professor in a house of ill-fame. The next my seat was empty.[10]

He gave three reasons for leaving the 'live' shows, although previously he had managed to sit all the way through 'blue films'. Firstly, because (although, he admits, so, too, were the films) 'they were utterly horrible, pornographic and unfit to be allowed in any well conducted city'. Secondly, because the required audience participation was unforeseen by himself, and lastly, a feeling of 'self-preservation' was added to deep abhorrence – that in some sense, he felt in some personal 'danger'.

All these reasons may, of course, be genuine, but Gyles Brandreth had a different interpretation of the situation. He believed that Longford used the situation very carefully, and that it was his intention that everyone should believe that he left because he couldn't stomach the scenes he was being forced to view:

I, on the other hand, think that the gartered Earl is a bit sharper than that. At the show he was attending, naked ladies mingled with the tiny audience, offering to sit in their laps and play with their persons. Lord Longford allowed a whip to be foisted on him. Imagine what might have happened had a young lady landed in his lap! Click, flash and hey presto, around the world in eighty seconds go stunning photographs of the sixty-five-year-old English Milord with a Danish dolly in the raw giving him a friendly fumble. Gerald Scarfe did powerful things with that whip sequence. Think what he might have been able to do had Lord Porn had hotter stuff to handle.[11]

The responses to the trip by those who went were mixed as to its value and, indeed, public response was broadly similar. Much of the national press was sceptical about the trip, and much of the published criticism came from the pen of Gyles Brandreth. The much-maligned excursion received support in the pages of the *Sunday Times* from the literary critic and campaigner against pornography, David Holbrook, who, writing of Longford at the time, said:

> I still think he's an excellent fellow. It was right to go and see the pornography in Denmark, and to advertise it by a shocked reaction. To my mind, that kind of stuff is madness, total madness. We've got to realise that, even if it means we display a mad reaction to it. I mean – it is necessary for us to stop being urbane and calm about pornography. We've got to vomit in response – then we can begin improving the situation.[12]

Holbrook here seems to be displaying the emotions that Devlin suggested would be the necessary basis for using the criminal law to enforce morals – i.e. intolerance, indignation and disgust. The honourable Lord also found support from the *British Medical Journal*[13] and from the editor of the *Daily Telegraph*.[14]

The *Report* was published on 21 September 1972, and dominated the media for a good time afterwards. To say that it caused a fair amount of debate is to put it at its mildest. It was published as a paperback by Coronet Books, and was on sale to the general public for 60 pence. The word 'pornography' was printed in large red letters on the front, and underneath in much smaller grey letters was printed, 'The Longford Report'. It is about 500 pages long and is divided into four sections: firstly, Pornography Today (an outline of the situation by the committee); secondly, contributions from individual members; thirdly, Reports and sub-committees (there were eight of these); and finally, conclusions and recommendations.

The main suggestion of the *Report* was that the Obscene Publications Act, 1959, should be amended in several areas, including the definition of 'obscenity'. The *Report* also includes a draft of a proposed new Bill. It recommends, firstly, that an article or the performance of a play would be obscene 'if its effect taken as a whole, is to outrage contemporary standards of decency or humanity accepted by the public at large'; secondly, that the existing defence of obscenity in terms of being in the 'public good' should cease; thirdly, that the Act should be extended to cover cinema and television broadcasting; and fourthly, that the penalties for publishing obscene material should be increased. The Bill would also make it illegal to display in a street or other public place 'any written, pictorial or other material which was held to be indecent'.[15]

The parallel between the proposed new definition of obscenity, 'to outrage contemporary standards of decency or humanity accepted by the public at large', and the essence of Lord Devlin's theorisation of the relationship between law and morality should be immediately apparent. In common with Devlin, and with the proposals of the Society of Conservative Lawyers considered below, this definition assumes a moral consensus. Indecency or obscenity is seen as an absolute, not as something which is likely to be variably defined. It would be something, it is argued in the *Report*, that a jury would be able to establish objectively, as they would be randomly chosen members of a society which had agreed-upon moral standards. The implications of using such a definition in a society in which the assumed moral consensus does not exist were brought out by Dworkin:

> that means that an obscenity trial will be a lottery, all over bar the shouting once the jury is picked. Prosecution and defence will be desperate to have the jurymen chosen who give conventional signs, at least, of the right morality: it will be a case of trial by sensible shoes and short hair, or mini-skirts and tie-dyed jeans.[16]

The abolition of the 'defence of public good' is also consistent with a 'seamless web' conception of morality. Thus anything which sufficiently outrages contemporary standards is, by implication, a threat to society's well-being, and thus not to be protected because it may have some redeeming social, artistic or cultural value. That is to say, the defence of public good allows for the obscene qualities of an article to be mitigated by other qualities that it may possess.

The Longford Report not only recommended a narrowing of the law in these ways, but also two additional offences. The first would punish the public display of 'indecent material', though it did not define what was meant by 'indecent'. It also recommended that a new offence should be created to 'punish those who, for purposes of gain, induce others to take part in any obscene or indecent performance to be shown to the public, or as models for any photographs or films of a similar kind produced for a like purpose'.[17] Taken on their own, these two recommendations are closer to Hart's than Devlin's formulation (although the concept of indecency would probably be rather wide), but in conjunction with the other recommendations, they formed part of an attempt to extend rather than narrow the ambit of the law.

Following the main proposals and recommendations, were the reports of the various sub-committees which also figured very largely in the ensuing debates. The broadcasting sub-committee, chaired by Malcolm Muggeridge, caused the biggest uproar and there is, in fact, a rejoinder by Frank Gillard, a former Director of Sound Broadcasting at the BBC, immediately after the chapter. Many television programmes and cinema films came in for severe criticism from Muggeridge *et al.*[18] First of all, the IBA:

It seems fair to say that the programmes shown are, for the most part, vulgar rather than vicious, smutty rather than specifically pornographic, infantile rather than pernicious. It would be difficult to think of any form of human entertainment more intrinsically fatuous and demeaning than give-away programmes like 'Double Your Money', an ostensibly 'religious' programme like 'Stars on Sunday' or that weary old biographical number, 'This is your Life'.[19]

and the BBC:

It is ironical now to recall that the strongest argument used against the introduction of commercial television was that it would sully and vulgarise a screen that the BBC had maintained in purity and at a high cultural level since its inception.... Today the most ardent champion of the BBC and opponent of commercial television would ... hesitate to take up this position in the light of programmes like 'Steptoe and Son' and 'Up Pompeii' which, whatever merits they may have, are full of smut, vulgarity and double meaning rapturously received by the studio audience.[20]

These two quotations, although they are more specific in their attack than the rest of chapter, probably adequately reflect the broadcasting subcommittee's consistently castigating tones. The breadth of Muggeridge's attack on television gives some clue to the real nature of what was being attacked. In the first paragraph of the sub-committee's report, we are told what the 'problem' is: 'it would seem to be abundantly clear that, in abandoning what is today fashionably described as 'traditional morality', our society ... is set upon a Gadarene course towards self-destruction'.[21]

The question Muggeridge sought an answer to is that of the extent to which broadcasting had contributed to this moral decline? The sub-committee attacked the 'give-away' programmes, advertising and consumerism, the secular nature of most broadcast material, nudity and so on. They explicitly criticised 'modern' values and argued that if the BBC had maintained its earlier Reithian values broadcast material would be considerably more acceptable. The essence of the problem for the sub-committee was what they perceived to be a lack of attachment in modern society to traditional Christian morals, and, as an example of this lack of attachment, the policies of those with authority in the BBC:

The truth is that, apart from the Christian ethic, our way of life has no moral basis whatsoever, and since, at any rate among the great majority of communicators, Christianity is no longer acceptable, they are in practice operating in a moral vacuum.[22]

This broad attack on modern culture and on what, conceptualised socio-
logically, was perceived as a state of anomie, pervades the whole report.
The sub-committee reporting on cinema and the theatre singled out *The
Devils, Straw Dogs* and *A Clockwork Orange* as three films which provoked
a considerable amount of disquiet amongst the cinema-going public. Their
main recommendations were that performers should receive protection
against the possibilities of exploitation, and that the British Board of Film
Censors should no longer be responsible solely to the industry. This would
be changed with the appointment of the President and Secretary by the Home
Secretary, and with the inclusion of representatives from industry and the
local authorities, as well as 'suitable' members of the public. As for the
theatre, *Hair, Oh Calcutta!* and *The Dirtiest Show in Town* were cited as
deliberately challenging accepted standards, and the recommendations
concerning performers in films were also to apply to the stage.

The next section of the *Report* deals with books, magazines and newspapers. The section on books largely covers the proposed revisions to the
Obscene Publications Act. The section on magazines goes into great detail
about the types of magazines, the size of circulation, etc. One brand they
identify are the 'small format, largely textual presentation ... based on
"scientific" exposure of sexual problems, mostly in the shape of correspondence columns'.[23] Referring to the leading publication of this genre, *Forum*,
they say: 'However sincerely conceived as a beneficial service to those
with problems or inadequate sexual knowledge [it] cannot avoid appealing
also – we would suggest, largely – to those whose interest is salacious,
prurient or fantasist.'[24]

Two other magazines modelled on *Forum* were produced by Goldstar
Publications, namely *In Depth* and *New Direction*. Goldstar will be
discussed in the discussion of the debate which followed the publication of
the *Report*. The rest of this section in the *Report* covers all types of
magazines from the well-known: *Mayfair, Men Only, Penthouse*, to the not
so well-known: *Heat, Relate, Intro* and *Open*. The *Report* even mentions
Cosmopolitan, of which they say, it

> Believes that women like to see 'this kind of woman who is being
> idealised for men' and it is one of the new magazine's aims to show the
> sophisticated 25–35 year old 'how to get, keep, and if necessary get rid
> of her man'. That this involves keeping up the sex-war, by offering
> nudes and instructions on seduction techniques, might be considered a
> strange response to the sexploitation of the magazine market.[25]

As far as newspapers were concerned, the sub-committee recommended
'that the Press Council should explicitly reveal itself much more conscious
than hitherto of its responsibilities in regard to pornography'.[26]

The advertising sub-committee recommended that 'the public should be more widely informed of the code of advertising practice and encouraged to draw to the attention of the Advertising Standards Authority any advertising material that is felt to be offensive or indecent'.[27] It was also recommended that any unsolicited pornographic material received through the post by members of the public should be immediately brought to the notice of the Director of Public Prosecutions or the police. Finally, the authors of this section recommended that tougher legislation should be introduced to curb the activities of the underground press such as *OZ*, *Rubber Duck*, *IT* and *Rolling Stone*. (Events in the following two years suggest that the existing legislation was tough enough for combating the underground press.) According to the sub-committee, these types of magazine displayed advertisements for sexual apparatus or 'treatments' designed to prolong the act of intercourse and the sensation of orgasm and advertisements for homosexual and lesbian clubs and holidays. Its attitude towards these advertisements was that they should be controlled, and that this would need new, tougher legislation, although they felt some fringe publications such as *Penthouse* might well respond to the threat of sanctions from the advertising industry.[28]

The last sub-committee was concerned with the subject of sex education. The committee criticised two articles, one a book, one a film. The first, the film called *Growing Up* by Dr Martin Cole from Aston University, was described by the sub-committee as 'disturbing'. The second, the book entitled *The Little Red Schoolbook* was intended to produce in children, it was suggested, 'a mentality which can only be stigmatised as corrupt'.[29] The sub-committee made three main recommendations. Firstly, 'that no local authority will have the right to arrange programmes of sex education without full consultation with parents in the area concerned'. Secondly, 'that any parent who objects to a sex education programme shall have the statutory right to withdraw his or her children from such a programme', and lastly that 'it shall be made illegal to show children in school or elsewhere in private any material which may not be shown in a more public place'.[30]

Although Longford had received much publicity during the twelve months or so in which the *Report* was being prepared, particularly when he and other members of his team had visited Denmark, it certainly did not decline after publication. Nor did the heat of argument cool. In surveying the debate, it is very seldom possible to provide both arguments for and against each particular point. On the whole, the media contained only replies to and denials of allegations and arguments made in the *Report*, very little being said in defence of the central proposals. In fact, on the Sunday after publication, J.W.M. Thompson wrote in the *Sunday Times*: 'So far, hardly a single word has been heard in favour of the central recommendation of the Longford Report on Pornography.'[31] This was very much the case, although Mary Whitehouse, in her capacity as Honorary General Secretary of the NVALA, said that four-fifths of the population probably supported the committee's recommendations, and the NFoL also welcomed the *Report's* attempt to tackle 'this social evil in depth'.[32] Professor Norman Anderson, Vice-Chairman of the Committee, defended its proposals, saying that 'the present law defining obscenity is hopeless'.[33] In stating this, he was obviously aware of the Home Secretary's reply to the Arts Council just two years previously, in which he suggested that, although the law was flawed, it was hard to see how it could be replaced.

One of the first groups to reply to the *Report* were the Defence of Literature and the Arts Society (DLAS). They claimed that the proposals were 'a threat to freedom of speech and expressions of non-conformist opinion',[34] and that if they were implemented in their present form, there was the possibility of controversial work of real artistic and literary merit being judged to be obscene by a jury that didn't have the benefit of guidance from experts. Mrs Marion Boyars, secretary of the society, stressed this point arguing that 'one might have a judge who is not particularly well read in literature and the arts, although he may know his law very well, and a jury from backgrounds not familiar with literature'.[35]

Also in disagreement with the proposed abolition of the 'defence of the public good', was Mr Michael Havers QC (later to be Attorney-General), although he suggested that he was in favour of the new definition of obscenity. Joining in the debate, the National Secular Society said 'the whole idea of obscenity is tied up with an unhealthy belief in sin which most ordinary people in this country have now rejected along with other superstitions of the past centuries'.[36]

Implementation of the recommendations would, the National Secular Society authors felt, give rise to a large black market, breeding blackmail and fear. The National Council for Civil Liberties called the *Report* 'obscene to suggest the suppression of ideas by law, absurd to attack sex education, and wise to proclaim the basic irrelevance of pornography'.[37]

Gyles Brandreth, already a thorn in Longford's side, entered into the arena again, saying that the *Report* was neither a valid scientific document nor an independent assessment of pornography:

> The Report may be valid as a document expressing opinions. An investigation might be valid, but not a crusade like this to chart the declining moral standards of the nation. The atmosphere of the whole thing is a fight against sin. I would not be surprised if they felt that *Chick's Own* was pornographic.[38]

Those who were directly attacked in the *Report* were the next ones to join the debate. Hughie Greene whose programme, *Double Your Money*, was criticised as 'fatuous and demeaning', said he believed Lord Longford was a 'sick man': 'He has made himself look like a dirty old man. The definition of pornography does not cover quiz shows, but it seems Lord Longford is determined to find filth in everything.'[39] There is a certain truth in this, of course. Not that Longford was determined to find filth in everything, but rather that, setting out with his world-view (all sex outside marriage is immoral), it was almost inevitable that he would discover things that he and others of like mind, such as Malcolm Muggeridge, disapproved of, almost everywhere they looked.

A number of correspondents made rather more 'methodological' criticisms of *The Longford Report*. Jeffrey Simmons, Managing Director of W.H. Allen and Co. Ltd, the publishers, described his experiences with Longford as follows:

> My evidence to the Longford Committee ... consisted of a genial discussion with Lord Longford himself, assisted by the organising secretary of the inquiry who took shorthand notes and asked a few questions while Lord Longford was on the telephone. I never saw one of the remaining fifty or so members of the committee, and the final report of what I said, although accurate as far as it goes is highly selective, as is the Report as a whole. Indeed not only is the evidence selective, but huge chunks of it are provided by the Committee members themselves.[40]

Two other men who corroborate this experience of a 'Longford interview' are Bernard Hardingham and David Sullivan who, in 1972, were running a sex book mail order business. Hardingham said that they 'could have told him a lot but it seemed he didn't want to know. He didn't approach the interview like an investigator. His approach seemed like one of idle curiosity'.[41] Sullivan agreed, saying that Longford had not really wanted to see them. 'When we did see him the interview lasted only fifteen minutes. We thought we would be questioned by a panel, but only Lord Longford was there.'[42]

The *Report* was criticised for a similar lack of professionalism by Derek Hill, the film critic and founder of the New Cinema Club. In the report, he was quoted as having said that he 'was forced to offset losses on an audience of perhaps 50–150 people by also putting on "sexploitation" films which would attract perhaps 5,000, and he told us, most of the national critics'.[43] Mr Hill suggests that he felt uneasy when he was giving information to Longford and particularly 'that he didn't appear to be listening to anything I said'.[44] In the next programme at the New Cinema

Club, there was an apology from Longford, accepting that the club didn't
select sexploitation films to offset losses, and that Hill never said they did,
despite being quoted to the contrary. Hill's comment on one of the films he
was showing at that time, *La Fée Sanguinaire* by Roland Lethem, was that
'it would presumably make us liable to up to three years' imprisonment if
the Longford draft Bill were ever taken seriously'.[45]

As has already been suggested, Longford's general moral position was
that sexual relations should be confined to marriage and that homosexuality
was to be condemned by definition. It is not altogether surprising, therefore,
that the *Report* also attracted criticism from the Gay Liberation Front for
maligning 'homosexuals in a way that has not happened since the early
debates on the Wolfenden Report'. *The Longford Report* consistently refers
to homosexuality as a 'perversion', they suggested, and as something
intrinsically pornographic. This, critics argued, is reinforced by the fact
that: 'this wholly private statement of personal prejudice should be received
with massive publicity and the respect due to a Royal Commission'.[46]

The most damning criticisms were contained in the *Observer* and came
from the pen of Bernard Levin:

> This vast brantub, the contents of which are a thousand parts chaff to one
> part wheat, is not only useless, it has effectively ruined the market for a
> serious study, by some such means as an academic team or a Royal
> Commission.... The book has many faults, but two are crucial; one is
> methodological, the other, conceptual. The first is the almost total
> absence of intellectual rigour in the way Lord Longford and his
> colleagues went about their work.... [The second is that] pornography
> and obscenity are confused again, until the reader's head swims with the
> effort to look two ways at once.... And the whole ragamadoglio ends in
> a fine flourish of crazy illogic, with a draft Obscene Publications Bill
> that would abolish the defence of 'public good' thus at last making clear
> in so many words what has been visible between the lines throughout,
> that Lord Longford and his group are simply concerned to ban what they
> find disgusting, even if what they find disgusting does more good than
> harm.[47]

After the Arts Council, Longford was not the last to try to amend the
obscenity laws. The third and final set of recommendations aimed at
amending this almost universally unpopular legislation came from the
Society of Conservative Lawyers. A small committee of members, chaired
by Sir Michael Havers, was appointed in May 1971 to consider the statutory
definition of obscenity. Their recommendations (the report was sent to the
Home Secretary in December of the same year) were a mixture of
approaches. On the one hand, they proposed an offence of 'public

indecency', and by implication accepted that there were private areas that were not the law's business. 'Public' was to be defined as 'any place to which the public has access or where they have the opportunity of seeing the material on display'.[48] However, the new offence would involve no reference to harm and defined material as indecent 'if it is grossly offensive to the public at large', a most Devlin-like definition. This approach was reinforced by their re-definition of obscenity as something which 'grossly affronts contemporary community standards of decency, and the dominant theme of the material taken as a whole appeals to a lewd or filthy interest in sex or is repellent'. The 'public good' defence introduced by the Obscene Publications Act, 1959, was to be retained. The Society's proposals received little support, and were even criticised by the *Economist* for their lack of reference to harm. Referring to the new definition, it argued that: 'It is not lewdness or indecency that makes criminal hardcore obscenity but its potential use as self-stimulation towards sexual and violent crime.'[49]

The committee's new definition, although based on a test of indecency rather than obscenity and thus potentially widening the scope of the law, also included, probably through oversight, a potential new limitation. By picking on the dominant theme of a 'prurient interest in sex' as a method of distinguishing material that is obscene, the Committee effectively defined out material which encouraged drugtaking. Thus *Cain's Book*[50] would have been unlikely to have been successfully prosecuted under the new terms. It was in this way narrower than the 'depraves and corrupts' formula.

The importance, particularly of underground magazines like *OZ, IT,* etc., lies not simply in the fact that they were considered obscene enough to be prosecuted, but rather that the whole debate signifies a clash between two bitterly opposed groups: those wishing to preserve the status quo (or like Longford to reverse it, to take us back by means of what one might call a kind of 'retrogressive progress' to the 1950s or earlier), and those who wished to change it. Those belonging in the latter group wished to change the way people organised their lives by removing from society what they believed to be its most apparent injustices. In this light, then, sexuality, sexual behaviour and relations often became a major bone of contention between the two groups, one of which was hankering after the morals of a bygone age, the other attacking what they conceived of as the inequality, hypocrisy and prudery of the present age. *OZ* is central in this debate for, as has already been suggested in Chapter two, its editors undoubtedly considered sexuality to be a powerful tool (although only one of many) to be used in bringing about the revolutionary change in social relations that was their principal goal. *The Longford Report* describes Richard Neville's (one of the editors of *OZ*) views as follows:

in his view, sex was one of the revolutionary weapons with which he hoped to change society; promiscuity, provided the dangers of VD and the need for contraception were pointed out, was one beneficial way of breaking up the family structure that had led to women becoming appendages and children the property of parents. For him, sexual repression and political repression were part of the same tradition, and therefore, the post-pubertal child should regard any voluntary sexual relationship as freedom and therefore therapeutic.[51]

The trial of *International Times* (*IT*) began the period during which the 'underground' press was in and out of court, a situation which constituted what Mary Whitehouse described as a 'moral backlash'. A case such as this had been anticipated by Lord Simonds in the Shaw case in the early 1960s. He said:

Let it be supposed that at some future, perhaps early date, homosexual practices between adult consenting males are no longer a crime. Would it not be an offence if even without obscenity such practices were publicly advocated and encouraged by pamphlet and advertisement? Or must we wait until Parliament finds time to deal with such conduct? I say, my Lords, that if the common law is powerless in such an event, then we should no longer do her reverence. But I say that her hand is still powerful and that it is for Her Majesty's judges to play the part which Lord Mansfield pointed out to them.[52]

On trial in the *IT* case were three of its directors: Peter Stansill, David Hall and Graham Keen. They were charged with 'conspiring to corrupt public morals and to outrage public decency'. This was seemingly contrary to the assurance given by Sir Peter Rawlinson, the Solicitor-General, that these types of charges would not be used in order to circumvent obscene publications legislation. Whatever the status of any undertaking given, the use of the conspiracy charges once again was clear evidence of a desire on the part of the legal establishment to attack the underground press with vigour.

At the focus of legal attention on the magazine were a set of advertisements described as a 'gentleman's directory' (an obvious parallel with Shaw's directory in 1960). The column in which the advertisements were contained was entitled, 'Males', and carried the warning that 'it is illegal for minors to place ads in this classification, or for advertisers to seek to contact minors (under 21).'[53]

The advertisements were of the type that may now be found in 'contact' magazines, and it was shown by the prosecution that they had been answered by homosexuals. Robertson gives several examples of the type of advertisement to be found:

Alert young designer, 30, seeks warm, friendly pretty boy under 23, who needs regular sex, reliable and beautiful surroundings. If the cap fits and you need a friend, write.

Good-looking boy, 28, desperately wants pretty younger boyfriend. All photos, letters answered.

Male (32) seeks younger male for genuine friend. Versatile/passive phase. Looks immaterial, but must be virile, quiet disposition. I have own house, would suit working boy, of boyish nature, for weekends or share house together.

Young gay male desperately needs to earn £40 as soon as possible. Will do anything legal. Genuine replies only please.

Pretty dolly boy wanted for sex and travel by boy, 21. Ample bread.[54]

According to Peter Stansill, the editor at the time, the intention of this section of the magazine had been to provide a public service for a minority of individuals who had been continually discriminated against, harrassed and victimised. He said that the staff of *IT* believed that, as a newspaper with a special conscience, they could make a positive and practical contribution to the welfare of homosexuals.[55] On 10 November 1970, at the Central Criminal Court under Judge Sutcliffe, the company, Knuller (Publishing, Printing and Promotions) Ltd and the three men were convicted on the first count, conspiracy to corrupt public morals and conspiracy to outrage public decency. Knuller Ltd were ordered to pay a fine of £1,000 on count one, and £500 on count two, and to pay up to £500 costs. The three men were sentenced to concurrent terms of 18 and 12 months, suspended for 2 years, and ordered to pay up to £200 costs each.

They decided to appeal against what they felt was a harsh decision, firstly, on the grounds that an agreement by two or more people to insert advertisements in a magazine for the purpose of committing acts that were no longer an offence between consenting adults over 21 would not amount to a conspiracy to corrupt. The Court of Appeal dismissed the appeals, but admitted that important points of law were at stake, and gave leave to appeal to the House of Lords. The Lords decided that conspiracy to corrupt public morals could be committed whether the advertised actions were legal or not, as long as the jury were to decide that their encouragement struck at the nation's moral fibre. Therefore, the appeal on count one was dismissed, although on count two it was allowed, as the Law Lords agreed that a serious misdirection had taken place. The three men, then, were effectively convicted of conspiring to induce people to commit acts that were quite legal. Presumably it was still felt by some that overt homosexuality was a threat to the nation's moral fibre. This was not the last time that conspiracy charges were to be used in the 1970s. Indeed, at this point in time, Roy Jenkins *et al.* must have wondered why they had bothered at all in 1959 to try to reform the law.

Not long after the *IT* case came the prosecution of Paul Abelman's 'study of human orality', *The Mouth and Oral Sex*, published by Running Man Press. Sutherland describes the publication as a 'manual with instruction, history and various diverting material relating to the hitherto hole-in-the-corner business of fellatio and cunnilingus'.[56] Christopher Kypreos, on behalf of Running Man, bought a mailing list of half a million names and, according to figures mentioned later in court, sent out 100,000 postal circulars by way of advertisement. The police obtained a copy of the list which, it seems, contained the names of several schoolchildren. Children were to figure centrally in a number of trials at this time (inter alia *OZ, The Little Red Schoolbook*) and, as was shown in Chapter two, have been an ever present concern of moral reformers such as Mary Whitehouse and the NVALA. Several thousand copies of the book were ordered, but complaints were received by both the police and MPs and, after due consideration, the Director of Public Prosecutions decided to prosecute. In early 1970, a magistrate decided there was a prima facie case to answer before a jury, and lines were once again set for battle. The trial began in March 1971 at the Old Bailey before Judge Alan King-Hamilton. Kypreos was charged with possessing an obscene article for publication for gain, and sending obscene articles through the post. Although the Defence of Literature and the Arts Society (DLAS) offered support, the publishers had great difficulty in finding witnesses ready to testify to the book's literary or other merits. In the event, *The Mouth* was defended by the novelist Margaret Drabble, as well as by a sociologist, a social worker and a doctor. They testified to the effect that the 'allegedly corrupt behaviour' described in the book had, by this time, received wide acceptance from the community at large, and that, rather than being likely to deprave and corrupt, it was actually more likely to enlighten its readers.

This defence was used to contradict the prosecution's argument that the book was encouraging deviant activities by failing to criticise or condemn them. This seemed not to convince Judge Alan King-Hamilton who protested 'why is it important to read about it now? We have managed to get on for a couple of thousand years without it.'[57] The judge also suggested at one point in the trial that lessons might be learnt from studying the decline of the Roman Empire. He argued that contemporary decadence as illustrated by 'the increasing number of illegitimate births, abortions, cases of venereal disease and increasing homosexuality' were the contemporary equivalents of the causes of that historical downfall. The 8-day hearing, however, ended with the book being found not to be obscene. Nevertheless, Kypreos' circulars were found by a ten to two majority to be indecent under the Post Office Act, 1933, and the publishers were fined £250 with £150 costs.[58]

Possibly the best known of all the underground magazines was next to be prosecuted. *OZ* magazine had its origins in Australia (it was originally called *Oztralia*), the home of its founder, Richard Neville. It had a contentious history there, and its life in Britain from 1967 onwards was to be similarly eventful. Its beginnings in this country were dominated by competition with *Private Eye*, the more established satirical journal in Britain. David Tribe has described its publishing history thus:

> *OZ* had a colourful, if at first unspectacular career.... Apart from its 'Beautiful Breast Competition' ... No 3 provoked concern with its photomontage of camped-up beefcake. No 5 was banned by the Australian customs ... No 20 on the Hell's Angels led to a police visit to the printer, who pulped 6,000 copies. As a *Homosexual OZ*, No 23 was certain to attract attention, not least from the police, who removed all copies still with the publishers and formally warned the editors at Scotland Yard ... *Acid OZ* No 27 moved explicitly into the dangerous world of drugs, but No 28 brought the real nemesis.[59]

As Tribe suggests, it was *OZ* 28 that incurred the wrath of the authorities, and it was not long before the editors found themselves in court.

The trial, which began in June 1971, lasted 26 days and thus became the longest obscenity trial in British legal history. The accused were Richard Neville (29), James Anderson (33) and Felix Dennis (24). Richard Neville chose to defend himself, Anderson and Dennis were represented by John Mortimer QC, and Keith McHale defended 'Oz Publications Ink Ltd'. Brian Leary appeared for the prosecution and the judge was Michael Argyle QC. The defendants all pleaded 'not guilty' to five charges. That:

1 they had 'conspired with certain other young persons to produce a magazine' that would 'corrupt the morals of young children and other young persons' and had intended to arouse and implant in the minds of these young people lustful and perverted desires.
2 that between 1 May 1970 and 8 June 1970 they had published an obscene article, *OZ* No 28 known as the 'Schoolkids' Issue'.
3 that between the same dates they had sent a postal packet containing a number of indecent or obscene articles, in *OZ* No 28.
4 that on 8 June 1970 they had possessed obscene articles, 252 copies of *OZ* No 28 for publication for gain.

5 and that on 11 June they had possessed 220 copies of *OZ* No 28, also for
publication for gain.[60]

OZ 28, or the *Schoolkids' Issue*, was 48 pages long, made up largely of
cartoons, reader's letters and articles concerning school, sex, drugs and
discipline. It began with an editorial which described what *Schoolkids'
Issue* meant:

> *OZ* has been put together with the help and inspiration of about 20
> people, all 18 and under, mostly still at school who came from various
> parts of London and England [sic] in answer to our appeals for injections
> of youthful vigour in our ageing veins.[61]

It also contained profiles of some of those who answered the appeal for
help:

**Charles Shaar Murray, 18,
Reading.**
He's a Jewish Pantheist. Doesn't turn on because he has weak lungs.
Says he is a clumsy lover. 'I have all the sex appeal of a mouldy sock'.
Believes in the brotherhood of man and the dawning of the age of
Aquarius. Starts a journalism course in the autumn.

**Viv Kylastron, 16,
Aries.**
Smoked at 9, first tripped at 11. Owes this to the Roundhouse and
Bradford. An anarchist, trying to dissolve it and replace it with a living
school. Came to *OZ* to meet Richard Neville and the others, also inter-
ested in the workings of *OZ*. Interested in mysticism.[62]

This trial began with Neville's opening speech in his own defence. He
explained why No 28 had been called *The Schoolkids' Issue*. Already there
had been a *Homosexual OZ*, edited by homosexuals for the usual *OZ*
readers, a *Women's Liberation OZ*, edited by Germaine Greer, and
similarly, there had been a *Flying Saucer OZ*;

> So we advertised in issue 26 for any schoolchildren between the ages of
> 14–18 to come and edit *OZ*. We offered them freedom from editorial
> interference, and we kept our promise. There was no coercion of any
> kind and our assistance and advice was confined almost to technical
> matters.... 'Schoolkids Issue' it says on the cover which means of
> course, the issue edited by schoolchildren, not aimed by others at them.[63]

This, however, proved to be a major source of confusion. *OZ* 28 was
continually presented during the trial as being aimed at the young and

innocent. As has been noted before, the defendant is entitled to an acquittal if it can be shown that the publication is for the public good, i.e. in the interests of 'science, literature, art or learning, or of other objects of general concern'. Once this defence is raised, according to Robertson,[64] the merits may be canvassed by experts for either side, although the onus is on the accused to establish the defence on the balance of probabilities.[65]

Neville's first 'character' witness was George Melly, the author, critic and jazz musician. Being interviewed by Neville, he described what he considered to be the main characteristics of the underground and 'pop-culture', the contributions that these were able to make to society as a whole and, in particular, the qualities of *OZ* magazine. In reply to the prosecution's question, 'What brings you here today?', he said 'My belief that something which I think is valuable is up for judgement, and I felt it necessary to stand up and be counted.'[66] The defence also called expert evidence on the use of drugs and the effect of sex on the minds of school-children. The first expert called was Caroline Coon, a founder member of 'Release', an organisation providing relief work and welfare services for the young. It had apparently been set up in the first instance as an organisation to help those who had been arrested for drug offences but, according to Coon, had rapidly expanded to cover all sorts of problems. She said of *OZ's* attitude to drugs, that it 'had actually prevented the problem from getting worse, simply by refusing to moralise or dogmatise about the various forms of drug addiction'.[67] The other side of this coin of course, would be to see *OZ's* presentation as lacking in firm moral principles and guidelines. The question of sex came to the fore again, though, with the next witness, Dr Lionel Haward, a psychologist, who said of *OZ* 28:

> It has a number of beneficial features which I would like to see incor-
> porated in many school magazines. I found many of the drawings rather
> disturbing, because as a psychologist, I could see what was going on in
> the minds of the people who drew them, but I think the text matter is
> basically good.[68]

Several of the drawings in the magazine played a prominent part in many of the exchanges in court. One in particular depicted Rupert Bear having sexual intercourse with an old woman, described as 'gypsy granny'. Commenting on the cartoon, Haward said that he felt its message was a critique of the lack of dissemination of sexual education. He was also asked to comment on the front cover of the magazine which depicted the lesbian poses of a number of black women. This, he felt, would only have a small impact on children, although it might induce them to look and see what was inside. 'I think it would have a greater impact on an adult who, knowing more about lesbianism, might see more in it.'[69]

Next in the box was Michael Schofield, a social psychologist. His opinion of the magazine's possible impact on children was that it could possibly 'surprise and shock' but certainly not harm. When questioned about the 'Rupert' cartoon, he suggested that 'it would have absolutely no effect on young people at all. It is intended to be humorous'.[70]

The final part of the defence rested on section 4 of the 1959 Act, and to this end, four 'experts' were called upon. Firstly, John Peel the BBC radio disc jockey spoke about the level of musical criticism in the magazine. According to Palmer's account of the trial, the judge and Mr Leary both seemed more interested in the fact that Mr Peel had once confessed to his listeners that he had contracted VD, than they were in his comments on the merits of *OZ*. Marty Feldman, the comedian, who was next in the stand also failed to impress, despite suggesting that there was more obscenity in the Bible than in *OZ*. He also voiced his concern that the judge was not interested in his testimony by referring to him as 'a boring old fart'.[71] Felix Topolski testified as to the artistic merits of *OZ* and like many other witnesses was questioned about the contentious 'Rupert' cartoon. The cartoon, he argued, brought together unexpected elements, and was thereby an act of creation. Last of the 'experts' was Mervyn Jones, former assistant editor of the *New Statesman*, who testified to *OZ's* literary merits. The only parts of his testimony that directly concerned 'sexual' matters, were his defence of the use of the words 'bollocks' and 'cunt', and his agreement with Mr Leary that the magazine lacked tenderness, although he qualified this by saying that there were many expressions of love which were probably more important. Having brought the defence to a close, all that was left was the closing speech by Mr Leary, who made clear what he felt the problems with modern society were. He used an argument derived from Lord Devlin and suggested that morality is essential to the health of a community. He then said to the jury that it was for them to set a standard, and continued

> ask yourselves, members of the jury, what alternatives are before you, *dropping out* of society, expecting the State to provide for you, and by that I mean, by you and me, and those of us who do not mind work.[72]

Two elements of Mr Leary's summing-up are worth highlighting. Firstly, his insistence on the importance of firm, unified and, above all, *unitary* moral standards. That is to say, the jury were asked by him to set *the* standard. Secondly, he moved on to a brief outline of what he took to be the sort of standards that might be suitable. This included such traditional criteria as hard work and discipline, which he compared with the general desire to 'drop-out' advocated, he implies, by the defendants amongst others. In his summing-up, Justice Argyle reminded the jury that the case was not a trial by experts, but a trial by jury. Referring to the evidence given by Michael Segal, the former probation officer and freelance film producer, he said 'I thought he was a jolly good witness. He wasn't prepared to whitewash all of *OZ* like some of the other so-called experts and I can't say fairer than that.'[73] On the other hand he felt that the evidence given by Mr Dworkin, a Professor of Jurisprudence at Oxford, was not as reliable, saying that he found it interesting 'that such a man could have walked into this court, and without having heard any of the evidence, tell us that the entire prosecution was a corruption. So you can attach what weight to his evidence as you wish'.[74]

The broadcaster, Jonathan Dimbleby, had the following to say about Justice Argyle's summing-up:

> The Judge's summing-up was stunning. Suddenly the defence witnesses became 'so-called defence experts', some of whom members of the jury, you may think reached the position where they either had to admit they were all wrong or tell a lie: If *OZ* was a window on the hippy world – 'well, windows sometimes need cleaning don't they?' As he finished with a witness, he would toss his copy of *OZ* disdainfully down on the table, and with it, one felt, the case for defence. It was a distressing and perhaps crucial exercise. For after constant 'exposure to' (a favourite expression of the prosecutor's) 'fucking in the street' 'masturbation' 'deviation' 'lesbianism' 'corruption' and 'cannabis', this middle-aged group of British householders – the jury – was asked quite simply to 'set a standard'. What an invitation.[75]

The jury considered their verdicts for almost four hours and eventually found all three defendants not guilty on the charge of conspiracy, but guilty on all other counts. They were remanded in custody pending full prison, medical, psychiatric and social reports. During this time they were also required to have their shoulder-length hair cut to 'standard prison length'.

The public reaction was varied. Mrs Whitehouse suggests in a book written in 1977 that the press were on the side of the defendants all the way through. A thorough reading of reports at the time, however, suggests otherwise, although the following two were rather harsher than was the norm. The *Daily Telegraph* commented:

> So, Mr Neville and his two colleagues have been found guilty of publishing a dirty magazine.... Judge Argyle remanded the three in custody saying that he wanted 'social, medical and mental' reports about them, before pronouncing sentence. That, in our view, just about puts the

matter in the right perspective. These people, and others like them, may not be potty in a technical sense, but their state of mind almost certainly requires expert examination.[76]

On a similar line, the *London Evening News* wrote:

It was appropriate you may think that the Judge in the *OZ* case sent the defendants for medical examination. There must surely be something wrong with the minds of men who not only produce such a magazine like that for children, but enlist the help of children in producing it.[77]

It is worth noting once again that the magazine was presented as being *for* children. On 5 August, Neville, Anderson and Dennis reappeared in court for sentencing. The *Guardian*, reporting on the precedents for sentencing in this type of case, examined the court reports for the twelve previous years. They showed that fines imposed ranged from £50 to £2,000, and that the longest prison sentence was two years but subsequently successfully appealed against. Furthermore, the directors of *IT* were given suspended sentences of eighteen months. According to the *Guardian*, all the prison sentences that had been given had been suspended or quashed on Appeal.[78]

Passing sentence, Judge Argyle said that, as all three accused were over 21, 'probation would be inappropriate' and, as they were comparatively poor, so would a fine, which left him with no choice but a custodial sentence, although it could be suspended. Citing an earlier statement made by Felix Dennis in which he had said that he would certainly continue his activities, he sent them all to gaol, Dennis for nine months, Anderson for twelve, and Neville for fifteen, as well as recommending the latter for deportation. Oz Publications Ink Ltd was fined a total of £1,000 and ordered to pay one-quarter of the prosecution costs not exceeding £1,200.[79] If the verdict went off relatively quietly, apart from the demonstrations that had been going on outside the Old Bailey all through the trial, the passing of the sentences certainly did not.

The very same afternoon, thirteen Labour MPs put down a motion in the House deploring the severity of the sentences. Three of these were former Ministers: Tony Benn, John Stonehouse and Dick Taverne, who said that they considered that the English system of justice had been discredited by this treatment of first offenders of good character and integrity. The motion said that the sentences would be regarded by many 'as an act of revenge by the Establishment against dissenting voices'.[80] Two other Labour MPs, Stanley Clinton-Davis and Bruce Douglas-Mann, said 'we were outraged by the severity of these sentences which are totally inappropriate in our judgement to the offences for which these defendants were arrested'.[81]

The outcry over the forcible cutting of the trio's hair gave rise to a statement from the Home Secretary, Mr Reginald Maudling, in which he said he proposed to amend that particular rule at the first opportunity.[82] The National Council for Civil Liberties described the sentences as 'an official declaration of war by an establishment that sought to destroy everything it feared or did not understand'.[83] The Young Liberals said the sentences were 'savage' and the outcome of a 'sordid and snivelling little political trial'.[84] Mary Whitehouse was, however, standing firm, and her statement in reaction to the sentences had a somewhat xenophobic ring to it:

> I think it is a very good thing that the line has been drawn and drawn effectively. The sentences were about right. It was absolutely essential for them to be long enough to make them effective. The line had to be drawn because children were at risk and the people of this country will not take that kind of thing. The country suffers a lot from people who come into it.[85]

A group of people who had also come from the same place as Neville, all being notable Australian journalists, wrote to *The Times* to protest about both aspects of the sentence:

> We would like to join the protest against the severity of the prison sentences passed on Richard Neville and his colleagues.... To banish him to Botany Bay adds to the weight of imprisonment the further punishment of ruining his career in London.... To Australians the whole sad business brings to mind the absurd literary morals trials, together with rigid censorship that have always marred Australian intellectual life.[86]

The reaction of the newspapers was broadly similar, with most stressing their shock, although some did voice their agreement. This voice was to be found in the *Sunday Telegraph*, for example:

> Obscenity for political purposes ... employs deliberately disgusting or shocking language and pictures to degrade and so damage the social order. This is what the editors of *OZ* ... can be accused of practising. Last week's sentences were presumably intended as a decisive declaration that this type of verbal violence is no more acceptable than the more familar physical kind. Again there is little doubt that the large majority supports a declaration to this effect, and that it cannot be depicted as an attack upon radical unorthodox ideas as such.[87]

It has already been argued that the main focus of the prosecutions of the underground was, in fact, the lifestyle, culture and morals of those associated with it. Brian Leary made this explicit when he talked of Richard

Neville's advocacy of 'dope, rock'n'roll and fucking in the streets'. Mrs Whitehouse, Lord Longford, the prosecution in this case and the Sunday Telegraph editorial quoted above all make much of the underground's suggestion (most usually put forward by Neville yet again) that obscenity was a prime weapon in the battle for social and cultural revolution. To the extent that the prosecutions of *OZ, IT, The Little Red Schoolbook* and later, *Nasty Tales* and *Libertine*, were aimed at stemming or reversing the process of cultural attack, the perceived challenge to the 'moral order' that they were alleged to contain, they were political in character. The use of the conspiracy charges in order to circumvent the Obscene Publications Acts reinforces this view.

Not all newspapers took the view held by the *Sunday Telegraph*. The *Observer* commented:

Whatever view is taken of the law that makes the publication of obscenity a crime, it is surely unacceptable to send those found guilty of it to prison – all the more so when the men concerned are first offenders … it is not necessary to be young, or to go along with the heady talk about the 'revenge of the establishment' or 'the persecution of *OZ*' to deplore the severity of the sentences that Judge Argyle thought fit to pass last week.[88]

Similarly the *Sunday Times* said that it was 'not necessary, however, to endorse Mr Neville's view of society to find the sentences passed on him and his colleagues quite unjustifiable'.[89] Bernard Levin, writing in *The Times* two days later, was in agreement saying, 'the *OZ* trial was a national disgrace. It served notice on the young that we will listen to them, but not hear; look at them, but not see; let them ask but not answer'.[90] The sentences were even criticised in the *New Law Journal* which described them as '… indefensibly severe … bearing little recognizable relevance to the objectives of sentencing nowadays generally accepted as valid'.[91]

On 9 August the three were released from Wormwood Scrubs on bail, pending appeal which eventually began on 3 November. John Mortimer, appearing for Neville, Anderson and Dennis, had three main points to make about the course of the trial. Firstly, he alleged that Judge Argyle had misdirected the jury as to the definition of obscenity; secondly, that the judge had not given sufficient weight to the evidence given by experts on the likelihood of a tendency to deprave and corrupt, and the possibility that the effect of some of the articles would be one of aversion; and thirdly, he criticised the judge's denigration of some of the expert witnesses.[92]

The Appeal was heard by the Lord Chief Justice, Lord Widgery, as well as by Mr Justice Bridge and Mr Justice James. In a significant legal judgement they upheld the appeal against all the charges except under the

Post Office Act 1953. The implication is that an article may be found to be not guilty under the Obscene Publications Act 1959, i.e. not obscene, yet guilty, i.e. indecent, under the Post Office Act. The six-month prison sentence under this Act was upheld, but suspended for two years, and the recommendation for Neville's deportation was cancelled. Explaining the judgement, Lord Widgery said that the trial judge had seriously misdirected the jury on the definition of obscenity in the 1959 Act and that, for the future, there must be no widening of the formula to introduce colloquial notions of obscenity or concepts imported from the less serious indecency offences.[93]

The Lord Chief Justice also argued that Mr Justice Argyle had failed to put across fully the defence argument that articles on sex and drugs in the magazine could deter people rather than encourage them. 'These two matters put together form a very substantial and serious misdirection.'[94] The Court of Appeal were also in agreement that 'the Judge was biased against experts as a group and was inclined to make little of their evidence whenever he got the chance to do so'.[95] Although the convictions were thus quashed, Lord Widgery had a warning for those who in the future might be convicted under the Obscene Publications Act:

> We would therefore like to make it quite clear in general terms that any idea that an offence of obscenity does not merit a prison sentence should be eradicated. There will be many cases in future in which a prison sentence is appropriate if the court imposing the sentence thinks fit, and any general impression to the contrary should not be retained.[96]

The ruling was criticised by Mary Whitehouse, who called it a 'disaster':

> I do not have anything personal against the three men but I think it is an unmitigated disaster for the children of our country. If they cannot be protected by the law from this kind of material then the law should be tightened up. The first thing I am going to do is get on to the Attorney General.[97]

In line with these sentiments the appeal decision stirred Mrs Whitehouse into action. She instituted what became known as the 'Nationwide Petition for Public Decency' which eventually amassed well over a million signatures and was presented by her and the Bishop of Leicester to the Prime Minister.

At almost the same time that Neville, Anderson and Dennis were being prosecuted at the Old Bailey, the less salubrious surroundings of Lambeth Magistrates' Court housed a similar affair. Richard Handyside, the sole proprietor of 'Stage One' publishers, was being prosecuted under the Obscene Publications Act for the production of a book, aimed at children and containing advice on school, sex, drugs, teachers, etc. It was entitled *The Little Red Schoolbook*[98] and was 208 pages long. The book contained bits of advice under its varying headings.

On homework:

Homework shouldn't be just a routine duty, set because it says so in the timetable. It should give you a chance to work on things on your own, and develop the ideas discussed in class. It's important for you to learn to think things out for yourself and to express them clearly.[99]

On teachers:

If you're dissatisfied with a certain teacher and he [sic] refuses to talk to you, organize a boycott of his lessons. Try organizing your own lessons on the subject he teaches badly.[100]

On sex:

When a boy puts his stiff prick into a girl's vagina and moves it around it is called intercourse, or making love, or sleeping together (even if they don't sleep at all). The usual word for intercourse is fucking.[101]

and:

The only way to avoid unforeseen consequences in sexual relationships is for both peple to be honest with one another about what they are looking for. Someone seeking security rarely finds it with someone who only wants sexual satisfaction. Someone who feels under pressure to have a sexual relationship may not find sexual satisfaction.[102]

On drugs:

If you haven't started smoking (tobacco) don't. Some of your friends or other people at school may smoke themselves and encourage you or dare you to try it. Saying no is sensible, not cowardly.[103]

Mrs Whitehouse was again instrumental in these proceedings, bringing the book to the attention of the DPP. Despite the widespread view at the time that it was Mrs Whitehouse who had initiated the prosecution, Detective Chief Inspector Clifford Turvey said that the Obscene Publications Department, of which he was chief, had been looking at the book before Mrs Whitehouse's campaign against its appearance in Britain. On the witness stand, he justified prosecution by describing the book as 'hard-core pornography'.[104]

The prosecution argued that the book ignored the importance of self-control and that it passed over the bad effects of promiscuity. Indeed, they argued, it was also very close to an incitement to commit offences in breach of the Sexual Offences Act, as it was a book basically aimed at the over 11s and only in part did it warn that sexual intercourse was unlawful for people under 16. Although many of the prosecution witnesses were called to back up these ideas, other criticisms of the book were made, two of which deserve special attention since they might well have had a substantial influence on the case. Even if they did not do so, they are typical of the kinds of ignorance that tend to pervade obscenity trials.

Firstly, Dame Mary Green, Headmistress of Kidbrook Comprehensive School in Greenwich, said that she felt that there was a need for informed sexual instruction but not the way it was given in the book. As an example of this, she cited the words 'orgasm' and 'masturbation', and said that she thought these might have an unpleasant effect on children under 16. Next was Dr Ernest Claxton, a former secretary to the BMA's committee on venereal disease and young people (and coincidentally a member of the NVALA). His objection was to the section on masturbation:

> It is harmful to masturbate. An occasional act cannot cause any harm, but masturbation is like a drug and many children become addicted. The result is a degeneration in their physique and their character. It gives a sense of unreality and division from his family because it is a secret thing, and this begins to cause the generation gap.[105]

In the event, Richard Handyside was found guilty and fined £50 with £110 costs. Reactions to the decision varied greatly, but the divisions were again clearly recognisable. After the decision Handyside commented that he was 'truly amazed by the decision, but not really surprised'.[106] The *Daily Telegraph* was also unsurprised:

> It can hardly be a cause of surprise that the publisher of the English version of *The Little Red Schoolbook* should yesterday have been found guilty in a magistrates' court under the law relating to obscene literature. ... What does give cause for wonder is that the publisher of a book of this kind should escape with a fine of £50 and costs of £110. His consequential financial losses may be great but where writing is both potentially corrupting and explicitly addressed to children, the case for exemplary punishment is strong.[107]

In criticism of those who rallied to the defence of the book, Ronald Butt said that he could not imagine how one parent in a thousand could really consider the book suitable reading for children, adding that what the book's advocates were really trying to establish was that there was no such thing as 'childhood'.[108]

The book was also criticised in the *Guardian* for aiming at 'juniors' when it was more relevant for 'seniors', and for failing to discuss the importance of respect. However, the *Guardian* suggested that 'neither of these defects makes the book obscene. In our view its condemnation was not justified. Nor is it as revolutionary as some critics have suggested, even though it advocates a healthy scepticism towards authority'.[109] The notion of the revolutionary quality of the book was given support by Mary Whitehouse. Tracey and Morrison, in their book on Mrs Whitehouse, argue that although the case revolved around the book's sexual content, this was merely a strategy adopted by those campaigning to have it banned by concentrating on its weakest point. 'The wider issues were in fact raised in a letter to the *Guardian* by Ross McWhirter, in which he argued: "The real issue, in my submission, is that the book is not only obscene but also seditious."[110] Indeed, as was shown in Chapter two, Mrs Whitehouse backs up this idea in her book, *Whatever Happened to Sex?*, with a general argument that owes much to Reich and Marcuse: 'It is part of our thesis that sexual and political revolution go hand in hand and that indeed the first is prerequisite of the second. That *The Little Red Schoolbook* was a revolutionary primer there can be no question.'[111]

The traditional battlelines had formed in anticipation of the result of the appeal. On the one hand, the defendant was backed by the underground press, the NCCL, the Defence of Literature and the Arts Society (DLAS), and particularly Richard Neville through his column in the *Spectator*, as well as various assorted 'humanists' and 'radicals';[112] against him on the other hand were what was often referred to as the 'establishment': the enforcers of law and order, the censors, or would-be censors, and the more conservative sections of the national press.

The hearing took place in late October and lasted for 5 days ending with the appeal being rejected. The reason given was that the publisher had failed to show that the publication was for the public good, and Handyside was ordered to pay costs of over £1,000.[113] Geoff Robertson described the appeal as follows:

> The court seemed as much concerned by the book's political bias as by its sexual content. The judge deplored the suggestion that children might organize demonstrations or strikes, and condemned the book as 'inimical to good teacher/child relationships.... Subversive not only to the authority but to the trust between children and teachers ... the influence of parents, the church, youth organisations and other adults with whom they come into casual contact will be very seriously affected in the face of a very considerable portion of the children who read this book'.[114]

Despite this setback, Richard Handyside published a revised version of the *Little Red Schoolbook* later in the year. Twelve lines in the offending 23-page section on sex had been rewritten, and one other paragraph, condemned as 'obscene', was covered by a supposedly non-removable sticker. A copy was examined by the DPP but no action was taken.

The case did not stop here. It was eventually taken to the European Commission of Human Rights, where Handyside claimed that the conviction violated his freedom of thought and expression as defined in the European Convention on Human Rights. The Commission, however, ruled against him. Judge Mosler, however, made the point that 'in this case it is difficult to understand why a measure that was not thought necessary outside England and Wales was deemed to be so in London' (no action had been taken against the sale of the *Little Red Schoolbook* in other parts of Great Britain, except in Glasgow and Edinburgh where it had been acquitted).[115] For those who know a little more about the background of the opposition to and critics of *The Little Red Schoolbook*, *OZ*, etc., the reason is clear enough.

Pressure on the underground continued when a comic entitled *Nasty Tales* found its way into court. At the date mentioned in the charge, June 1971, the publishers of *Nasty Tales* were also the owners of *IT*. The trial actually started on 15 January 1973, at the Old Bailey. Charged were Bloom Publications, Mick Farren, Edward Barker, Paul Lewis and Joy Farren, with having had in their possession obscene articles for publication for gain, namely 275 copies of a magazine entitled *Nasty Tales* No1. The prosecution case concentrated on three of the pages in the magazine which contain cartoons about sex and drugs. Of apparently particular note was a full-page drawing by Robert Crumb entitled 'Great Continental Fuck-In and Orgy Riot'. Michael Coombe, prosecuting, suggested that the magazine promoted sex, drugs and violence (a remarkably similar argument to that made by Brian Leary in the *OZ* case, that *OZ* 28 promoted 'dope, rock 'n' roll and fucking in the streets'). For the defence, expert witnesses appeared in the form of George Perry, a co-author of the *Penguin History of Comics*, and Germaine Greer. What they suggested was that, by ridiculing what they considered to be society's obsession with sex and drugs, the comic might make the truth about them clearer.

In this trial, as in other obscenity cases, the judge's summing-up caused some debate. He told the jury that they would have to ask themselves whether there was anything in the magazine that could be said to be good for anyone except the publishers:

> You may have been surprised that anyone could say that anything in the magazine was of literary or artistic merit, but the world is full of

surprises ... how could it be for the public good for hippies to go and live in communes?[136]... You may think that it would have been more for the public good if *Nasty Tales* was designed to make the hippies come to terms with us and understand what is wrong with them.[116]

This final statement, according to the *Sunday Times*, brought a gasp from the mainly young people in the audience. Nevertheless, the jury came down on the side of the defendants, with a ten to two verdict for acquittal. The judge's summing-up in the *Nasty Tales* case is perhaps the clearest illustration of the attack on 'lifestyle' that underpinned all the prosecutions of the underground press. Although quite clearly, it was never suggested that being a hippy or living in a commune (itself anti-nuclear family) could be considered to be criminal offences, such lifestyles were nevertheless at the root of the 'establishment's' indignation. Writers and publishers such as Neville, Dennis, Anderson, Stansill, Farren and others were being accused by the authorities of being subversive. As the judge said, 'it would have been more for the public good if ... (they had) ... come to terms with us and understand what is wrong with them'.

It was suggested in Chapter three that the debate in jurisprudence in the early 1960s provides a useful method of analysing changes in the law in areas such as obscenity, particularly with regard to the question of the enforcement of morals. Part of the reason for its usefulness is that it was itself triggered by proposed legislative change in another area: homosexuality. Crudely put, Devlin and Hart represented two fundamentally opposed positions, one which defended the state's right to intervene in questions of morals, the other which thought that such a right should be restricted to cases in which individuals required protection from harm. The Wolfenden Report – which is generally seen as being the embodiment of the philosophy which underlay most of the legislative changes in the 1960s – was based on an approach which was closer to that of Hart than Devlin. Chapters four and five have considered the laws relating to obscenity in some detail and have attempted to relate these changes, and the ways in which the law was implemented in the period, to such jurisprudential distinctions.

The period under discussion began with the prosecution of major British publishers under the archaic nineteenth-century censorship laws. The response to these partially successful prosecutions was, indirectly, the introduction of new legislation: the Obscene Publications Act, 1959. This involved a compromise between alternative approaches to obscenity. Roy Jenkins *et al.* were only able to get part of what they wished to see by way of protection for literature in return for far stricter controls over what was called 'pornography', but which included written as well as pictorial literature. Although the new law of 1959 was the product of an essentially utilitarian initiative, it was constrained by the desires of what Devlin might have called a 'legal-moralist' establishment for increased controls over pornography. Thus the 'deprave and corrupt' definition taken from the Hicklin judgement of 1868 was embodied in the new law, and it was generally used in a most un-utilitarian manner. In the *Chatterley* trial, Mr Justice Byrne used the OED definition, 'to make morally bad, to pervert, to debase or corrupt morally', and refused to allow the defence counsel's argument that the reader's character needed to have changed, thus impelling the reader to commit acts that he would not otherwise have done. Similarly, and echoing Devlin, Lord Simon in the *IT* case suggested that the charge of 'corrupting public morals' suggested conduct that would be damaging to the social fabric. The first case under the new legislation was a victory for the so-called liberals, but was qualified almost immediately by the imprisonment of Federick Shaw for 'conspiring to corrupt public morals'. This use of the common law as a method by which the terms of the Obscene Publications Act could be circumvented hardly lends support to the idea that the law was being implemented in a 'permissive' manner.

The trial of *Fanny Hill*, which was being prosecuted for the first time after 215 years of free publication, continued this trend. Not only this, but the intentions of the law were again by-passed to the extent that the case was brought under section 3 rather than section 2 of the 1959 Act, thus denying the defendants a trial by jury. Again, a conviction was secured. The whole affair caused an uproar culminating, finally, in the passing of new legislation, not to extend the protections afforded to literature, but rather simply to tighten up the controls over what might and what might not be published.

The next major trial, that of *Last Exit to Brooklyn*, came about through pressure from two Conservative MPs, despite the fact that the Director of Public Prosecutions had read the book and had refused to take any action. After a long drawn-out process, the book was finally condemned as obscene, only to escape in the Appeal Courts on two points of law – a victory finally for the supporters of 'permissiveness' – 'only by default' suggested Mrs Whitehouse.

These were the major relevant events of the 1960s, and it is indeed hard to see how these might be described as 'opening the floodgates to obscenity'. This would seem to be the same conclusion that the NCCL and the Arts Council came to, as, such was their concern, they got together to form a working party to investigate the operation of the obscenity laws. The report they produced included the recommendation that the censorship laws should be scrapped. Barry Cox, in his book on civil liberties,[117] suggests that this was a triumph for the 'liberals', yet even he notes that opinion was soon to change. Cox, however, misrepresents the situation. It was not that public opinion was about to change, as an important sector of public opinion was already against such proposals. The report received very little support from the public, and Parliament, when not apathetic, was hostile.

If the 1960s are usually seen as embodying the 'permissive' age, then the early 1970s are generally characterised as a time when censorship returned to stem the tide of the 1960s. Sutherland argues that 'decensorship' was far advanced by the late 1960s and that works generally agreed to have literary merit were no longer prosecuted. Whilst this was generally true, it must be remembered that this was only what a very respectable pressure group (the Society of Authors) had been trying to achieve in the mid to late 1950s, and it was a very fragile achievement anyway, as cases such as *Gay News* (cf. Chapter two) were later to illustrate. The Arts Council Report was swiftly followed by *The Longford Report* on pornography which, although it commanded the type of respect that a man like Longford would have expected, received no more support than did the Arts Council's. The report produced by the Society of Conservative Lawyers also sank without trace.

Thus begins the 'harassment of the underground' or whatever term one might care to use. The first in the dock was Ableman's *Mouth*, which escaped, although his publicist Kypreos fell foul of the Post Office Act. *IT* followed, and they were prosecuted (thanks to the verdict in the Shaw case) of conspiring to corrupt public morals and outrage public decency. The fact that the acts they were supposedly conspiring to incite people to commit were not, themselves, offences, made little difference to the final outcome, and they were found guilty. Conspiracy charges were used again in the *OZ* trial, but were thrown out, although the trio were found to be in breach of the Obscene Publications Act, a verdict which was only reversed on appeal. *The Little Red Schoolbook* was also condemned, although a revised version with twelve lines having been censored, was reissued within months, and was not prosecuted. The final case was that of *Nasty Tales*, which, unlike the others, managed to escape, and effectively brought to a close the battle between the underground press and the 'establishment'. Neither side had won for, as Sutherland points out, all that really happened was that the issue ceased to be historically relevant.

In conclusion, it may be argued that there were significant events in the 1960s that may more easily be described by the phrase 'a movement towards regulation' rather than as a 'movement towards permission'. In fact, events corresponding to both these types may be identified as occurring simultaneously in the period. As we have seen, Hall refers to this as a 'double taxonomy'.[118] The 'movement towards regulation' provides the other side of the coin to the one that caught the public's imagination at the time, and now infuses sociological description of the period. What then of the early 1970s? A backlash? Although there has probably never been a more concerted attack upon any part of English literature, the permissive gains that *had* been made in the previous decade, ensured that the attack would not be completely successful, and, in the light of the above argument, the 'repressive movement' identifiable in the 1970s can only be understood insofar as it arose out of similar but less concentrated strategies in the 1960s. It is both untrue to say that the law was simply altered in a 'permissive' direction, or was only or mainly implemented in a 'permissive' manner during the period 1960–75. To the extent that changes such as these may be identified, they are accompanied by changes that seem to show the law moving in precisely the opposite direction. What were involved, in other words, were shifts in the *balance* between permission and regulation.

6   A woman's right to choose?

Abortion and the law in post-war Britain

For opponents of abortion law reform, the 1967 Act is, like the case of pornography and the 1959 Obscene Publications Act, considered to be 'the opening of the floodgates'. We are presented by them with a picture of a once relatively abortion-free Britain in which the operation was only necessary when there was grave physical danger to the life of the mother. As Professor Hugh McLaren might have put it, there was nobody 'murdering little babies'.[1] On the basis of press cuttings collected by the Abortion Law Reform Association (ALRA) in the late 1930s, Madeleine Simms is able to provide fairly strong evidence to suggest that, far from an abortion-free country, illegal backstreet operations, carried out in, for the most part, dangerously unhygienic conditions were numerous:

> The press cuttings ... suggest that criminal abortion was widespread in London and the major provincial cities, and that criminal abortionists, medical and lay, if they had a reasonable reputation, had large catchment areas in the country districts around the cities and in neighbouring smaller towns less well served in this respect. Some very notable abortionists like Dr Powell of Tooting, evidently attracted clients from all over the country.[2]

One will never be able to discover the actual number of abortions that were carried out each year in the earlier parts of this century but, whatever it was, it was sufficiently large and dangerous to prompt the formation of a pressure group, the ALRA, in 1936, whose aim was to campaign for liberal law reforms and more public information.

The first major piece of legislation dealing with abortion in this country was the Offences Against the Person Act which was passed in 1861. Section 58 of the Act made it a felony for anyone, including the woman herself, unlawfully to procure an abortion. The offence was punishable with life imprisonment. Section 59 of the Act made it a misdemeanour to supply any instrument, poison or 'noxious thing' for an abortion. This was punishable with imprisonment for three years.[3] During the later stages of the nineteenth century, it was slowly accepted that the operation was necessary if the mother's life was at stake, and the techniques of abortion were both explained and illustrated in medical textbooks.

Although this was the case, public knowledge and access were extremely limited, and there were several prosecutions of people who dared to publish and disseminate contraceptive techniques, among them, Annie Besant in 1887. The fact that abortions were performed 'legally' in certain cases at this time, was largely the result of a loophole in the 1861 Act created by the continued use in it of the word, 'unlawfully', implying, as it did, that there could, theoretically at least, be 'lawful' cases. The strides that were made at this time in various medical techniques made the operation safer, reinforcing this situation in which abortions were carried out to save life. The introduction of the 1929 Infant Life (Preservation) Act protected this practice, and also introduced the notion of 'viability' – the stage at which the foetus could be expected to live independently of its mother. The point was put at twenty-eight weeks. Up until this point, then, the only situation in which a doctor could perform an abortion and stay within the law, was in order to save the life of the mother.

During the 1930s, women's organisations, the newly formed ALRA and others placed a great deal of pressure on the government to set up an inquiry into the state of affairs regarding abortion. This the government did in May 1937, under the chairmanship of Mr Norman Birkett, as he was then. Its terms of reference were to 'enquire into the prevalence of abortion, and the law relating thereto, and to consider what steps might be taken to secure the reduction of maternal mortality and morbidity arising from this cause'.[4]

The Committee took two years to report, and it recommended that the law should be changed in order to make it more certain, so that medical practitioners should know under what circumstances they were acting legally. As regards the prevalence of abortion, the Committee estimated that well over 100,000 abortions were carried out annually, of which at least 40 per cent were 'illegal'. The Birkett Committee recommended that the law should be amended to make it clear, despite the fact that, during the two years it sat, there came before the courts a very important case that was to have a profound effect on the practice of abortion in the following thirty years. In 1938, a young girl aged 14 was forced into their barracks by a group of Guardsmen who assaulted and raped her, as a result of which she became pregnant. Her Roman Catholic doctor refused to terminate her pregnancy, and she was eventually referred through the ALRA to a Consultant Obstetrician at St Mary's Hospital, where he performed the operation, though not before some careful study:

After getting the consent of her parents, I admitted her on June 6th 1938. I kept her in bed in the ward for eight days to be sure of the type of girl I was dealing with; many of the prostitute type or those of low intelligence are completely undisturbed by pregnancy, except that for the first of these groups it is an obvious nuisance, but nothing more.[5]

He decided to try to establish the legality of the operation he was to perform and informed the police of his intentions. He was charged and eventually tried at the Old Bailey. The trial was national news for several days, and his eventual acquittal was greeted with approval by most of the national press. The summing-up by Mr Justice Macnaghton led to a considerable liberalisation of the abortion laws:

The defendant is charged with an offence against s.58 of the Offences Against the Person Act, 1861 ... my direction to you in law is this – that the burden rests on the Crown to satisfy you beyond reasonable doubt that the defendant did not procure the miscarriage of the girl in good faith for the purpose only of preserving life.... What then is the meaning to be given to the words 'for the purpose of preserving the life of the mother'.... As I have said, I think those words ought to be construed in a reasonable sense, and, if the doctor is of the opinion, on reasonable grounds and with adequate knowledge, that the probable consequence of the continuance of the pregnancy *will be to make the woman a physical or mental wreck*, the jury are quite entitled to take the view that the doctor who, under those circumstances and in that honest belief operates, is operating for the purpose of preserving the life of the mother.[6]

As can be seen, Justice Macnaghton extended the definition to cover not only 'physical' but also 'mental' health, thereby widening the conditions under which doctors could legally perform abortions. Despite this new protection, similar cases were brought against doctors in the 1940s and 1950s. In 1948, two practitioners, Dr Mary Ferguson, a psychiatrist, and Dr Elizabeth Bergmann, a surgeon, were charged under the 1861 Act at the Old Bailey. The judge in his summing-up, endorsed the findings in the Bourne case, and the jury duly acquitted. Nevertheless, two highly respected members of the medical profession found themselves in court for four days, and faced prison if convicted.[7]

Ten years later, two doctors found themselves in the Central Criminal Court. One, a Dr Stungo, was charged with being an accessory before the fact to using an instrument to procure a miscarriage; the other, a Dr Newton, was charged with manslaughter. The case arose when a pregnant woman was admitted to hospital in a very agitated condition. Having been referred by Dr Stungo to Dr Newton, she was given an inter-uterine injection of utus paste and sent back to her hotel, where she later died. The judge's summing-up in the case followed that laid down in the Bourne case, and Dr Stungo was found not guilty. However, Dr Newton was found guilty of manslaughter by unlawfully using an instrument to procure a miscarriage and sentenced to consecutive terms of three and two years imprisonment respectively. Thus although the law had seemingly been clarified by the Bourne case and Mr Justice Macnaghton's summing-up had been subsequently reinforced in several cases, doctors were still unsure of their legal position and this undoubtedly led to inconsistency in treatment.

Five years before the Newton case, the first attempt was made in Parliament to alter this situation, and it was the start of at least twenty-five years of almost continuous parliamentary debate on the subject of abortion – a history which is well documented elsewhere. There were a number of important events which increased the pressure for change. In 1958 Glanville Williams' influential book, *The Sanctity of Life and the Criminal Law*, urged a more liberal approach to abortion, as did Roy Jenkins in *The Labour Case*. The most glaring defect in the contemporary situation, it was held, was the inequality that existed. Abortion on 'social' grounds was denied to most women, particularly the working classes, whereas it was fairly common knowledge that private abortions by specialists in Harley Street and similar areas could be relatively easily obtained by those with enough money to pay. This situation was well documented by Alice Jenkins in her book, *Law for the Rich*, published in 1961, in which she quotes from Glanville Williams:

> No one wants the publicity of a jury trial and even an unsuccessful prosecution may be professionally ruinous.... Whilst the ordinary practitioner is frequently reluctant to involve himself in an abortion, some practitioners make a profitable speciality of it, giving abortion to allcomers on pretence of therapy, protecting themselves by working in teams, and charging fees commensurate with the risk they consider themselves to run. Hence the law of therapeutic abortion tends to be one for the rich and another for the poor.[8]

The policing of the law at this time was highly selective. During the Second World War there was a fourfold increase in the number of crimes of procuring abortion known to the police and the 1940s and 1950s saw the continued reporting of criminal abortions.[9] Brookes suggests that along with this, after the war, there was an increase in police surveillance of the activities of the so-called 'professional abortionists'. However, few of these professionals were prosecuted. Dickens shows that only 5 per cent of the women, and 17 per cent of the men convicted could be classed as 'professionals'.[10] There had emerged during the course of the century an unresolved conflict between law and practice, and Brookes quotes one police official who said that 'there are so many abortions procured every day, and the law on the subject is so sticky, that we could not hope to clean up the situation'.[11]

Although there is little accurate evidence that would enable us to judge the number of abortions taking place in this period, most authors agree that the numbers were high. Nevertheless, the numbers of prosecutions were low, and the law was widely regarded as being obsolete. It is possible, however, that far from being a spur to reform of the law, its widespread disregard may have had the opposite effect. In this vein, Smith has argued that the general ease of access to safe abortion that was enjoyed by the middle classes may have actually slowed down the impetus for reform.[12]

The thalidomide 'epidemic' which began in 1961 was the turning point in the fortunes of the ALRA, and perhaps the major factor in the declining influence of the Catholic Church in the abortion debates in Britain. The birth of a large number of deformed children, usually having ill-developed limbs, generally the arms and shoulders, was first noticed in Australia, followed by Germany and Britain. The only factor that was common to these cases was the drug, a sedative, thalidomide taken by the mothers during pregnancy. Although the pro-abortion pressure group did not take advantage of the tragedy at the time, the thalidomide saga had an immense effect on public opinion and the press, and there can be little doubt that it was the single most important factor in modifying public opinion. There were a large number of well-publicised cases in the media which had the effect of moving public opinion in favour of therapeutic abortion. Brookes has described the situation at the time:

> Distillers withdrew the drug on 3 December 1961. In May 1962 the Ministry of Health sent a memorandum to Medical Officers of Health stating that 'every possible effort should be taken' to prevent the birth of deformed babies. Doctors were advised to identify from their records any patient for whom thalidomide had been prescribed. The meaning of an unwanted pregnancy, long understood by women, was dramatically brought home by doctors who had prescribed with such devastating effects. Many may have felt, as the *BMJ* suggested, that they had 'failed to keep their contract' if the mother and baby were anything but normal. The Ministry of Health did not even attempt to estimate the numbers of abortions performed to prevent the birth of deformed children.[13]

Over the following two years, this position was reinforced by the large number of congenitally abnormal babies that were born during the rubella epidemics of that time. There was no getting away from abortion as an issue.

In the mid-1960s two other important events took place, both of which had significant effects on the abortion 'debate'. The first was the intervention of the Church of England. The Church Assembly's Board for Social Responsibility published a report entitled *Abortion: An Ethical Discussion*, in 1965, in which it was argued that abortion could be justified where 'it could be reasonably established that there was a threat to the mother's life or well-being'. The important part of the Report as far as those in favour of reform were concerned was that health and well-being were 'seen as integrally connected with the life and well-being of the family'. Effectively, then, the Church Assembly was in favour of the inclusion of a 'social' clause in future attempts to reform the law, and it was such a clause that first saw the light of day in a Bill introduced in the House of Lords in late 1965 by Lord Silkin. This was the first of two Bills introduced by Lord Silkin, and to a great extent it was much the same as earlier Bills which had been presented by Renee Short, Joseph Reeves and Kenneth Robinson. The similarity is largely explained by the fact that all three were drafted by Glanville Williams. The major difference was the inclusion in the Bill of Clause 1(c) which proposed that abortion should be lawful, on the ground that:

> the health of the patient or the social conditions in which she is living (including the social conditions of her existing children) make her unsuitable to assume the legal and moral responsibility for caring for a child or another child....[14]

In discussing this clause, Lord Silkin said that he felt that it was less likely to receive the sympathy that certain of the other proposals had commanded. The Bill, nevertheless, received an unopposed third reading and was due to move on to the Commons when a General Election intervened. At the beginning of the next session, Silkin, seeing little chance of the matter being taken up in the Commons, decided to reintroduce his Bill, in exactly the same form, in the Lords. At this point, a group that was to play an important role in future discussions of abortion law reform, the Royal College of Obstetricians and Gynaecologists (RCOG), published their report on the subject.[15]

They argued in the Report that any radical alterations in the law should wait until there had been time to set up an interdepartmental committee to collect official figures concerning abortion both from this country and abroad, and subject them to impartial study.[16] The publication of the Report did cause Silkin to amend his Bill in one important respect, however – and this was the first point at which the terms of the debate started to be set by the medical profession. Silkin took account of their wish that one of the doctors in charge of the operation should be a consultant gynaecologist, as opposed to the registrar with a gynaecological appointment who had been specified in the First Bill. Silkin's Bill was to go no further, as in the following month the ALRA were able to persuade one of the MPs who had drawn a high position in the Private Members' ballot to take on board Abortion Law reform as his cause.

From the 1930s onwards, the question of women's access to abortion was a fairly constant theme outside Parliament, and reform of the law in this area can rarely have been out of the minds of MPs from the early 1950s onwards. As the years passed, it had become progressively clearer that abortion was a common operation and that, in many cases, it was considered to be quite legal. It also became clear that for those with money, abortion was not a difficult operation to obtain, even if one's reasons were outside what was generally considered to be 'legitimate'. Also clear was the fact that certain sections of the medical profession were not only willing to perform the operation under these circumstances, but were willing to become rich on it as well. By this time, a growing number of women were becoming more vociferous in claiming what they regarded as their right. The ALRA began to find its voice again in the early 1960s after some reorganisation and a change of leadership, spurred by the thalidomide tragedy in 1961–3 and the rubella epidemics of that same period. The renewed efforts of the ALRA and their supporters in Parliament, together with the impact of thalidomide, seemed to transform public opinion (the opinion polls at the time showed that anything up to 75–80 per cent of the public were in favour of reform), and the constant chipping away inside and outside Westminster brought the Church, and perhaps in this area more importantly, the medical profession into the arena. This is the backcloth upon which David Steel entered the fray in May 1966.

David Steel was placed third in the Private Members' ballot and was therefore in a good position to get a fairly lengthy hearing for whichever Bill he decided to sponsor. His first inclination was to go for something that would clearly benefit his constituents, such as a Border Development Bill, but he was told by the Scottish Office that they could not spare any time to help him and that the government anyway was against such a measure. Of a more national nature, two avenues of legislation were presented to him: homosexuality and abortion. He was strongly recommended by the Earl of Arran to take on board the Sexual Offences Bill which Lord Arran had just successfully piloted through the Lords. However, Steel found that his constituents were strongly against him introducing such a Bill, and after consultation with the ALRA he therefore chose abortion.

The second reading of the Bill was on 22 July 1966, and was to be the first full-scale debate on abortion in the House of Commons. The Bill as presented to Parliament read as follows:

1 Subject to the provisions of this section, a person shall not be guilty of an offence under the law relating to abortion when a pregnancy is terminated by a registered medical practitioner if that practitioner and another registered medical practitioner are of the opinion, formed in good faith:

   (a) that the continuance of the pregnancy would involve the serious risk to the life or of grave injury to the health, whether physical or mental, of the pregnant woman whether before, at or after the birth of the child; or

   (b) that there is a substantial risk if the child were born it would suffer from such physical or mental abnormalities as to be seriously handicapped: or

   (c) that the pregnant woman's capacity as a mother will be severely overstrained by the care of a child or of another child as the case may be; or

   (d) that the pregnant woman is a defective or became pregnant while under the age of sixteen or became pregnant as a result of rape.

In his opening speech, Steel said that he was unhappy with some of the wording of the Bill, and that he would be happy to accept amendments to it. His greatest concern was with section 1(c), but his interpretation of what might happen if the clause was changed, showed, as will become clear, great insight into the future of 'his Bill'.

> One could say that it would be better to drop subsection (1,c) altogether and leave the continued operation of the law based solely on the definition of physical or mental health, which any doctor may choose to make. But to do this is to leave too great an uncertainty still in the law. *It would leave open far too much the interpretation of the law by medical practitioners and would place too great a responsibility on them.*[17] (my emphasis)

As it was to turn out, this was almost precisely what happened to the original Bill.

In the previous attempts that had been made to change the law, only two had included a 'social' clause, i.e. had attempted to extend the range of reasons under which an abortion could be legal, and in both those cases (Silkin's two Bills) the clause had been considerably tightened. Steel addressed himself to this problem of 'where to draw the line'. He said in the Commons 'we want to stamp out the back street abortions, but it is not the intention of the Promoters of the Bill to leave a wide open door for abortion on request'.[18]

The first line of criticism came from William Wells QC who argued that the Bill contained no safeguards against the destruction of potentially healthy babies, undermined respect for the sanctity of human life, and, perhaps most interestingly, he suggested that it threatened the independence of the medical profession. The position of the medical profession was one of the central themes of the debate, and opinion ranged from that expressed by Williams Wells to that of Dr John Dunwoody, who argued that quite the opposite was true and that the Bill would give greater independence of action to the doctors. What was not contested was the degree of importance given to the opinions of the medical profession, and the reports published by the RCOG and the BMA were constantly cited as reference points. Where the two reports were in agreement was that subsection 1(c) was not the sort of proposal that should be supported. What they wanted was to enforce the position that already existed in Case Law and to stipulate more stringently the qualifications needed in order to perform the operation, i.e. to secure a greater degree of control over the implementation, as well as the shape, of the law.

Surprisingly, given the general outcry about 'permissiveness' that was becoming common at this time, there was relatively little discussion along the 'declining morals' line in the debate, although Jill Knight, MP for Birmingham, Edgbaston, did make the link between the morals of the young and abortion:

> For goodness sake let us bring up our daughters with love and care enough not to get pregnant and not let them degenerate into free-for-alls with the sleazy comfort of knowing 'she can always go and have it out.'[19]

After the Bill had received its second reading, it was time for the involved parties to decide exactly how best they would be able to achieve their aims. It is at this point that it is easiest to judge who were the most influential groups in determining the final outcome. Hindell and Simms[20] claim that the 'liberalisation' of the abortion laws in Britain came about largely as a result of the activities of the Abortion Law Reform Association. Whilst one cannot deny the influence of this pressure group on the debates at the time – they were, for instance, vital in organising and disseminating information about abortion and the intentions of the proposed legislation – to accord to them the position of 'moral entrepreneurs' is to ignore the role of a similar if not more significant lobby in this debate, the medical profession. Using Gusfield's notion of 'status politics', Victoria Greenwood[21] has outlined a persuasive argument that suggests that the involvement of the medical profession in the abortion law debate came about as a result of a perception on their part of a threat to their interests and autonomy. This becomes clear if one looks at the Committee stage of the Bill where the influence of groups like the BMA and the RCOG played a significant part in shaping the Bill:

> Officially these organisations were not opposed to reform, but merely opposed to particular sections of Steel's Bill. In the event the influence exerted by both organisations on Parliament and on the Government served to jeopardise the very life of the Bill, and almost wrote into it a clause which might have made it worthless, namely the consultant clause.[22]

In November 1966, the BMA and the RCOG published a joint report in which they sought to stress the dangerousness and difficulty of abortion as an operation. They did this by stressing that terminations should only be carried out under the supervision of a consultant or a doctor approved by the Minister of Health. They argued that it should be stipulated that 'at least' two medical opinions should be required, and that abortions should only be permitted in registered nursing homes approved for that purpose by the Minister of Health.[23] The Report also objected to clauses 1(c) and (d) on the grounds that they might well lead to an excessive demand for termination on social grounds and that this would be unacceptable to the medical profession. The BMA and the RCOG were not only trying to build in clauses that they wished to see included, but were, as a consequence, attempting to place greater control over the operation of the proposed legislation in their own hands.

Strong pressure was put on Steel, not only by the medical profession, but also by the ALRA who urged him to retain the 'social' clause. In late December, however, he tabled an amendment which withdrew clauses 1(c) and (d), and widened 1 (a) to make an abortion permissible if the continuance of a pregnancy involved risk to a woman's 'well-being' as well as to her physical and mental health. The clause also allowed a doctor to take into account 'the patient's total environment, actual or reasonably foreseeable'. The medical profession won the day. Some of the press described the amended Bill as 'watered down' and, as Hindell and Simms reported, 'many of the leading reformers regarded Steel's action as a betrayal'.[24] Nevertheless, Hindell and Simms do later point out that:

> In view of the tremendous effort which was later needed to get even the amended or watered down version through Parliament, it is very difficult to fault Steel's political judgement. At the time, however, many of the reformers were extremely critical of it.[25]

In his foreword to their book, Steel explains the reasoning behind the change:

In their desire to have retained a clear and separate 'social clause', I believe the authors underestimate the importance of the growing school of medical thought (of which Sir Dugald Baird is surely a founder member) that social conditions cannot be and ought not to be separated from medical considerations.[26]

What Steel is explaining here is that, during the course of the passage of the Bill, he was slowly persuaded by people like Sir Dugald Baird and Malcolm Millar that the so-called 'social' considerations that might be taken into account could only be fully understood by those qualified to decide upon the 'technical' aspects of each case, i.e. the medical profession itself. If one were to move towards a situation approaching 'abortion on demand', then it would be the pregnant woman who made the decision as to whether an operation was necessary or not. By incorporating a watered down version of clause 1(c) within clause 1(a), the medical profession were able to maintain a position in which they were effectively the sole arbiters and decision-makers.

That this was the case can be seen from Hindell and Simms's description of the Committee's discussion over the possible removal of clause 1(d) from the Bill:

> For the benefit of those who supported the original clause Steel stated that the medical profession has assured him that doctors would in any case take these conditions into account.... David Steel, the medical profession and the Government were propounding the view that the law must not be made too clear lest the public read it and begin to demand their rights. Much better to leave it vague and fuzzy so that doctors would have total discretion in the matter of abortion and so that patients would be unable to argue.[27]

Despite the continued tailoring of the details of the Bill to suit the wishes of the BMA and the RCOG, both organisations still objected to, or at least had two major criticisms of, the Bill. At the end of the committee stage, the first clause read that an abortion would be legal when two doctors thought that 'the continuance of the pregnancy would involve risk to the life of or injury to the physical or mental health of the pregnant woman or the future well being of herself and or the child or her other children'. The Ministry of Health objected to the phrase, 'future well being', which, after consultation, Steel was forced to withdraw as time was already getting short. The BMA and the RCOG also wished a 'consultant' clause to be reintroduced, but not only were Steel and the ALRA against such an amendment (a similar one had been defeated in Committee), but so was the Home Office.

The report stage did not begin until July 1967, and, in his opening speech in the debate, Steel was quick to point out the changes of a restrictive nature that had been made:

> Finally, I submit that it is necessary in a Bill of this kind, to introduce certain safeguards, and that we have done. For the first time there is a legal requirement of a second opinion; no one doctor can act on his own. Secondly, there is the requirement for notification of the operation to the chief medical officer of health. Thirdly, and importantly, the Committee inserted a further safeguard which was not present when the House gave its approval to the Bill on Second Reading in that there is now in the Bill ... a provision for control over the place where the operation may be carried out. These are three essential and new safeguards which do not exist in the present law.[28]

The Report Stage took three days and was a long hard battle for the reformers and their opponents. After a long debate, the House gave the Bill its third reading and it went on to the House of Lords. In the long term, the most important change to the Bill was made in the Lords. Lord Dilhorne had continually pressed for the inclusion in the Bill of a definition of the element of risk that would justify a termination. The Lord Chief Justice came up with a solution which was accepted almost without debate by both sides and inserted. Under the new definition, abortion was legal when the 'continuance of pregnancy would involve risk to the life of the pregnant woman ... greater than if the pregnancy were terminated'. Few seemed to realise the importance of this amendment at the time, but the critics were effectively confounding their own aims for, if abortions were as safe as the pro-abortionists claimed (and through technical advances they were becoming safer all the time), then, statistically, abortion could be safer than normal childbirth, where there is always a small degree of risk for the pregnant woman. The logic of this is that, in almost all cases, abortion would therefore be legally justifiable.[29] This has two consequences, of course. Firstly, it provides the basis for a situation in which doctors could effectively supply 'abortion on demand', something which they, in particular, but also both reformers and opponents alike, had always seen as undesirable. Secondly, it provided almost complete legal protection for doctors and, at the very least, ensured that the availability of abortion would be governed by medical ethics rather than legal principles.

Why, then, was the passage of the Bill successful? A number of authors[30] have pointed to the importance of the number of new young MPs in parliament and effective pressure group politics. This, and the lack of an effective opposition, have been singled out by others[31] as crucial factors in the success of Steel's Bill. Equally important, perhaps, was the thalidomide tragedy, which was undoubtedly a turning point as far as public opinion was concerned. The Abortion Act was ostensibly a response to increased calls, in particular from groups like the the ALRA, but also from women in general, for fair and equal treatment under the law. As we have seen, the 'one law for the rich, another for the poor' theme may have been the focal point of criticism of the situation as it was then, but the final outcome of the debate had far more to do with the strength of the medical lobby than it did with that of the women's movement. The medical profession sought through this question to reassert its monopolistic power of diagnosis against a perceived, yet undoubtedly real, threat from the increasingly powerful section of women in British society who wanted to play a greater part in deciding whether or not they wished to give birth. That the medical profession won this battle is, in retrospect, hardly surprising, as even reformers like the ALRA never considered, nor wanted, 'abortion on demand'. If the question of 'a woman's right to choose' was never really aired, it was because, at that point, it was never a serious consideration. The major question was how to enact a piece of legislation that would allow abortion for the minority without creating a situation in which women could ask for termination as by right. Seen in this light, the closing speech made by Christopher Price MP was somewhat ironic:

> When I have mixed with people both inside and outside the House who want the Bill, it has often occurred to me that this is not about abortion at all – it is part of the process of emancipation of women which has been going on gradually over a very long period. The public opinion behind the Bill is millions of women up and down the country who are saying 'We will no longer tolerate this system whereby men lay down, as though by right, the moral laws, particularly those relating to sexual behaviour about how women should behave.'[32]

As has already been argued, there can be little doubt that the pressure for change came partially as a consequence of 'women's emancipation' or rather, from their increasing relative power potential in Britain, just as there can be little doubt that, in the form it finally took, the Bill continued to place in the hands of the male-dominated medical profession the power to determine whether or not women should be allowed to terminate their pregnancies.

The Abortion Act came into force on 27 April 1968, and was subjected to an almost immediate attack. Its opponents were out to destroy it before there was a chance to see how it worked in practice. In July 1969, Norman St John Stevas introduced an amending Bill under the 10-minute rule which would have required one of the two doctors who recommended an abortion to have been a consultant in the NHS or a doctor of equivalent status. This attempt to restrict abortion by limiting the number of doctors that can authorise the operation had little chance of success, but the rationale of the opponents was that the longer time went by without a debate on the issue, then the more difficult it would be to get the law amended. As we shall see this was a consistent tactic. Just as the pro-abortionists kept plugging away in Parliament from the early 1950s to the passing of the Steel Bill, so the opponents of the 1967 Act have kept the issue alive in the Commons ever since.

After the successful passage of the Bill, the ALRA went into something of a decline. Most authors are agreed that this was the result of a general feeling within the organisation that the battle had been won and that it was time to move on to other issues. In particular, this meant the Birth Control Campaign to which the ALRA pledged much of its reserves in 1970. The reason for this was explained in the Association's 1969–70 Annual Report:

> The executive committee believes that the abortion problem will assume a proper perspective in the eyes of many members of the public only when it is seen as part of an overall campaign to avoid unwanted pregnancies. This suggests that the best course for ALRA, both from the point of view of reducing the need for abortion and of defending, and perhaps later extending, the Abortion Act, lies in a campaign for better facilities in the whole field.[33]

With the passing of the Act and the decline of the ALRA, the opposition started to grow. Not only did abortion become visible for the first time, but the numbers of reported abortions rose steadily. Francome suggests that the anti-abortion movement was also prompted into action by the fact that Britain was the first major European country to relax its abortion laws, and this prompted fears that Britain, and London in particular, was becoming the abortion capital of the world.

Not long after the defeat of St John Stevas' Bill, a Conservative MP, Bryant Godman Irvine, introduced another amending Bill which also included a 'consultant' clause. Again, he was unsuccessful, his Bill being easily talked out.[34] This was followed by a Bill by John Hunt which would have prohibited the charging of fees for referring or recommending women to doctors or clinics for treatment. Whilst his Bill failed even to reach a second reading, a more successful attempt was made by Michael Grylls, who introduced an Abortion (Amendment) Bill in May 1974 along the same lines as Hunt's. It successfully completed its second reading before a General Election intervened and the Bill fell. When the new Parliament sat, Michael Grylls obtained permission to reintroduce his measure, and it got to the committee stage, whereupon supporters of attempts to change the law withdrew their support, walking out and leaving the Committee without a quorum. Their reason was that they felt Grylls' Bill did not go far enough. They wanted a more thorough reform of the 1967 Act! The three years in between the attempts by Hunt and Grylls to change the law seem, in retrospect, to have saved the 1967 Act. After the defeat of the Medical Services (Referral) Bill in 1971, the then Secretary of State for Social Services, Sir Keith Joseph, appointed a committee 'to review the operation of the Abortion Act, 1967'. He stressed at the time that the enquiry was only concerned with the working of the Act and not the principles that underlay it. The committee could not engage in moral or ethical debates, but simply suggest ways in which the law could be operated more efficiently. It is an established convention of Parliamentary procedure that no attempt will be made to change the law whilst such a committee is sitting, and the three years that the Lane Committee took to produce its Final Report undoubtedly saw the 1967 Act through what may well have been its 'stickiest' period. During those three years, the abortion rate levelled off, and it is generally suggested that both the medical profession and the general public adjusted to and accepted legal abortion.[35] After the three years' consideration, the committee unanimously supported the 1967 Act and its major provisions, arguing that any abuses that did exist were a product of maladministration rather than ineffective legislation. The one legislative change that they did recommend was the reduction of the upper time limit for abortion contained in the Infant Life (Preservation) Act 1929. The committee also recommended the introduction of controls over commercial abortion bureaux, recommendations which were implemented almost immediately.

The fact that the Lane Report supported the Abortion Act so whole-heartedly and that it received generally favourable comment upon publication seemed to have very little effect after 1974. It was not long before the anti-abortionists were back trying to amend the law in ways not suggested by Lane. The first Bill after that of Michael Grylls was introduced by James White, a Labour MP for Glasgow. Although White's Bill was ostensibly not 'anti-abortion' in that it concentrated on the 'abuses' of the system such as 'touting' rackets, it nevertheless went far further than this in that it attacked the 'social' aspect of the Act by inserting words like 'grave' and 'serious' into the clauses dealing with the woman's physical and mental health.[36] It would have restricted the decision-making process to two doctors who were not in practice together, and required that one had been registered for five years or over. In this way, it would not only have restricted women's access to termination, but would have also interfered with 'medical freedom', that elusive property that had caused so much debate over the 1967 Act. The Bill received a very large majority on second reading, and went to select committee. This large majority and a small but perceptible swing in public opinion at the time is generally explained by the effectiveness of the anti-abortion campaign which, if not organised around, was in no small part prompted by, the publication in 1974 of a book with the emotive but descriptive title, *Babies For Burning*.[37] The book was based on a series of articles originally written for and published in the *News of the World* by two journalists, Michael Litchfield and Susan Kentish. They set out to investigate the workings of the 'private abortion industry' – not the NHS – and to attempt to prove the effective existence of abortion on demand. They did this by posing as a couple seeking pregnancy advice. In the book, they claim that, on numerous occasions, Kentish was informed that her tests were positive and that she was pregnant, when in fact she was not and never had been. They further claim that she was told that abortions were easily arranged without her being examined by two doctors as required by the Act. Perhaps the most shocking claim in the book, and the source of its title, was that the authors had encountered one gynaecologist who had agreed to sell Litchfield aborted foetuses for soap manufacture. Asked how he would arrange this, the gynaecologist replied:

> I would not have to know officially what was going on ... the foetuses, as far as I'm aware, are prepared for the incinerator, then they just disappear. I don't know what happens to them. They just vanish. You have to make all the arrangements for a van or lorry or something to come to the rear entrance. Times and so forth would have to be arranged later.... You see, I get some very big babies. It's such a shame to toss them in the incinerator, when they could be put to so much better use. We do a lot of late terminations. We specialise in them. I do ones that other people won't touch. I do them at seven months without hesitation. The law says that twenty-eight weeks is the legal limit, but it is impossible to determine at what stage a termination was performed after the baby is burned, so it does not matter when one does it, really. If the mother is prepared to take the risk, then I'm game.
>
> Now many of the babies that I get are fully formed and are living for quite a time before they are disposed of. One morning, I had four of them lined up crying their heads off. I hadn't the time to kill them there and then because we were so busy. I was loathe to drop them in the incinerator because there was so much animal fat that could have been used commercially.[38]

Many of the doctors, including this one, also had Nazi sympathies, the authors claimed. The same gynaecologist was quoted as having said the following:

Hitler may have been the enemy of this country, but not everything about his policies was bad. He had some very progressive ideas and philosophies. Selective life has always appealed to certain elements of the medical world. I've always been drawn to the possibility of selective breeding and selective elimination. But that's another matter.... Many, many gynaecologists doing terminations in London and elsewhere think the same way as I do. But you have to be a man of science and not of emotion, to see through the fog of sentimentality. Human life is just a matter that can be controlled, conditioned and defused like any machine.[39]

Many of the book's claims are extreme and unproven. Others have been discredited. Potts, Diggory and Peel point out that 'even a second-trimester foetus has no subcutaneous fat to act as a raw material for soap',[40] and the authors were also successfully prosecuted for libel by, amongst others, the British Pregnancy Advisory Service. Substantiated or not, the claims in the book were readily used by anti-abortionists and, in such an already emotive area, it is hardly surprising that some of the mud stuck. Other factors existed to help the Bill on its way. The ALRA had gone into a period of steady decline, whereas the anti-abortionists, reeling from defeat, grew in number and got themselves better organised. The Society for the Protection of the Unborn Child (SPUC) formed in 1967 to try to prevent the passing of the Steel Bill, was joined in 1970 by LIFE, an organisation which saw itself as an alternative to voluntary pregnancy advisory services. Although the ALRA was in decline, opposition to attempted amendments to the 1967 Act was vigorous, and demonstrations against the White Bill led to the formation of the National Abortion Campaign (NAC). Working with groups like the ALRA and the Labour Abortion Rights Campaign, the NAC was an essentially grassroots organisation building on local feminist activity and trades union support. As Lovenduski suggests,[41] the trades union base in local branches to some extent enabled the defenders of the 1967 Act to counter the organisational base that the opposition groups had in the parishes. Despite the opposition's degree of organisation, the White Bill was not successful, as parliamentary time ran out. However, the size of its majority at second reading gave encouragement to its supporters and they began a renewed assault on the 1967 Act in the forthcoming months.

In 1977, William Benyon, Conservative MP for Buckingham, introduced a Private Member's Bill, largely based on the report of the Select Committee that had been reconvened after the fall of the White Bill. The Benyon Bill fell when the government refused to allow it extra time to complete the report stage. Soon after, Sir Bernard Braine introduced a Bill under the 10-minute rule along similar lines to Benyon's but, as with St

John Stevas' Bill seven years earlier, it was largely a tactical move and had little chance of progressing. The result of the General Election of 1979, returning the Conservative Party to power, gave the anti-abortionists the chance they were looking for. Towards the end of the life of the Labour government, during the voting on the Benyon and Braine Bills, the House had looked as if it was fairly closely divided. The changing balance of power in Parliament, including the retirement or defeat of several of the most distinguished pro-abortionists, must have filled the opponents of the 1967 Act with confidence. John Corrie won the Private Member's ballot in the first new session, and decided fairly quickly that it was the Abortion Law that he would direct his intentions at.

The main elements in the Bill were a reduced time-limit of twenty weeks for abortion, a tightening of the argument in the 1967 Act that allows termination if the risk were less than the continuance of the pregnancy: the so-called 'statistical' argument. This was to be replaced by the phrase 'where there was a *substantial risk* of serious injury to the physical or mental health of the pregnant woman'. The Bill – a very restrictive one – was particularly popular in Parliament, and received its second reading by 242 votes to 98, the largest majority at this stage of the passage of a Bill, or of any amendment, relating to abortion. After its committee stage, the Bill went on to the report stage where it received a very long hearing in the Commons, four Fridays in all, an exceptional amount of time. Yet, despite this, it still failed.

Perhaps the most important and influential attack on the Bill came just a week before the report stage was due to start. In a letter to the *Lancet* on 1 February 1980, seventy leading doctors, surgeons and professors of obstetrics and gynaecology launched what Marsh and Chambers describe as a 'devastating' attack on the Bill:

> ... which they regarded as 'a most swingeing attack [on the 1967 Act] which would, according to one of its supporters, cut abortions by two-thirds and destroy the charities'. It would they went on, result in a return to the 'scourge' of septic abortion, which had been greatly reduced by the 1967 Act. The signatories included Sir George Godber, former chief medical officer at the DHSS, Sir Richard Doll, Professor of Medicine at Oxford University, Dame Josephine Barnes, president of the BMA and the presidents of all but one of the Royal Colleges of Medicine.[42]

There can be little doubt that this, along with the general attitude of the medical profession towards the Bill, was one of the major reasons for its defeat. Lovenduski has argued that the Corrie Bill failed for two basic reasons: the attitude of the medical profession and Corrie's general unwillingness to compromise in order to get his Bill through. She suggests that it was generally agreed at the time that a reduction of the upper limit to twenty-four weeks rather than twenty would have got the measure through parliament.

Almost before the dust had settled, David Alton, the Roman Catholic Liberal MP for Liverpool, Edge Hill, introduced a Bill under the 10-minute rule for the sole purpose of reducing the time-limit to twenty-four weeks, but it received little support as the anti-abortion pressure groups were still hoping for something more comprehensive. More recently, Alton has again attempted to amend the law, this time proposing to reduce the time-limit to eighteen weeks. The more recent, and generally non-controversial, reduction of the time-limit to twenty-four weeks seems likely to have postponed further attempts at repeal or reform of the 1967 Act for some time.

What does the politics of abortion tell us about 'permissive' and 'postpermissive' Britain? Were the ethics and morality of abortion law reform, or could they ever be, described as an area where attitudes and behaviour moved in a 'permissive' direction during the 1960s? The 1967 Act was the product of many years campaigning by pro-abortion and women's groups. Indeed, one has to go back to at least the 1930s to discover the roots of the changes of the 1960s. To the extent that this is true, and that the train of legislative change was started in the early 1950s, it would be a mistake to see the 1960s as somehow self-contained; to think of them as a 'permissive' age somehow separate from other ages. That the backlash against the Act started as soon as it was on the statute book must also make one question the efficacy of using such unidimensional terms to describe complex social processes. Indeed, 'backlash' is undoubtedly also the wrong type of word to use, in that it, too, tends to convey a rather unidimensional picture. Whilst it is true to say that there was heightened criticism after the passing of the 1967 Act, it would be wrong, as the above discussion shows, to underplay the opposition to the Bill that existed in the 1960s. Perhaps the situation is better described by saying that the balance of power in the ideological battle over abortion swung in favour of the anti-abortionists after 1967, partially because the reformers undoubtedly felt by that time that they had won the 'war'.

What about the Act itself? As has been suggested, the entry of the medical profession into the arena tightened up many of the clauses in Steel's Bill, yet much of this was undone by the clause that was inserted at the last moment by the Lord Chief Justice which gave the Act a much more 'liberal' sheen than it had had before. To this extent, the Act certainly had 'permissive' elements, but ones included almost by accident. Indeed, had the 'permissive' clause formed part of the original Bill, and had its full implications therefore been digested and understood, it seems very unlikely that it would have survived the journey. For whom, then, was the Act permissive? Women? It certainly opened the doors to many women who would have previously been denied abortions, or who at the very least would have been forced to the 'back-street operator'. This 'permissiveness' was, however, a tightly restricted and regulated freedom. The medical profession saw to that. The BMA and the RCOG in particular, through their powerful lobbying position, were able to persuade those who were framing the Bill to structure it in such a way that control over the decision-making process, even with the wider 'social' conditions that might have to be taken into consideration, would continue to lie in the hands of the medical profession. Ironically, as Madeleine Simms[43] points out, the BMA and others originally objected to a change in the law as they felt it would infringe medical freedom. There can be no doubt that David Steel felt the full pressure of the medical lobby for as Hindell and Simms suggest 'at times the medical hierarchy came near to demanding that Parliament accept their word as final'.[44]

Not only did the medical profession shape the 1967 Act but, because control of the decision-making process continued to lie in their hands, the implementation of the Act has also been controlled by them. Thus the 'abuses', inequalities and discrepancies in the working of the abortion laws that were noted, not only by the critics but also by the Lane Committee, and which are described as 'administrative' problems, if they are not a product of bad law, can only be the responsibility of the administrators, who are in this case the GPs and gynaecologists who control the provision of abortion in Britain. The regional variations in abortion provision which still affect women in this country[45] are one illustration of these 'administrative' problems. They are also an effective reminder of the limits of 'permissiveness', limits that were written into the 1967 Act under pressure from the medical profession and which that profession still applies. Brookes has summed up the situation thus:

> The 1967 reform of the law does not recognise a woman's right to abortion which Stella Browne had so forcefully claimed in the 1930s. The law does not take into account the woman's expressed desire for an abortion, but rather the effect of a pregnancy on her physical or mental health, or that of her children.[46]

One final interesting change that ought to be noted here is that one of the major reasons that the anti-abortionists have not, as yet, been successful in repealing or amending the 1967 Act, is the 'change of heart' that the medical profession had *vis à vis* the abortion laws in the early 1970s. It could be argued, of course, and Hindell and Simms among others do argue, that this change is due to doctors and gynaecologists becoming aware of the necessity and justice of the new Act. Whilst one would not want to deny this possibility, it might also be argued that part of the change may be due to a dawning realisation on the part of the medical profession that attempts to amend the 1967 Act might have the effect of diminishing or at the very least interfering with, their 'administrative' control of the Abortion Act. The 1967 Act, while it may have certain features with which they were not in full agreement, had at least been put into operation in a way in which there was no threat to the professional status and power of the doctor or the gynaecologist. Through the terms of the 1967 Act the medical profession secured considerable power and responsibility in the area of abortion. David Steel recognised this possibility and in the early debates in the House of Commons prior to the removal of the 'social clause', said that he thought the likely effect of such a change would be to 'leave too great an uncertainty still in the law. It would leave open far too much the interpretation of the law by medical practitioners and would place too great a responsibility on them.'[47] Quite clearly the 1967 Abortion Act contained a 'double taxonomy' of permission and regulation similar to that contained in the 1959 Obscene Publications Act and the Sexual Offences Act, 1967. Although abortion on demand was neither sought nor achieved, legal access to abortion within the NHS was opened up to a considerable degree. The extent to which the anti-abortion movement grew after the passage of the Act is a testament to the latter's liberal qualities. However, its limitations are also clear. As with other areas of legislative change in the period, much of the debate over abortion centred around the question of individual freedom and the limits of state intervention.

Part of the pressure towards reform resulted from the number of women who were able to secure abortions prior to the passing of the Act, despite its status as a crime. This general availability to those who could pay was reinforced by selective policing of the offence and the general sympathy of juries to abortionists. Indeed, certainly in the early part of the century, abortion was viewed as one of many methods of birth control, and there was not the distinction now made between methods used before and after conception. Brookes has suggested that 'resort to abortion was the most significant female-initiated method of fertility control contributing to the fall in the birth rate from the 1870s to the 1930s'.[48] The development of the welfare state, the growing commercialisation of birth control and the development of new technologies such as the pill, heightened awareness of the possibilities of fertility control through prevention. Whilst social historians have made much of the 'liberating' effects of developments such as oral contraception, there has been less discussion of the effect of this 'liberation' on the changing nature of abortion. Whereas abortion was previously a 'vital female-centred form of fertility control'[49] which allowed (some) women to take decisions for themselves about family limitation, and thus provided them with a limited degree of authority, during the course of this century abortion has become a 'medical event, closely monitored by the state'.[50]

The availability of abortion, though extended, has been subjected to a reordered modality of control. No longer is abortion a back-up contraceptive method for those respectably married women who most frequently resorted to it[51] but has become an operation underpinned by notions of health care, with the decision-making process now tightly controlled by the medical profession. Access to abortion has become less a question of finance, and more a question of convincing medical practitioners of need. The 1967 Abortion Act was essentially a piece of paternalistic legislation. Few rights or powers were given to women, and the whole question of abortion was medicalised. It is the medical profession which now operates as the gatekeeping agency which sets the boundaries or limits of the normal, moral and permissible in this area.

7 Morality, the law and contemporary social change

> Indeed the entire Wolfenden strategy may be read as a complex discourse on the subject of sexual vulnerability, anxiously protecting those held to be at special risk from potential 'corruption'. Thus a normative yet somehow ever-threatened heterosexuality is inscribed at the heart of the institution of law.[1]

At the core of this book is an examination of legislative change in four areas: obscenity, abortion, homosexuality and prostitution. The law was altered in all four areas during the period in recent British history which has become known colloquially as the 'permissive age'. Not only has the law been reformed, but it has been argued by many commentators that it was reformed in a specific, i.e. permissive or liberal, direction. In basic terms we may conclude that in all four areas the use of a term such as 'permissive' or indeed 'liberal' in relation to the changes identified, is at best overly simplistic, at worst misleading. Nevertheless, it would be fair to say that legal reform in these areas was characterised, partially at least, by a distinctive principle. This principle was based on a distinction between public and private behaviour and has become known as the 'Wolfenden strategy'.[2] It has also been suggested that the debates surrounding legislative change in the four areas of obscenity, abortion, homosexuality and prostitution have centred around concern for what are perceived to be vulnerable groups or institutions, in particular the young, women, the 'family' and the 'Church'. Why was it that the critical areas of debate at this time focused upon these particular, supposedly vulnerable, groups and institutions? And why, although the term 'permissiveness' is not an entirely satisfactory one for analysing social change in the 1960s, does it continue to retain such considerable ideological resonance and continue to be so widely used? Politicians are still able to criticise the 1960s for their permissiveness without having to substantiate what they actually mean and seemingly without fear of challenge or contradiction.

To some extent the answers to these questions can be found by looking at the changing structure of post-war Britain. It appears, in general terms, that the twentieth century, and particularly the period after the Second World War, has witnessed a lessening of the power inequalities between adults and youth, women and men, and the middle and the working classes. The lessening of these power inequalities has meant increased possibilities and opportunities for the less powerful in these dyads, if not to control their lives, then to articulate their wishes, aims and objectives – what might be termed their 'cultural position'. One of the major consequences of this process has been to raise the visibility of differential moral values. It has enabled modern youth, for example, to express desires and aspirations which are not necessarily in accordance with adults' values, in ways that had not been available to preceding generations. The corollary of this has been that the heightened volume and visibility of 'alternative' ways of behaving and styles of living have progressively undermined long-established beliefs in the existence of, and the necessity for, a single and uniform morality. Increased debate over values has made it progressively more difficult to sustain the impression of moral consensus. A further consequence of this process has been the rise of moral entrepreneurial groups. The process of structural realignment of the social classes and, more particularly, the diminution in the power inequalities between the middle and working classes that occurred during the second half of the twentieth century disturbed those members of the lower middle class who stood at the margins, and felt the threat from such changes most strongly. In post-war Britain, at a time of rapid social change, in an attempt to defend their relatively powerful social position from encroachment from below, the lower middle classes in particular were attracted to forms of protest dedicated to the idea of reversing threatened changes and upholding traditional prescriptive norms and values. The opening up of opportunities for debate on morals and values by means of restructuring power relationships simultaneously problematised the supposed existence of a uniform morality. Thus at just the time that moral entrepreneurial groups were acting to preserve a particular set of (relatively) dominant cultural values, that is preserve the status quo or return to the status quo ante, the very idea of a consensus of moral values was losing credence. In essence, a potential 'cultural threat' was added to the perceived 'status threat'.

At the heart of the theories of Gusfield and Wallis is the idea that, in times of social upheaval, certain social groups search for avenues of certainty, reassurance and fundamental truth. This general idea might usefully be expanded. In times of relative social calm – ignoring for present purposes the argument that a real or perceived, external, common enemy may be a unifying influence – it seems a degree of dissensus and conflict is more easily tolerated than during times of rapid or fundamental social upheaval. So, conversely, signs of dissensus, conflict or lack of order appear more frightening, more challenging or more undermining at times of rapid and/or major change, when there is already upheaval. The two decades after the Second World War were just such a time and they were characterised by considerable concern over what appeared to be the rise of moral pluralism (through the increasing visibility of competing 'ways of behaving') and the threat that this posed to moral fundamentalism.

All these transformations were linked to the parallel process of secularisation with which they were interdependent. Post-war British society witnessed the continuing decline of the influence of organised religion. Traditional Christian ethics had formed the basis of the (perceived) extant moral consensus. However, the declining force of religion merely highlighted the developing cracks in such orthodoxy. Indeed a clear gap was evidently opening up between the 'dominant value system' and traditional Christian beliefs. The idea that there was some degree of 'fit' between the two was becoming less and less tenable. Contemporary morality appeared to be increasingly independent of religious doctrine. Perhaps this, however, is itself somewhat simplistic. For, just as one is over-generalising when using generic terms like 'culture', rather than speaking of 'cultures' or referring to a dominant culture and subordinate or local sub-cultures as is more usual, it must be recognised that the use of phrases such as 'morality' and 'value-system' also tend to exaggerate the degree of consensus that exists in a society at any time.[3] It must be recognised that some degree of conflict concerning the rules and norms that guide everyday conduct exists, and has always existed. Therefore, commentators must expect and learn to recognise in all historical periods the existence of a number of 'contending moralities', or to put it another way, a range of values and mores that vary from group to group, class to class. Our society, our history, is characterised by a continual conflict between groups which hold different moral positions and values. The ability of any group to impose its 'morality' on any other, obviously depends on its relative power potential at a given time. The declining acceptance of traditional Christian ethics occurred alongside, and partly as a result of, the diminution of power inequalities between certain social groups and in doing so it served to heighten the visibility of their 'contending moralities'. This process of relative equalisation reduced the ability of any one social group to impose its morality on others.

These fundamental changes can also be linked to the general direction of legislative change in the period in two ways. Firstly, the legislation considered earlier, and the debates that were associated with that legislation, appeared to reflect a growing (if limited) acceptance of moral pluralism. That is, in contrast to the legislation of earlier periods, it was generally influenced less by notions of firm or uniform moral rules and, in particular, was less dependent upon conventional Christian mores which had to a large degree underpinned the traditional framework of the law. For example, the post-war legislation regarding homosexuality and prostitution did not centre around questions of sinfulness or any other moral absolutes which could be used to distinguish 'right' from 'wrong'. Thus, although the practices of homosexuality and prostitution were fairly widely condemned, the legislation decriminalised homosexuality and ensured that prostitution was legal though highly circumscribed. In this way, the existence of social groups with moral values distinctly at odds with what was felt to be the 'dominant morality' were recognised, and to a limited extent protected, by the law. With regard to abortion, the inclusion in the 1967 Act of grounds for abortion beyond strictly medical ones, entailed an acceptance of differing attitudes toward procreation, motherhood and the sanctity of life. The Obscene Publications Act of 1959, through its 'defence of the public good' clause, rejected absolute notions of propriety and was, on the contrary, based on the assumption that certain forms of obscenity could, theoretically at least, be deemed to have social worth and be of legitimate interest to certain social groups. Moral absolutes were largely absent from much of the legislation in this period and this, it might be argued, to some extent reflected the (limited) public acceptance of moral pluralism at this time.

The second connection was through an increasing emphasis on self-control. Two pieces of legislation, the Street Offences Act, 1959, and the Sexual Offences Act, 1967, took their form from the stance adopted by the Wolfenden Committee in the late 1950s. This 'philosophy', as it has been termed by Hall,[4] derived from J.S. Mill's utilitarianism (via H.L.A. Hart), restricted state intervention in matters of morality to those instances where *harm* to others was likely, on the basis that self-control, rather than state-control is preferable so long as the well-being of others is not put at risk. The practical corollary of such a stance is that as the boundaries of what is considered to be *private* behaviour are extended and the areas of public behaviour are more minutely defined and subjected to increased surveillance, a change in the balance between reliance on self-control and external control also occurs. In this way, the increasing visibility of 'contending moralities' and the increasing emphasis on self-control in private formed part of the social backdrop or context of the legislative changes of the period, and appear to have influenced the nature of the legislation.

The general process described above had, if anything, a more profound effect on the *debates* over morality in the post-war period. As has been argued the restructuring of power relationships was related to the rise of moral entrepreneurial groups. These groups wished to promote a morality based on moral absolutes or fundamental truths, and thus vigorously resisted those forms of legislation which sought to recognise, in however limited a fashion, the existence of moral pluralism. The search for a supposedly lost moral orthodoxy by entrepreneurial groups like the NVALA centred around two major themes: concern over the perceived, and perhaps actual, process of secularisation, and concern over the welfare of the family. For the NVALA, concern for the welfare of the family was manifest in their ever-present worries over the vulnerability of the young. For many other groups (and on occasion the NVALA), the focus was the changing role of women, and in particular the role of 'mother'. On the other hand, the NVALA's essential *raison d'être* was to attempt to (re)create a society in which the Church (followed closely by the family) would be the central unifying institution. Underneath all their arguments lay a pre-occupation with the loss of a perceived Christian moral consensus, though their initial and continuing focus has been standards on television. Colin McCabe, talking about the parallel process of 'cultural pluralisation', explains just such a preoccupation:

> The Reithian news announcer, clothed in his dinner-jacket and articulating the precise tones of received pronunciation can serve as an image of that unified national culture and the terms of that unification. We might be forgiven for thinking that, with the advent of broadcasting we could finally see regional speech forms disappear, and Professor Higgins rule all our tongues. But the reality is that broadcasting in Britain has led to an ever greater diversity of accents and speech patterns and an even more fragmented national culture. In the fifties and sixties a nation gathered to watch its own transformation. Television, although by no means the only, or most important cause of this transformation, became its focus.[5]

These concerns, however, were not confined solely to groups such as the NVALA. As will become clear worries about 'the family', the role of women, in particular mothers, and the fate of modern youth, were widespread in post-war Britain.

SEPARATE BUT EQUAL? WOMEN AND THE IDEOLOGY OF PERMISSIVENESS IN POST-WAR BRITAIN

Concern that 'the family' is in a state of crisis is not a new phenomenon. It was of grave concern to many middle-class legislators and reformers of various political hues in the nineteenth century; it was a concern during the inter-war period and in the past decade has re-emerged as a contentious political issue. It causes most concern during periods of economic recession, when there is a change in the rate of population growth, and/or times when fear of political unrest and upheaval is acute. The three, of course, often go together, and all provide an insight into why 'the family' becomes a political issue during such periods.[6]

During the post-war period – particularly the late 1950s and early 1960s – as the class-based inequalities of British society appeared if not to disappear completely then at least to diminish considerably, inequalities of age seemed to gain a prominence far greater than in previous decades. The young, whilst becoming slightly better-off, slightly more vociferous in their demands for freedom from parental control and slightly more visibly distinguishable in terms of style and dress, also, and by no coincidence, became the focus of many of the fears and anxieties abounding at this time. Interestingly enough, although women were also greatly affected by changes in the post-war economy, fears about their changing position did not become *directly* linked to 'permissiveness' until the late 1960s. Nevertheless, concern about the role and position of women was inextricably tied to concern over youth, through the role of the family. Indirectly, therefore, much of the concern over Britain's supposed moral decline, and much of the legislative activity of the 1960s, can be – and was at the time – explicitly linked to the changing position of women, and concerns with female sexuality, the family and therefore, once again, the young.

It would be a mistake to underestimate the importance of the war in focusing attention on certain issues. It had, for example, a very definite effect on ideas of motherhood. The number of absent males as a result of conscription, the rapid increase in women's employment during the war, and the problems associated with evacuation, concentrated attention on the relationship between mother and child. After the Second World War, the 1950s were identified as a period of stabilisation, and the institution upon which this stability was to be built was the family. Since the 1930s, there had been worries about the possibility of a continuing decline in the population. The birth rate reached its low point in 1933, and concern was fuelled by the losses sustained during the war, and the nationalism fuelled by the conflict. In 1942, the Beveridge Report suggested that, 'with its present rate of reproduction the British race cannot continue'.[7] During the war, the Royal Commission on Population was set up. In 1949 it reported, on the one hand, anxiety about the effects of declining population on Western values, and, on the other, called for official recognition of, and advice on, voluntary birth control. In this way the Report reinforced fears about the decline of the family in modern Britain, and yet contributed to the legitimisation of contraception. By the late 1940s, despite a general rise in the birth rate, and a short-term 'baby boom', the fact that family size was undergoing a process of continued decline could not be concealed. These changes in family size were linked to other worries such as the rising numbers of illegitimate births and, perhaps more importantly, divorces.

There was a high divorce rate in the late 1940s, though much of this may have been due to hasty wartime marriages and lengthy separations. Although, later, the divorce rate started to drop (slightly and temporarily) the concern with the possible effects of divorce started to increase. A Royal Commission (Morton) on Marriage and Divorce was set up in 1951, and for a while it appears that there were hopes that the divorce laws would be liberalised. However, when it was published in 1956, the Report resisted any such temptations. The Committee were clear and direct about what they took to be the importance of family and marriage, stating that 'the Western World has recognised that it is in the best interests of all concerned – the community, the parties to a marriage and their children – that marriage should be monogamous and that it should last for life.[8] The Morton Commission, although it came out in favour of a 'conservative' approach to the divorce laws, was by no means unanimous in its conclusions. However, both 'conservatives' and 'reformists' were concerned that they should be seen to hold a position that viewed marriage as an important, continuing, central and stabilising institution. The affirmation of 'the family' as the central organising unit in British society was the aim of both.

The positions held by the two opposing groups in the debate over divorce reform and the positions staked out in debates around other areas of legislative change in the 1950s and 1960s are similar in some respects. The 'conservatives' represented in the Report used key words like 'duty' and 'responsibility' to outline a position which saw firm and immutable moral rules as the only barrier against 'social anarchy'. The liberals or 'reformists', whilst occasionally caricatured as desiring the destruction of those institutions the 'conservatives' felt they were trying to protect (in this case primarily the family), not only appeared to wish for quite the opposite, but felt the need for a change in the law in order to protect certain members of society (in this case the partners to a 'dead' marriage) from 'harm'. One might compare this with supporters of homosexual law reform who were vehemently in favour of strict controls to protect the young, yet expressed the opinion that homosexuality was sinful and that monogamous heterosexual marriage would continue to be the 'norm', whilst wishing to alter the law to protect this 'deviant' group from undue harm.

The rising divorce rate, the rising rate of illegitimacy, together with the fairly steady decline in family size and fears about the population, gelled to form a climate in which 'the family' was held up as the institution within which 'normal' and 'healthy' relationships could grow. This emphasis on the family had important and far-reaching implications for women in 1950s

Britain, particularly with regard to that area which most clearly differentiated women in the 1950s from women in the 1930s – employment.

As has already been suggested, the war provided opportunities of work for women that had not previously existed. Although there was a temporary drop after the end of the war in the numbers of women working, by the early 1950s the number began to increase once again. Despite the ideological pressure to stay at home, there were pressures in the opposite direction from a booming economy and full employment. Industry and domestic work were the two largest areas of employment for women in the period and, by the late 1950s, over 40 per cent of married women were working. The consequences of this move back to work were important, for they could have provided women with a feeling of affluence in a way similar to that experienced by the young in the same period. It was the better-off working-class wives who tended to go out to work, as Rowntree noted,[9] and the style of consumption was very different from that of young males, in that it was much more heavily dominated by 'the family' with all its 1950s ideological overtones.

Whereas consumption had been held back by rationing and wage-restraint until the early 1950s and the first post-war Conservative government, from the mid-1950s on, such restraint was lifted and post-war optimism was fuelled. Along with the safety net of the recently installed 'welfare state', nationalistic high points like the Festival of Britain and the Coronation, together with a growing emphasis on commodity consumption, set the tone for the decade. Although this commodity consumption was organised essentially around the family, it was focused primarily upon women. Indeed, the push towards consumption was effectively made possible by women, not only because they had the jobs in the commodity-producing industries, but because it was their wages, or the increased spending power of families as a result of women's wages, which enabled them to buy 'consumer' goods. The growth of consumption was matched by the development of mass advertising extolling the qualities of the newly available commodities. Women were not only in a new role here as wife, mother and earner, but also as Abrams argued that as 'home has become the centre of most of his activity and most of his earnings are spent on or in the home, his wife becomes the chooser and spender and gains a new status and control – her taste forms his life'.[10] As Janice Winship has suggested, women were in this way established as 'individuals' through the individuality of their homes, not necessarily from having money of their own as wage-earners.[11] It was in this way that the conflict between the roles of housewife and wage-earner became organised in the 1950s.

The role of women and the ideological emphasis on the family were sustained in other ways during this period. One of the major factors, and one that has already been touched upon briefly, is what the authors in the Birmingham Feminist History Group have referred to as the 'compressed fertility' increasingly characteristic of this time. This came about as a result of the increasing number of marriages, the earlier age of marriage, the reduced size of the family and, crucially, the increased availability and use of contraceptives.[12] Although contraception had gained a degree of respectability by this point, it only reached as far as married women, and control over family size. Legitimate sexual relations were confined to 'the family'. Consequently the higher divorce and illegitimacy rates, together with perceived changes in sexual behaviour, were widely interpreted as being attacks upon the family and the defence of this crucial ideological totem was central to much of the 'panic' and subsequent moral campaigning in the period.

Contraception was by no means universally available until well into the 1960s, and the pill, which is widely held to be a key to understanding changing attitudes towards sexuality in the post-war period, was widely mistrusted for many years. However, the pill may have had a crucial influence not simply because of its increasing availability but also because as Cartwright (1970) argues, it enabled a less embarrassed discussion of contraception than those methods related to the penis, vagina or to sexual intercourse. It is possible, therefore, that the effect of the pill was, at least in the first instance, on attitudes towards, or the discourse surrounding, sexuality, rather than on sexual behaviour *per se*. Such a process was part of what Edward Shorter referred to as 'the eroticisation of the family' – the weakening of the link between sex and reproduction, although as Smart argues, whilst there was perhaps a slightly more open acceptance of the possibilities of women's sexuality, around this time, this was itself restricted within the boundaries of the monogamous nuclear family. She suggests that 'a wife was allowed, even encouraged, to be sexual but her sexuality had to be functional in terms of family stability, and was consequently still constrained within very narrow limits'.[13]

Although one of the results of women's changing roles was to 'problematise' the family, this did not push women into the front line of moral concern in the same way that the changing position of young people created moral anxiety. Part of the reason for this was the belief in many quarters that 'equality' between the sexes had actually been achieved. It is clear that the economic position of some women had improved. Similarly, the legal and political position of women had improved quite considerably in the earlier half of the century. However, as Smart documents in great detail, there was a great difference between what she describes as 'formal' and 'substantive' equality.[14] She argues that although formal legal equality did not guarantee actual social equality, it did have the ideological function of fostering the idea that men and women were equal at the same time as it shielded the continuing material disadvantage of women from view. The type of equality that women were widely believed to have achieved is described by the phrase 'equal but different'. Women were believed to have separate spheres from men – homes and families – which afforded them the opportunity to assume particular caring and service roles for which they were thought ideally suited, whilst at the same time, if necessary, entering paid employment. The emphasis upon motherhood was also linked to concerns about the young and was supported by the writings of the neo-Freudians and others. Through the works of authors like Bowlby and Spock, and the use of emotive phrases in the media like 'maternal deprivation' and 'latch-key children', concern was focused on the young in post-war society, and the centrality of the woman's role as mother and home-maker was reinforced and reproduced. Bouchier, commenting on such pressures, suggests that 'a monstrous weight of guilt was thus heaped on working mothers whilst those who stayed at home were assured that their child rearing task was more challenging and worthwhile than the vain pursuits of any career woman'.[15] In summary, in the 10 to 15 years after the Second World War in Britain, the role and position of women was the centre of fears about population decline, the rising number of divorces and illegitimate births, increasing numbers of women taking up paid employment, and revelations provided by American researchers about so-called 'normal sexuality'. These fears, however, were displaced in two directions so that attention was focused instead largely upon the importance of the monogamous nuclear family and the problems associated with post-war youth. Fears about moral decline may have stemmed in part from the changing position occupied by women in Britain at this time, but stigmatisation was generally reserved for the far more discernibly different – and therefore worrying – young. Equality for women was in large part believed to have been achieved by the 1950s, and it was not until the cracks became more visible when the feminist movement re-emerged in the latter half of the 1960s (and in particular in the 1970s and 1980s), that women once again became the focus for moral outrage and protest. Hutter and Williams, writing in the 1980s, argued:

> We would suggest that in Britain and the USA we are witnessing a similar 'moral panic' over the apparently new phenomenon of women seeking to free themselves from traditional classifications. In this anti-feminist backlash, the liberation of women is linked with a cluster of social themes: the 'permissive society'; the breakdown in law and order and public morality. Abortion, pornography, sexual promiscuity, drugs and public acceptance of homosexuality are linked together. The

'blackboard jungle' of the comprehensive school, rising crime and general 'lack of discipline' are variously blamed on women's 'failure' to continue in the voluntary caring roles and to promote a 'traditional morality' within the home. In all this, women are seen as contributing to a general lessening and removal of civilised standards.[16]

'DOPE, ROCK 'N' ROLL AND FUCKING IN THE STREETS': PERMISSIVENESS AND POST-WAR YOUTH

An understanding of youth as a category is central both to the fundamental changes that have taken place in British society since 1945, and more specifically to an understanding of the discourse that came to surround sexuality and morality in the so-called permissive age. This is perhaps the one area of debate on the subject of 'permissive Britain' where politicians, moral entrepreneurs, social commentators and sociologists find something about which they can agree. Almost all argue that the young, or 'youth', underwent a fundamental transformation after the Second World War.

As young people became relatively more autonomous in the post-war decades, so they also became increasingly vocal in their demands, increasingly visible and therefore separable from the rest of 'society' in terms of their 'cultural insignia', and, because of their newly extended relative autonomy, increasingly difficult to silence. Thus they were an obvious target for those groups concerned about what were perceived to be declining moral standards, and indeed they became a major focus of concern.

What formed the basis of this increased autonomy? The major and most often cited change in the post-war period is the increasing affluence that the young experienced from the mid-1950s onward. Indeed, this has been characterised by many authors as the point at which 'youth' first gained economic independence. Colin MacInnes' much-quoted book, *Absolute Beginners*, is set in this world of the newly and conspicuously affluent youth:

> The teenage ball had a real splendour in the days when the kids discovered that, for the first time since centuries of kingdom come, they'd money, which hitherto had always been denied to us at the best time in life to use it, namely, when you're young and strong and also before the newspapers and telly got hold of this teenage fable and prostituted it as conscripts seem to do to everything they touch. Yes, I tell you, it had a real savage splendour in the days when we found that no-one couldn't (sic) sit on our faces any more because we'd loot to

spend at last, and our world was to be our world, the one we wanted and not standing on the doorstep of somebody else's waiting for honey, perhaps.[17]

Here, encapsulated by MacInnes, is a world of affluence, optimism, excitement and expectation which, if not absolutely new, was felt at least to be quite distinct from that of earlier periods. This is not to suggest that Pearson's argument, for example, that such fears can be found at almost any point in the last few hundred years[18] is unfounded, simply that post-war youth was *perceived* to be quite distinct from that of the preceding generations. The importance of affluence was reinforced by the recent experience of the war and the austerity of the immediate post-war years. Despite post-war austerity and recurrent economic crises, it was firmly believed that Britain in the 1950s was entering a period of economic boom and high consumption that had been most usually associated with the United States. A relatively affluent younger generation had developed, for as Abrams pointed out 'compared with 1938, their "real" earnings (i.e. after allowing for the fall in the value of money) have increased by 50 per cent (which is double the rate of expansion for adults), and their real "discretionary" spending has probably risen by 100 per cent.'[19] It was not just spending-power of course, there was a style to this consumption. It was the conspicuous consumption of what Frith (1983) called 'leisure and pleasure'.

As Clarke *et al.* point out,[20] after 'affluence', perhaps the other most important series of changes were those associated with mass communications, and in particular what was to become known as 'mass culture', the apogee of which for many commentators was youth culture. Although there were many ways in which the 'separateness' of youth was communicated, perhaps the clearest were in terms of style and music. The mid-1950s are always cited as the point at which distinct subcultural styles first emerged in this country, at least on a national basis.[21] This was the moment when rock 'n' roll began to get a grip of the younger elements of the nation. Elvis, Little Richard, Gene Vincent and countless others offered a sense of freedom and possibility that, until then, had not been provided for the young. Although the adult population was spared the more colourful of Little Richard's lyrics and the sight of Elvis' hips, the youthful hysteria that greeted the showing of Bill Haley's 'Rock Around the Clock' guaranteed a hostile reception from the 'adult world'. Rock 'n' roll was not only aggressive and explicitly sexual, it was also American and, as such, viewed somewhat suspiciously by those on the outside of this new teenage world.[22]

If popular music was one of the major means by which post-war youth communicated their autonomy, then it was also given expression by certain sections of the working class through the styles of dress that they adopted. Within a couple of years of its emergence, the Teddy Boy 'cult'[23] had spread far beyond its London origins. Whatever its intention, the style was viewed with hostility, and 'Teddy Boy' became, for the media at least, a term of abuse with John Osborne, for example, being described as an intellectual 'Teddy Boy' by a reviewer of *Look Back in Anger* in 1956. The assertiveness implied by the style, and often reflected in the behaviour of the 'Teds', was also found in many other areas of British social life into which the young were breaking at this time. Writers such as the previously mentioned Osborne, together with John Braine, Colin Wilson and Kingsley Amis, were collectively described as 'angry young men'. Actors such as James Dean and Marlon Brando were starring in cinematic celebrations of youth and its new aggressive outlook. The relative affluence of the 1950s and 1960s was an important factor in the growth of a variety of such subcultural groups in addition to the 'Teds'.

The emergence of rock 'n' roll in the 1950s, together with the development and spread of nationwide youth cultures, helped to foster the impression that, as Geoff Pearson has put it, 'young people were somehow more radically unintelligible to older people than at any previous time in history'.[24] 'Subcultural styles' were, of course, nothing new, as Pearson has documented. What was perhaps distinctive about post-war youth styles was the fact that they were no longer geographically circumscribed, but were to be found across the length and breadth of the country. As Dunning *et al.* have argued[25] the emergence of adherents across the country to the 'Teddy Boy' style and the fact that this was reported by the mass media, lay at the heart of adult concern over post-war youth. It was, however, not only working class youth that was 'rebelling' in the 1950s and 1960s. The middle class were also involved in a series of political protest movements. Thus, as Frank Parkin (1968) suggested

> nominal support for CND was for many teenagers a more or less commonly accepted feature of the youth culture; like the preference for folk music, outlandish clothes and the like, it was a way of drawing a line of demarcation between adolescent and adult values.[26]

Muncie (1984), following Parkin, argues that support for movements like CND was appealing for the young precisely because of its non-adult, anti-authoritarian character, and that much of the protest associated with such issues was in many ways a protest against 'adult society'. As such, there is a direct link (through the 'New Left' movement) with the bohemian subcultures which emerged later on in the 1960s. As the discussion of the *OZ* and *IT* trials showed this essentially middle-class and counter-cultural movement became the focus of attention by the authorities who were attempting in the early 1970s to stem what they perceived to be the increasing degeneracy of the younger generation. The prison sentences that the editors of *OZ* received before the decision was overturned on appeal leave one in little doubt of the fear that was created in certain quarters by the activities of those involved in the 'underground press'. Two of the major protagonists in the opposing camps of 'youth' and 'adult' society, Richard Neville and Mary Whitehouse, made much of what they saw to be the revolutionary qualities of the counter-cultural movement. To reiterate Mrs Whitehouse's anxiety:

> thousands of parents who had seen their children's lifestyle changed through the impact of the underground press were only too well aware of its significance. They knew Richard Neville not as some hard done by humourist, but as the author of the paperback *Playpower* which became the handbook of the international dropouts and bemused pot-smoking youngsters, persuaded to believe that society was rotten, life was too hard, and the odds stacked too heavily against them – the best thing to do was to drop out and bum around. The purpose of the underground press is 'not so much to dissent as to disrupt', and its editorial policies explicitly and implicitly seek to overthrow society as we know it, and of this it makes no secret.[27]

Mary Whitehouse had made much of this type of argument over the years. The young in her view were no longer governed by a strong series of moral imperatives (traditionally provided by the Church) and as such were but a step from 'sexual anarchy'. This lack of firm leadership was exploited by a few radical and, in her terms, unscrupulous individuals (such as Neville) to bring about the destruction of the existing political system, and, eventually, to secure the domination of atheistic communism. The sexual revolution that was believed to be occurring was viewed simply as the precursor of eventual political revolution. She and others felt that the only method to turn back this tide was to attempt to legislate in a variety of areas in which permissiveness was believed to have a stranglehold: obscenity, prostitution, abortion, drugs, etc., and to begin to work towards the re-emergence of the Church as a central institution in society. In a phrase, the aim was to rediscover Christianity.

'Youth', both as a category and in reality in post-war Britain, appeared to transcend class. Although, as has been argued, the sub- or counter-cultural styles adopted by the young in this period were distinctly class-based, nevertheless there was a wide concern over the group as a whole, and the development of notions like 'generation gap' give expression to the feeling prevalent at the time that it was the differences between age groups as opposed to classes that were the more problematic. This was given some support from sociological quarters by those who believed that traditional class divisions were being broken down by the affluence of the period.[28]

Whilst most studies of sexual behaviour appear to show that patterns of behaviour had changed far less than was suspected by some, most authors still appear to argue that a process of liberalisation had indeed occurred. How is one to account for this? It is possibly more helpful to think rather less about sexual behaviour, and perhaps even moral attitudes, and to concentrate rather more on moral authority. Gillis points in the right direction when he talks about 'freedom' for he suggests that by the 1960s 'there was a significant tendency for parents to place considerably greater trust in the peer group and to require less adult supervision for both their sons and daughters'.[29] A reflection perhaps on the increased relative autonomy of youth at this time? John Gillis points to a series of demographic changes which he links to what he sees to be the 'end of adolescence' in the 1950s and 1960s.[30] First of all, he points to the century-long decline in family size. Although there apears to have been a slight increase in family size in the 1950s, the overall trend was toward a decrease, and this 'seems to have percolated down to the lowest ranks of society, even though the restriction of fertility was still slightly less at the very bottom of the social order'.[31] The smaller, more privatised family was no longer dependent upon the wages of their offspring for survival; the young were ceasing to be dependent upon their families at an earlier age. Similarly, males and females continued to reach maturity at an ever earlier stage (three years earlier in the 1960s compared with the 1860s),[32] and also married younger. Gillis suggests that the trend toward earlier marriage is illustrative of the move toward autonomy, and similarly:

> While the movement toward women's liberation has encouraged some to delay marriage or even abandon it entirely, its effect with respect to the status of youth has been, nevertheless, to increase the autonomy of young persons from the authority and control of their parents.[33]

This trend toward greater (relative) autonomy, which may be expressed as a change in the 'power potential' of the young, resulted in the creation of a feeling of 'anxiety' in the adult population around the question of the control of the young. A variety of other anxieties connected to this increased relative autonomy (however tenuously) such as those over rock 'n' roll, dress and fashion, political protest, drug use and juvenile delinquency all contributed to the more general feeling that contemporary youth could either no longer be controlled or were well on their way to anarchy. This is, of course, not the whole story. The panics around the subject of 'permissiveness' were only in part a response to the change in the strategic position of youth in post-war Britain. Youth, as has already been argued, also became the focus for a series of other *'displaced anxieties'* concerning, in particular, the position of women in modern Britain, and therefore female sexuality. This attempted explanation of the politics of post-war morality would, nevertheless, be incomplete without some discussion of the role of organised religion in the period.

SECULARISATION AND POST-WAR SOCIAL CHANGE

There can be little doubt that one of the most significant trends in twentieth-century Britain has been the declining significance of the Church. Academics, in particular, have disagreed over precisely what the process generally known as 'secularisation' actually involves, or in which way, if any, one can chart its progress. However, there is little disagreement, either within or outside the Church, that religion plays a less central role in British society now than it did, say, one hundred years ago.

A process of secularisation was central to the complex of changes which were characterised as being 'permissive'. It was during the 1960s that this process of religious decline came to a head and many, both within the Church and outside, believed that religion was in a state of 'crisis', and that, consequently, it could only be through a process of radical change that the Church could re-establish itself, and regain the ground it had lost. In this increasingly secular society, many viewed religion as becoming less important, less influential and less relevant. Of particular concern were the new post-war generations who were growing up in a society where the Church's ability to provide firm moral leadership was seen to be in decline. This process was considered by Mrs Whitehouse and the NVALA to be particularly crucial, and they viewed the Church's inability to lead from the front in matters of (sexual) morality as the firmest indication of the insidiousness of the 'new morality' evident in modern Britain. In Chapter two, a passage by Paul Johnson, then of the *New Statesman*, which has been used by Mrs Whitehouse, was quoted as an illustration of the view held by Mrs Whitehouse and her supporters that the Church in the 1960s did not speak with one voice on the subject of morality. The focus of that particular passage was pre-marital sex, and whilst it is indeed possible, as it was there implied, that there had once been a time when answers to questions about pre-marital sex would have been eminently predictable, and would have been based on what Johnson described in that passage as 'orthodox' or 'traditional' Christian morals, by the early 1960s this was clearly no longer the case.

The Church was no longer in a position to provide, or to lay down, firm rules which would guide everyday behaviour. As British society had become increasingly secular and the Church had correspondingly undergone a relative decline in its importance and influence, so it became increasingly less able to dominate discussion of moral questions. It was not that moral rules were in some way disappearing or disintegrating but that the basis upon which the 'moral code' existed was changing. More particularly, it was becoming increasingly secular. This, however, is not the full picture. The 'crisis' that the Church was in, or was at least seen to be in, was in fact twofold. For at one and the same time, not only was the Church's grip on the 'nation's morals' being loosened, but it was also unable to present a united front on questions of ethics and morality. There was what might be termed on the one hand, an 'intrinsic' crisis where the Church itself saw its own declining influence in the moral sphere, and on the other hand, an 'extrinsic' crisis in which those outside the Church viewed as problematic its inability to agree on a method of responding to its declining fortunes. John Robinson, the Bishop of Woolwich, likened these problems the Church was facing to a 'currency crisis'. In this analogy the 'currency' is 'moral codes, doctrinal formulations, liturgical forms', and the problem for the Church was that 'in our generation people are increasingly beginning to question whether in fact they [doctrines, moral codes] mean anything or stand for anything real'.[34] Not only was the Church seen to be of declining significance, it was also unsure how to respond to its changing situation. Essentially, of course, there were two basic options, and continuing with the analogy of the 'currency crisis' Robinson describes them thus:

> One is to stress the value of the old money at all costs, to strengthen its purchasing power by internal reforms, and to try to extend its area of exchange. The other is to admit that it probably has a limited life and to set about seeing how it can be replaced, while there is time, by other currency, with as little real loss as may be managed.[35]

Looking at the publications of, and statements by, leading and influential members of the Church at this time, there is much evidence of both these strategies being utilised. Many attempted to reassert what they felt to be the fundamental or traditional Christian position, whilst others attempted to construct a 'new' or what they considered to be more realistic theological position for modern times. This was especially true of what was undoubtedly the most widely read, discussed and influential piece of theological writing in the period, John Robinson's *Honest to God*. In 1963, the Church was, in Canon Welsby's words, 'startled into full wakefulness' by the publication of John Robinson's unexpected bestseller, and it is clear in hindsight that his book and the publicity surrounding it was not only timely but also hit a nerve in the nation's consciousness.

Robinson's major argument, baldly put, is that the images, particularly of God, that the Church was using at that time were out of date or simply irrelevant in modern society. He argued in *Honest to God* that nothing of itself could be labelled as wrong, an argument which became associated with the school of thought known as 'situational ethics' and which, described more fully, suggested that 'our moral decisions must be guided by the actual relationships between the persons concerned at a particular time in a particular situation, and compassion for persons overrides all law. The only intrinsic evil is lack of love.'[36] This statement is, as will by now be clear, much closer to the type of argument that Hart used in his critique of Devlin, than the position Devlin himself adopted. That is, the position adopted in 'situational ethics' adheres much more closely to the views, for example, of the Wolfenden Committee on the relationship between law and morality in advocating that some judgement of 'harm' should be used to determine whether or not the criminal law should be used to intervene in the behaviour of adults, than the position adopted by Lord Devlin, Mary Whitehouse and others in which the decision was to be based on a set of firm traditional (essentially Christian) moral principles that outline those forms of behaviour that are condemned and those that are not.

It has been the argument here that what was actually being witnessed in the 1960s was a gradual movement away from the type of position articulated by Devlin and Whitehouse, and towards that expressed by, in this instance, the Bishop of Woolwich. For Mrs Whitehouse and the NVALA, the publication of *Honest to God*, although it was only one – albeit significant – event, was a key moment in the emergence of what she (and John Robinson) described as the 'new morality'. For Mrs Whitehouse this 'new morality' involved the gradual loosening of the Church's hold on mores and values, and implicitly here at least, a decline in 'authority'. She was and is by no means alone, of course, in this belief, for numerous commentators on the period have also assumed that the declining influence of the Church on questions of morality that they witnessed at this time meant that moral guidelines were being eroded, and that, because the authority of the Church was being questioned, all authority was disappearing. Christopher Booker, for example, commenting on *Honest To God* said:

> In no way was the disintegration of authority more subtly and pro-foundly reflected, however, than in a book published in March which was to sell more than three quarters of a million copies and which finally brought to a head all the doubts and insecurities which had recently been afflicting many leading members of the Church of England.[37]

It would appear that these 'doubts and insecurities' were not confined to the Church of England, for *Honest to God* was not the only piece of religious literature that caused a stir in 1963. Also in that year a group from the Friends' Home Service Committee published a pamphlet entitled *Towards a Quaker View of Sex: An Essay by a Group of Friends*, which was mainly devoted to a consideration of homosexuality and the Church's response to it. Although, viewed from the 1990s, it does not appear to be a particularly radical document, it must be remembered that it was published roughly four years before Parliament passed the Sexual Offences Act, 1967, and it is also clear that it was closer to the stance on morality adopted by Wolfenden than it was to a more 'traditional' religious position:

> we do not regard the standards of judgement relevant here as being different from those that apply to other sexual problems. Surely it is the nature and quality of a relationship that matters: one must not judge it by its outward appearance but by its inner worth. Homosexual affection can be as selfless as heterosexual affection and therefore we cannot see that it is in some way morally worse.[38]

Both *Honest to God*, and in a smaller way *Towards a Quaker View of Sex* were crucial 'signifying events' in the early 1960s. The Church found itself occupying an increasingly minor role in questions of morality, and had two basic polar positions that it could adopt in response to this 'crisis'. Robinson used the analogy of a 'currency crisis' to explain these conflicting strategies, the first involving a stress on the value of the old currency, the second a search for a new currency before the old one is finally declared bankrupt. The authors of *Honest to God* and *A Quaker View* sought a new currency that would bring theology into line with what were perceived to be the exigencies of the modern, more secular society.

These two publications are also significant in another respect. For Mrs Whitehouse, among others, they not only represented both the point at which the new replaced the old morality, but also served as the vehicles for change. They represented, and for her were part of, all the ills that she identified in modern Britain:

> 1963 was by any standards, an extraordinary year, a climactic year, the year of the Profumo scandal, *Honest to God*, kitchen sink plays, late night satire; the year in which Dr Peter Henderson, Principal Medical Officer of the Ministry of Education announced that 'it was not unchaste' to have pre-marital sex, Dr Alex Comfort defined (on television) a chivalrous boy 'as one who takes contraceptives with him when he goes to meet his girlfriend', and the BBC gave the 'full treatment' to the exponents of the New Morality and censored, by exclusion, the 'protagonists of established morality'.[39]

In this way, via traditional teachings on the one hand, and on the other publications such as *Honest to God, A Quaker View*, and the Church of England's recommendations on divorce reform, *Putting Asunder*, the Church was seen, by some at least, as being inconsistent in the moral debates of the day, and as being unable to present a uniform moral stance. Critics such as Mary Whitehouse viewed this lack of uniformity as a supreme indication of the effects of 'permissiveness' – the fact that even the Church was no longer *sure* where it stood on moral issues.

Part of the strength of religious doctrine in the past, and the centrality of the Church as an institution, has been its ability to establish an essentially 'hegemonic' position in the moral order – it has been almost universally accepted that 'morality', and in particular sexual morality, is religiously based; indeed this is forcefully argued by Lord Devlin. The declining importance of religious doctrine in the moral field, i.e. the erosion of this apparent theological hegemony, has resulted in the increasing visibility of what I have referred to as 'contending moralities'. MacIntyre, discussing the process of secularisation, makes a similar point:

> English society today is at best morally pluralistic in a way that makes the notion of authoritative moral utterance inapplicable; at worst it is a society in which the lack of a shared moral vocabulary makes the use of explicit moral assertion positively pernicious.[40]

What I have sought to argue is that the Church has been declining in importance and influence throughout the twentieth century, a process that accelerated after the Second World War. Its declining influence was perceived by those inside and outside the Church as a point of 'crisis'. Those inside the Church responded to this 'crisis' in two general ways: firstly, by what may be described as 'theological traditionalism' whereby an attempt was made to reassert conventional theological principles; and secondly, through what Dr Robinson himself described as 'theological radicalism', whereby an attempt was made to find a new religious currency more in tune with modern British society. On the other hand, some outside the Church viewed its declining influence, and the contrasting responses to this decline by its members, as being prime evidence of, and a vehicle for, the establishment of the 'new morality', and as heralding the 'permissive age' where 'anything goes'. The erosion of the Church's hegemony was in fact connected with the increasing visibility of 'contending moralities', a process interconnected with the decreasing power inequalities between men and women, adults and youth and the fracturing of traditional class boundaries. It became increasingly clear that British society ought more accurately to be described as 'morally pluralistic'. This pluralism was interpreted by some as indicating a lack of moral rules and regulations, when in reality, there were a variety of moral codes which were in competition (including traditional religious values); yet for a time at least, one moral code could not be identified as dominant. One further piece needs to be added to this jigsaw, however. Although it was difficult during this period to identify a dominant moral code, the preceding case studies which focused more closely on legislative reform nevertheless attempted to discover the possible existence of what might be referred to as an underlying philosophy. Stuart Hall, amongst others, has argued that what is generally referred to as the 'Wolfenden strategy' underpinned the major legislative transformations of the period. Most authors would now agree with Hall that:

> There was an underlying philosophy within Wolfenden which gave the *Report* and its proposals an underlying unity – a philosophy. This involved a new principle for articulating the field of moral ideology. Wolfenden identified and separated more sharply two areas of legal and moral practice – those of sin and crime, of immorality and illegality. In creating a firmer opposition between these two domains, Wolfenden clearly staked out a new relation between the two modes of moral regulation – the modalities of legal compulsion and of self-regulation. This set of distinctions constituted a new, if temporary, 'moral economy'. It marked a shift, however small and imperceptible at first, in what Foucault (1978) has called the micro-physics of power.[41]

Hall asks whether or not a dominant tendency can be identified in the direction of what he calls the 'legislation of consent'? What he identifies is a strategy which consisted in practice of what he refers to as a 'double taxonomy'. There are distinct parallels between the elements in this double taxonomy and the restructuring of the balance between external and self-control outlined by Elias and Wouters and referred to below. Hall describes the double taxonomy thus:

> In each domain there is an increased regulation by the state, a greater intervention in the field of moral conduct – sometimes making more refined distinctions, and often taking a more punitive and repressive form than previously existing mechanisms of regulation and control. At the same time, other areas of conduct are exempted from legal regulation – and so to speak, from the gaze of public morality ... and shifted to a different domain, to be regulated by a different modality of control: that of the freely contracting private individual.[42]

Although Hall's review does not cover the laws of obscenity, his basic argument would nevertheless appear to be applicable. Earlier, increases in both 'permission' and 'regulation' were identified within the Obscene Publications Acts of 1959 and 1964. These two movements correspond to what Hall called the double taxonomy which underpinned the 'legislation of consent' during the period. Similarly, the consideration of abortion law reform in Chapter six also pointed both to the existence of basic extensions of access to abortion as well as to the more finely articulated apparatuses of control contained within the Abortion Act of 1967. Hence, one basic conclusion, and one upon which a number of authors are agreed – Hall, Weeks, Greenwood and Young amongst others – is that the legislation of the period cannot profitably be described by a simple unidimensional word such as 'permissive'. The Wolfenden strategy, as was suggested in the quotation from Hall above, means more, however, than simply the legal articulation of a 'double taxonomy' of permissiveness and control. As Hall argues, it involves a new modality of control – what he refers to as that of 'freely contracting private individuals'. This involves a redrawing of the boundaries between state control and private morality. The argument outlined here, which is in essence derived from authors such as Hall and Elias, suggests that the historical process which underpinned changes in post-war moralities involves as one of its fundamental 'moments' progressive social pressure towards self-control.

Wouters, for example, has identified a process of 'informalisation' in which 'dominant modes of social conduct, symbolising institutionalised power relationships, tend towards greater leniency, variety and differentiation'. As part of this process, he notes the growth of 'individualisation', which is taken as clear evidence of the increased social constraint towards self-constraint. There has been a rise, Wouters argues, in 'mutually expected self-restraint'. A lessening of the power inequalities, for example, between men and women, adults and youth, is conducive to greater informality in relationships. These less formal relationships, based on lessened power inequalities, require more deeply established self-restraints than relationships of a more formally structured nature. This relates back to Hall's description of 'consenting legislation', and the 'Wolfenden strategy' which involved a restructuring of the boundaries between 'public' and 'private' morality. These did not, as some authors have argued, mean less control, merely (following Hall, Elias, and Foucault) a different modality of control involving a different balance between external and self-control. This argument may be taken one stage further for not only did the legislation of the period involve a new modality of control, but the period under consideration also involved the realisation that the law might not be the most appropriate means of securing control. As Bland *et al.* have argued:

Wolfenden's recommendations on homosexuality, while they opened up a privatised space in which adult male homosexuals could now operate without the threat of criminal sanction, in no sense advocated the abandonment of 'control' from that space. Power is no longer to be exercised through the operation of law, but what the Report recommends for homosexuality is the *diversification* of forms of control in the proliferation of new discourses for the regulation of male homosexuals. It explicitly marked out 'a course for treatment' for the homosexual which is distinct from that of the criminal model – henceforward medicine, therapy, psychiatry and social research are to form alternative strategies for the exercise of power. The state abandons legal control of the homosexual, only to call into play a network of discourses which constitute a new form of intimate regulation of male homosexual practice in the private sphere.[43]

Although Chapter three shows that this argument that the state abandoned legal control of the private sphere is somewhat overstated, the general tenor is accurate and is applicable to all the areas considered here, not just homosexual law reform. Side by side with the reformulation of legal controls were new discourses for regulation which involved explicit pressures towards self-control. It is worth repeating Abse's closing remarks as his Bill was about to pass its final reading, for they illustrate precisely this point:

I ask for those who have, as it were, been in bondage and for whom the prison doors are now opening to show their thanks by comporting themselves quietly and with dignity. This is no occasion for jubilation, certainly not celebration.... Homosexuals must remember, while there may be nothing bad in being a homosexual, there is certainly nothing good.[44]

8 Postscript

Thatcherism and the politics of morality

> We've been through a period where too many people have been given to understand that if they have a problem, it's the government's job to cope with it. 'I have a problem, I'll get a grant.' 'I'm homeless, the government must house me.' They're casting their problem on society. And, you know, there is no such thing as society. There are individual men and women, and there are families. And no government can do anything except through people, and people must look to themselves first.... A nation of free people will only continue to be great if family life continues and the structure of that nation is a family one.
>
> (Margaret Thatcher)

Although the central concern of this book has been with the period colloquially referred to as the 'permissive age' and, more particularly, with the direction of legislative change during the late 1950s and 1960s, much that has happened since that period throws an interesting light on those years. As the 1960s have become known as the permissive years so the 1980s are likely to be remembered as anti- or post-permissive years. However, just as it is inaccurate to use a blunt instrument like 'permissiveness' to characterise the complexity of changes incorporated in a decade such as the 1960s, so equally it is not enough, as some would have us do, to view the 1980s simply as a backlash or a repressive response to earlier times. Obscenity, pornography, 'indecent displays' – whichever term is preferred – were a central and almost ever-present concern in the 1980s just as they had been in the earlier decades. Whilst preceding the Thatcher era by a few years the nature of the Report of what became known as the Williams Committee signified that although the Wolfenden 'formula' or philosophy had gained a certain currency in the 1960s it was still very much open to challenge.

Although the government's intention to set up a committee to consider the workings of the Obscene Publications Acts was not made public until

1976, the decision to do so resulted from events in the earlier parts of the decade. In 1974 an Indecent Displays Bill was discussed in parliament and although it was not successful, it was a clear indication that the 'pro-censorship' lobby was becoming ever more organised and the establishment of a committee was one way in which the Labour Party could shelve the issue for a year or two. The intention to set up a committee was announced in the Commons in 1976 and the committee established in July 1977. Its terms of reference were to 'review the laws concerning obscenity, indecency and violence in publications, displays and entertainments in England and Wales, except in the field of broadcasting, and to review the arrangements for film censorship in England and Wales and to make recommendations'.[1]

The group of thirteen men and women were led by Bernard Williams, Professor of Philosophy at Cambridge, an appointment which did not please the pro-censorship pressure groups, in particular the NVALA, who felt that his 'humanism' was incompatible with the task at hand. The Report took two years to produce, eventually being published in November 1979. The major recommendations in the Report on the whole reject pre-censorship (except in the case of films) and advocate the *restriction* of certain classes of material. The formula that the Committee came up with to describe material that would be restricted was that which would be 'offensive to reasonable people by reason of the manner in which it portrays, deals with or relates to violence, cruelty or horror, or sexual, faecal or urinary functions, or genital functions'.[2] Such material did not include the written word which was, by the late 1970s, the Committee felt increasingly less at risk from criminal prosecution, certainly in comparison with pictorial matter. The Committee suggested that pictorial material, unless it involved bestiality or the 'exploitation' of people for pornographic purposes, should be available to those over the age of 18 in shops to which no-one under that age would be permitted access. As far as films were concerned, little would be changed except that a new statutory body would be set up to pre-censor and designate the code that each film should carry from U (universal) to 18R (restricted).

Both the philosophical basis of the Report and the responses that the Report engendered reflected similar concerns about the role of the criminal law that had resulted from the deliberations of the Wolfenden Committee twenty years previously. Firstly, the Williams Committee utilised the Wolfenden philosophy in its discussion of the limits of legal intervention in matters of morals: Williams agreed with the principle that 'no conduct should be suppressed by law unless it can be shown to harm someone'.[3] The major criticisms levelled at the Report of the Williams Committee stemmed from a more absolutist philosophy which rejected the essentially secular conclusions of the Committee.

In a book on the work of the Committee, one of its members, Professor Simpson, describes the press reaction to the Report as on the whole 'favourable', yet argues that the government, which was by now Conservative, decided even before the Report was published not to legislate on its recommendations, even though it was sympathetic to some of its provisions. This, he goes on to suggest, was not because it disagreed, but because it did not wish to be associated with the moral philosophy contained in the Report. The problematical character of the Report lay 'in its symbolising what may be presented as either rational application of liberal ideology to the problem of pornography, or a group of soggy minded progressives too clever by half, going soft on porn and hurrying the country into the mucky quagmire et cetera'.[4] The major moral entrepreneurial groups were, not surprisingly, highly critical of the Report; indeed, the better organised of these produced lengthy documents detailing their criticisms. The different philosophical positions of the Committee and its critics were evident with the NFoL, for example, criticising Williams' use of such terms as moral and cultural harm and going on to suggest that the 'importance of public morality and the function of the law in protecting certain institutions (especially marriage) and values receive no proper consideration'.[5] Moral entrepreneurial groups, however, were not forced to mount a particularly vociferous campaign for the Report was firmly resisted by successive governments and its conclusions were quickly buried. The Thatcherite 1980s were a period of increasing hostility to any views approaching the philosophy of the Wolfenden Committee and its child the Williams Committee. A number of legislative changes in relation to obscenity were made in the period and one campaign perhaps signified much that was typical of the era.

During 1983 the British tabloid press – and the *Daily Mail* in particular – spearheaded a campaign against what became known as 'video nasties': video films supposedly of an especially horrific or brutal kind. The legislative end product of this campaign was the Video Recordings Act 1984, which not only aimed to outlaw the best-known of the video nasties – which had titles such as 'Driller Killer' and 'I Spit on your Grave' – but also introduced classification of all video films. The campaign had all the classic ingredients of a moral panic: a stereotyped threat to societal values (the stereotype constructed by the mass media); the manning of the barricades by moral guardians or 'right-thinking' people; and the construction of a legislative 'solution' which allowed the panic to subside.

The 'panic' must be viewed against the backdrop of the introduction and spread of the new technology. In the early 1980s relatively few British homes contained video recorders. By 1983 there was not only a booming market for recorders, but also a quickly expanding video film industry which was brought to the local High Street by the entrepreneurial small business culture of the period. Video shops proliferated, the number of titles available seemed to increase exponentially and access to them was not controlled in the way, for example, entry to the cinema was. Relatively easy access to lurid horror and 'sexploitation' films led to the charge that obscene material was being made available not only to the population in general but to children in particular.

The tabloid press exercised its imagination to the full and invoked all the time-honoured stereotypes of innocent children being corrupted by freely available pornographic material whilst at best negligent, or at worst acquiescent parents stood by. With banner headlines such as 'SADISM FOR SIX YEAR OLDS' and 'RAPE OF YOUNG MINDS' the papers gave accounts of 'teenagers being left with the video-recorder for company' (the 1980s 'latch-key child'?) and suggested that the 'video nasty' had replaced games and conjurors as entertainment at children's parties. If by this point the reader was not convinced of the new evil that was threatening social order then a few quotes from children such as the *Daily Star*'s 'find', Stevie, could be inserted to make the point. In a section of a report entitled 'Could This Be Your Child?', Stevie was quoted as saying 'I like the *Driller Killer* where he puts a man up on sticks and then he gets his drill and puts it through his stomach and he screams for ages. Then he dies'.[6] Young Stevie and those like him, it was being implied, need our help and, if possible, our legislative help.

As with many other 'morality campaigns' in previous periods, the campaign against video nasties had at its symbolic heart innocent and defenceless children. It was for their sakes, we were told, that censorship was unavoidable. It is here, the core of the ideology of the video nasty panic, that the obvious parallels with earlier moral campaigns can be found. The central message of this latest campaign as with, for example, both the campaigns for new obscene publications legislation and for restrictions on broadcast material, was that there exists a class of person who will be 'depraved or corrupted' from contact with the particular material under consideration. The campaigners imply that whilst they themselves have not been corrupted by viewing the material they seek to restrict, it is nevertheless obvious that there are those who will be. What is usually unclear is who these people might be. Only occasionally are we given a glimpse of their identity and generally speaking it turns out to be those without the educational or financial resources to resist the pernicious effects of the dangerous material. Thus, for example, when Mervyn Griffith-Jones asked the jury in the *Chatterley* trial if it was the sort of book they 'would like their wives or servants to read' and Peregrine Worsthorne deplored the potential availability of *Fanny Hill* to 'any citizen with a few shillings in his pocket' they were expressing a traditional middle-class belief in the essential corruptibility of the working class. In all these cases, *Lady Chatterley's Lover*, *Fanny Hill* and 'video nasties', the central fear was that 'family values' were most at threat and, as Martin Barker argues,[7] the campaign to have 'video nasties' banned centred around the defence of a particular conception – a middle-class or bourgeois conception – of the 'family'. Given the centrality of the 'family' to such campaigns it is not surprising that 'children' and, indeed, a particular notion of childhood have such a crucial ideological function. 'Children' are central to such campaigns in two ways. Firstly, they are a central component, if not the *raison d'être*, of this ideologically constructed bourgeois family and, more specifically, they provide a central method of defining the role of women or the limits of acceptable behaviour for women and for female sexuality. Secondly, because it is difficult to isolate the class or type of person who is potentially corruptible by the material considered to be indecent, obscene, etc., children are a convenient screen onto which images of innocence open to potential corruption and degradation can be projected. The defence of the child is a particularly powerful motif and one which is resistant to easy attack.

At the centre of the controversy over 'video nasties' was the *Daily Mail* with its 'Ban The Sadist Videos Campaign'. In a feat of remarkable journalistic patience the *Mail* ran stories about video nasties on a consistent basis for over a year and was praised for its efforts by one of the leading campaigners in this area, Dr Clifford Hill. Hill, who was involved in a much publicised research project on 'video violence and children' commented in November 1983 that his research 'fully vindicates and bears out the *Daily Mail* campaign'.[8] The research, however, had a very controversial history and Brian Brown, an Associate Director of the enquiry, even went so far as to repudiate 'the framework, context and conclusions of the entire (report)'.[9] Brown went on to suggest that the final report of the enquiry had a pre-set frame, that the questions in the survey were anecdotal in character and that it sought specific conclusions. Indeed he argued that the report 'had the feel and used the vocabulary not of a research document, but of a campaigning pamphlet'.[10]

The Reverend Brian Brown's association with the video enquiry began when he was invited to a meeting at the House of Lords at which children's viewing habits were discussed and a paper was given by Raymond Johnston, the Parliamentary Research Director of CARE (formerly the NFoL). At the meeting it was proposed that a working party be set up to investigate the effects of violent or horrific video films with the intention of reporting within six months. At the same time that the working party was being set up plans were afoot in Westminster to introduce legislation to combat 'video nasties'. Graham Bright MP, who came top of the ballot for Private Member's Bills, announced that he would sponsor such legislation and although the government were careful to distance themselves from actually being seen to support the Bill he was, nevertheless, given assistance in drafting the Bill by the Home Office, and Martin Barker goes so far as to argue that 'Graham Bright may have put the Bill forward, but it was really a Government Bill, and increasingly it passed back into their hands'.[11] From this point on the Bright Bill and the working party enquiry appeared to run on parallel courses. The time-scale for the research was shortened to fit in with the progress of the Bill and one of the reports (there were three in all) from the enquiry was published to coincide with the committee stage in the Commons.

The results of the research were widely publicised and hotly disputed. For example, although major articles criticising the way in which the research had been conducted had appeared in *The Times* and the *Observer*, the majority of newspapers, including the *Guardian*, reported the findings of the research in stark and largely uncritical terms. The *Guardian*, for example, under a headline entitled '"Nearly half" children see video nasties', reported that results from the first report of the parliamentary video enquiry had shown that 40 per cent of youngsters had viewed video nasties 'but that figure had now been increased to 45 per cent'.[12] The findings of the research were publicly queried not only by Brian Brown, the one-time associate director of the project, but also by such experienced media researchers as Guy Cumberbatch and Michael Tracey. The effects of widespread public criticism of the conduct and nature of the research were enough eventually for Graham Bright to distance himself and the Video Recordings Bill from it. By this point, however, the media-centred panic over 'video nasties', fuelled by the report of the parliamentary video group enquiry, had sufficient momentum to carry the Bill through. Added to this was the fact that the Bill had effective government backing, so its passage through Parliament was relatively straightforward. It received Royal Asssent in July 1984.

Under the Video Recordings Act 1984, the Home Secretary can designate any person – in practice it is the BBFC – as the authority responsible for classifying video films. Thus a system similar in parts to that used to classify films for cinema release was introduced for video films. The Act also linked up with the Local Government (Miscellaneous Provisions) Act, 1982, by introducing an 18R certificate which allows for the supply of certain films only through licensed sex shops. Both pieces of legislation were fundamentally restrictive in character and yet such was the tenor of the period that they passed through Parliament with relative ease, the Local Government Act even being supported by some Labour MPs.

The political agenda in questions of morals in the 1980s has largely been set by what has become known as the 'New Right'[13] or what in the American context Denis Altman has called the 'new puritanism'.[14] In many respects the agenda has been heavily influenced by what those who belong to the 'New Right' perceive to have taken place in the 1960s. This is a reversal of the more usual 'golden age' justification for moralising about the need for change. In the 'golden age' model, a previous era supposedly characterised by harmony and good will is summoned up and then compared with the ills – be they moral, political or economic – of the current order. A return to the old order is then recommended. What is interesting about the New Right moral ideology of the 1980s is that it is posited in opposition to an age which is viewed uniformly as having been harmful, indeed largely as being without redeeming features. Just as the economic troubles of the 1980s were laid by the Thatcher administration at the door of previous governments and wider economic trends outside the control of the Conservative government, so similarly have the 1960s been held to blame for the supposed moral ills of the 1980s. Once the need for change was established in this manner, the 'golden age' model was then invoked. The golden age for the Thatcherite New Right incorporates all the characteristics of the moral order that the moral entrepreneurs of the Whitehouse mould also revere: a society characterised by supposed Victorian values, with the patriarchal family as the central institution. Although this agenda has dominated all discussions of morality in the 1980s, nowhere has this line of argument been clearer than in the discourses surrounding AIDS.

Simon Watney in describing the 'missionary model', one of the two models of contemporary AIDS education he suggests exist, says

> HIV is essentially understood as a kind of evil spirit, taking possession of its 'victims'.... The solution from this perspective is therefore sought in a return to the supposedly 'traditional' values of Judaeo-Christian morality, and its attendant institutions, above all marriage and the family.[15]

Indeed, he goes on to point out that AIDS from this point of view is often depicted as if it were a straightforward product of permissiveness; what was presumably being implied by the Princess Royal when she described AIDS as a 'classic own goal, scored by the human race on itself'[16] and by James Anderton when he said people at risk were 'swirling around in a human cesspit of their own making'.[17] In this view, AIDS is the product of a faulty morality, and the signposts which point the way out of the epidemic are labelled 'monogamy', 'heterosexuality' and 'family'. In this tautologous world where 'victims' are also the guilty, there is no room for pluralism or sexual variety – moral fundamentalism is the key.

If there was ever any doubt about the way in which the moral funda-
mentalists conceived of 'the family' – and the earlier chapters should have
made it fairly explicit – all becomes clear in that most symbolically significant piece of governmental drafting: Clause 28 of the Local Government
Act, 1988. In addition to stating that 'a local authority shall not intention-
ally promote homosexuality or publish material with the intention of
promoting homosexuality', the Act also made it illegal for local authorities
to 'promote the teaching in any maintained school of the acceptability of
homosexuality as a *pretended family relationship*' (emphasis added). As
Watney suggests, the central distinction here is between 'real' or 'pretended'. Lesbian and gay relationships are in this definition not *real* family
relationships.

As the quote at the top of the chapter made clear, in the individualised
social world that forms the heart of the Thatcherite *Weltanschauung*, the
social group which is viewed as ensuring security and responsibility, and
through which legitimacy is conferred, is the family. Consequently, the
language of Clause 28 was a major assault on gay culture for, as Watney
(1989) has argued, people with HIV infection and disease are essentially
viewed by the New Right as if they are not members of families at all.
Indeed, he further argues that much of the rhetoric of the New Right in the
1980s took as its target the gay movement, largely because the values of
that culture 'are so profoundly incompatible with the narrow, pokey vision
of the world, so eloquently defended by the then Prime Minister'.[18]

The process taking place in the 1960s, and described earlier in the book,
a process of increasing articulation of moral variety or pluralism or, put in
other terms, the increasing visibility of contending moralities, paralleled by
a process of resistance both by moral entrepreneurial groups and those on
the moral right in Parliament, can be seen with equal clarity in the 1980s.
AIDS arrived on an ideological stage on which the battle over the role of
the nuclear family was being played with an intensity perhaps not matched
since the early 1960s. In addition to the social groupings outlined in the
previous chapter in relation to the 1960s and 1970s, two additional and
important groups of players were added to the cast list in the 1980s: the New
Right and the gay community. The increasing visibility of diversity given
further impetus from the 1970s on by the burgeoning gay movement, was
resisted through the promulgation of 'Victorian values' by the New Right.
Clause 28, perhaps the definitive moral statement of the Thatcher administration, allowed no heterogeneity. In its terms either one is for 'the family'
or against it. There is no room in such a world for homosexuals, lesbians,
single parents and, more recently, 'runaway' fathers. The nuclear family (as
it was in the 1960s) remains the ideological ideal; it is, however, now being
fought for by the combined armies of a powerful and long-standing political

administration together with the moral rearmers of the entrepreneurial right. As Watney (1989) has so eloquently put it, it is

> homosexuality which is increasingly being used to justify an entirely new set of political and ideological alignments, which pose the state as the supreme guarantor of 'family values', now threatened not only by the 'queers', but by what is presented as their viral surrogate, AIDS.

The ideological battle over the nuclear family and legitimate sexual expression, which has been focused during the Thatcher era on homosexuality, has involved a number of other campaigns in addition to the specific political treatment of AIDS and the passing of Clause 28 of the Local Government Act. In particular, there was the repeated raiding and eventual prosecution of Gay's the Word bookshop in London, and the attempt by Winston Churchill MP to amend the Obscene Publications legislation. The campaign against Gay's the Word included the seizure by customs of large numbers of books destined for the shop, raids on both the shop and the homes of some of its directors and prosecutions of directors and the shop manager under the Customs Consolidation Act of 1876 – despite the fact that at around the same time Winston Churchill was justifying his Private Member's Bill on the grounds that 'we like up-to-date legislation rather than relying on judgements made 130 or 140 years ago'.[19] Charges against Gay's the Word were eventually dropped, but not before considerable costs had been incurred.

Just as the charges against Gay's the Word were eventually withdrawn, so the Churchill Bill never made it onto the statute book. Despite its failure, the Bill was a further weapon in the attack on non-marital – particularly homosexual – sexual activity, and probably paved the way for the setting up of the Broadcasting Standards Council at the end of the decade. The Bill, which had the support of the Prime Minister and many Labour MPs, was a further step in the long-standing campaign to regulate the broadcasting media. Mrs Whitehouse, for example, had long argued for the extension of the Obscene Publications legislation to television along the lines of the Bill eventually sponsored by Churchill, including the redrawn definition of obscenity and the 'laundry list' of prohibited acts which it included. Many critics of the Bill were agreed that it appeared to have an expressly anti-homosexual purpose.[20] The broadcasting of two Derek Jarman films, *Jubilee* and the homoerotic *Sebastiane*, by Channel 4 was cited on many occasions by supporters of the Bill as being typical of the type of programme that they would like to see removed from the screens. Furthermore, the 'laundry list' was described in Parliament by Jo Richardson as having an almost 'obsessive concern' with the anus, and although its avowed aim was to limit the amount of violence on television, there was no mention of rape or other forms of violence against women.

As with many campaigns in the 1960s, legal intervention in this case was justified by recourse to the old standard: the innocent child who needs protection from the damaging influence of the television. What was important about this potential legislative extension was its avoidance of the public/private dichotomy characteristic of other post-war 'morals' legislation. Whereas the 'Wolfenden strategy' directed attention to the increased surveillance of the 'public' sphere and away from the regulation of the 'private', the politics of morality in the 1980s began to question the legitimacy of this distinction by refocusing attention on the 'private'. Television fits uneasily into the public/private dichotomy, and the Churchill Bill whose provisions would have obtained anywhere that 'persons under eighteen years of age have access' would thus have deemed every space to be 'public'. The surveillance of 'dangerous sexualities' was thus to be further extended, not only through the continual reinforcement of the policing role of 'the family' but also formally through legislative intervention by the state.

That 'the family' has been the central ideological totem under Thatcherism can also be seen in the debate that arose as a result of the intervention of 'concerned mother' of ten, Mrs Victoria Gillick. The overt issue was Mrs Gillick's challenge to the medical profession's right to prescribe contraceptives to girls under the age of 16 without seeking the permission of their parents. Embedded in the subtext again lay the features of 'family' and 'state'. Mrs Gillick's campaign aimed, in her terms, to reassert parental rights, encapsulated in the question: 'Would you like your teenage daughter to be prescribed the pill without your knowledge?'.[21] A right-wing Roman Catholic anti-abortion lobbyist, Mrs Gillick was backed by the Responsible Society, and was initially successful in persuading the Appeal Court to rule that the Department of Health's guidance to doctors concerning contraceptive advice was unlawful.

The Department of Health and Social Security in 1974 had first advised that contraception should be available to all young people at risk of pregnancy regardless of age. Mrs Gillick's argument was that the availability of undisclosed advice undermined parental efforts to care for their children's health and morals. Indeed, the Gillick argument was that offering contraception was tantamount to encouraging under-age sexual activity or even, it was implied, child sex.[22] As such the Gillick campaign was tailor-made for the New Right: a 'grassroots' movement that aimed to bring to the fore the rights and responsibilities of the privatised nuclear family at the expense of what Mrs Thatcher had called the 'interfering nanny-state'. Although she gained a significant short-term victory, in the end the House of Lords upheld the DHSS guidance (though only by a 3–2 majority). There is an important parallel here with the debates over the 1966

Abortion Act. Just as the partial liberalising of the abortion laws in the 1960s did not have at its heart the extension of women's rights over their own sexuality, so the Lords decision in the Gillick case did not involve the question of the rights of the child/young woman. In both cases, it was the power of the medical profession that was either upheld or reinforced.

The spectre of moral pluralism that had appeared – albeit only marginally – during the preceding decades, and which stemmed primarily from changes in the power structure (in gender, class and age relations and in the role and significance of religion) and which resulted in a reordered nexus of controls, was firmly resisted by the New Right grouping that held sway in the 1980s. The primary policing function was taken by 'the family', which signified all that was held to be legitimate or in Mrs Thatcher's terms 'right'. It was not surprising, therefore, that homosexuality became the focus for so much of the attack given that it was 'the developing gay way of life [that] ran radically counter to the received sexual norms which the New Right was busy mobilising behind'. Ironically perhaps, the supposed permissiveness and promiscuity of the 1960s and the response to it by moral campaigners who attempted to reassert absolutist values resulted – not necessarily directly – in new forms of sexual politics including, until the full meaning of HIV and AIDS became clear, a promiscuous gay culture. This latter development in turn fuelled the moral absolutists and legal moralists of the New Right, the campaigns of which have further politicised and strengthened the gay community. The increasing complexity of the politics of sex and the politics of morality is perhaps the key ingredient of the past twenty-five years.

The struggle for moral hegemony has appeared peculiarly intense during this period. The continued decline of the Church – at least in legislative matters – the emergence of politicised gay and lesbian cultures and, despite the best efforts of the moral entrepreneurial New Right, the continued 'problematisation' of the family[23] (which was particularly vivid under Thatcherism)[24] reinforced the necessity for us to come to terms with the reality of moral dissensus and pluralism, and the declining credibility of absolutism. The politicisation of sex[25] which was spurred on and reinforced by the activities of the New Right in the 1980s has at least some of its roots in the so-called permissive era which stretched from the mid-1950s to the mid-1970s. Although small legislative strides were made in that period perhaps, strangely, it was in the late 1970s and 1980s in Britain, with the enormous development and politicisation of the women's, gay and lesbian movements that the most crucial long-term transformations have been effected.

Notes

Introduction

1 Hewison, R. (1986) *Too Much!: Art and Society in the Sixties. 1960–75*, London: Methuen, p.76.
2 ibid.
3 Quoted in Masters, B. (1985) *The Swinging Sixties*, London: Constable.

1 Permissiveness: accounts, discourses and explanations

1 Gummer, J.S. (1971) *The Permissive Society*, London: Cassell and Co.
2 ibid. p.5.
3 ibid. p.7.
4 ibid. p.20.
5 ibid. p.181.
6 Booker, C. (1969) *The Neophiliacs*, London: Fontana.
7 ibid. pp.40–1.
8 Johnson, P. Hansford (1967) *On Iniquity*, London: Macmillan.
9 ibid. p.37.
10 ibid. p.18.
11 Masters, B. (1985) *The Swinging Sixties*, London: Constable, p.45.
12 McGregor, O.R. (1972) 'Equality, Sexual Values and Permissive Legislation: The English Experience', *Journal of Social Policy* 28: p.44.
13 In his book, *The Labour Case*, Jenkins suggested that a 'civilised' society would be characterised by "a climate of opinion which is favourable to gaiety, tolerance and beauty and unfavourable to puritanical restriction, to petty-minded disapproval, to hypocrisy, and to a dreary, ugly pattern of life".
14 Marwick, A. (1982) *British Society Since 1945*, Harmondsworth: Penguin.
15 ibid. p.149.
16 Cf. *inter alia* Sked, A. (1987) *Britain's Decline*, Oxford, Basil Blackwell. Sked arms himself with plenty of evidence to reject, quite forcefully, the suggestion that Britain has experienced any major change, in sexual behaviour at least, yet nevertheless still concludes by describing the 1960s as permissive.
17 Levin, B. (1972) *The Pendulum Years*, London: Pan Books, p.189.
18 Davies, C. (1975) *Permissive Britain*, London: Pitman, p.13.

19 Hall, S., Clark, J., Critcher, C. and Roberts, B. (1978) *Policing the Crisis*, London: Macmillan.
20 Becker, H. (1963) *Outsiders: Studies in the Sociology of Deviance*, Free Press.
21 Gusfield, J.R. (1963) *Symbolic Crusade: Status Politics and the American Temperance Movement*, Urbana: University of Illinois Press.
22 Clarke, J., Hall, S., Jefferson, T. and Roberts, B. (1976) 'Subcultures, Cultures and Class', in Hall and Jefferson (eds) *Resistance Through Rituals*, London: Hutchinson, p.73.
23 Hall, S. (1980) 'Reformism and the Legislation of Consent', in National Deviancy Conference (eds) *Permissiveness and Control*, London: Macmillan.
24 Hall's article on the 'legislation of consent' was, in some senses, the starting point for much of the thinking in this book. Hall's article is one of the few attempts to explore the complex character of 1960s legislation.
25 Tolson, A. (1975) 'The Family in a Permissive Society', *Working Papers in Cultural Studies*, CCCS: University of Birmingham.
26 Hall (1980) op. cit. p.21.
27 Clarke *et al.* (1976) op. cit.
28 ibid. p.72.
29 Hall *et al.* (1978) op. cit. p.260.
30 Weeks, J. (1985) *Sexuality and its Discontents*, London: Routledge & Kegan Paul, p.20.
31 ibid. p.22.
32 ibid. p.30.
33 Jeffreys, S. (1990) *Anticlimax: A Feminist Perspective on the Sexual Revolution*, London: The Women's Press, p.2.
34 Brownmiller, S. (1975) *Against Our Will*, Secker & Warburg.
35 See also Meiselman, K.C. (1979) *Incest*, San Francisco, Jossey-Bass and Russell, D.H. (1984) *Sexual Exploitation*, Beverly Hills: Sage.
36 Brownmiller, S. (1975) *Against Our Will*, New York, Simon and Schuster and Dobash, R.E. and Dobash, R. (1979) *Violence Against Wives*, New York: The Free Press.
37 Cf. Dworkin, A. (1981) *Pornography: Men Possessing Women*, London: The Women's Press.
38 Jeffreys, S. (1990) op. cit. p.93.
39 ibid.
40 Wouters, C. (1977) 'Informalisation and the Civilising Process', in Gleichmann, P., Goudsblom, J. and Korte, H. (eds) *Human Figurations*, Amsterdams Sociologisch Tijdschrift, p.437.
41 ibid.
42 See, for example the reading in Hall and Jefferson (1976) op. cit.
43 Wouters, C. (1987) 'Developments in the Behavioural Codes between the Sexes: The Formalisation of Informalisation in the Netherlands, 1930–85', *Theory, Culture and Society* 4; 405–27.
44 Quoted in Wouters (1977) op. cit. p.437.
45 ibid. p.441–2.
46 ibid. p.447.
47 ibid. p.449.

2 Permissiveness and moral protest: Mary Whitehouse and the National Viewers' and Listeners' Association

1 Whitehouse, M. (1982) *A Most Dangerous Woman?*, Lion, pp.14–15.
2 Whitehouse, M. (1971) *Who Does She Think She Is?*, New English Library, p.53.
3 Tracey, M. and Morrison, D. (1979) *Whitehouse*, London: Macmillan, p.47.
4 Whitehouse (1982) op. cit. p.72.
5 ibid.
6 Tracey and Morrison (1979) op. cit. p.61.
7 More about the Oxford Group and MRA can be found in Driberg, T. (1964) *The Mystery of Moral Re-armament*, London: Secker & Warburg.
8 Whitehouse said

> The often repeated suggestion that Moral Re-armament was behind our campaign was also meant as a smear, but as time went on the press, and everyone else it seems, came to accept what we ourselves came to say about the matter. My position was clear. I owed much to the Oxford Group and MRA for it was through these movements that I found again my personal faith and developed that concern for the country which along with my deep sense of responsibility for the children I taught, led me into this campaign.... At no time have we received any financial backing of any kind from MRA – or from anywhere else – and all our decisions and plans are made within our association without reference to any other body.
> (Whitehouse 1971: 66)

9 Caulfield, M. (1975) *Mary Whitehouse*, Mowbray, p.73.
10 ibid.
11 Whitehouse (1971) op. cit. pp.70–1.
12 ibid. p.15.
13 ibid. p.11.
14 ibid. p.239.
15 ibid.
16 Whitehouse (1982) op. cit. p.12.
17 Caulfield (1975) op. cit. p.93.
18 Quoted in Tracey and Morrison (1979) op. cit. p.111.
19 ibid. p.112.
20 Whitehouse (1982) op. cit. p.59.
21 Tracey and Morrison (1979) op. cit. p.115.
22 ibid.
23 Whitehouse, M. (1967) *Cleaning-up TV*, Blandford Press.
24 ibid. p.167 and quoted in Tracey and Morrison (1979) op. cit. p.82.
25 Whitehouse (1982) op. cit. p.120.
26 ibid.
27 Whitehouse, M. (1985) 'Obscenity that Fuelled the Brussels Brutality', *Guardian*, 10 June.
28 Palmer, T. (1971) *The Trials of OZ*, London: Blond and Briggs, p.25.
29 *Daily Telegraph* 6 November 1971.
30 Tracey and Morrison (1979) op. cit. p.135.
31 Whitehouse, M. (1977) *Whatever Happened to Sex?* London: Hodder & Stoughton, pp.256–7.

32 Whitehouse (1971) op. cit. p.46.
33 ibid.
34 ibid. pp.46–7.
35 ibid. p.145.
36 Whitehouse (1982) op. cit. p.137.
37 ibid. pp.137–8.
38 Tracey and Morrison (1979) op. cit. p.3.
39 Whitehouse (1982) op. cit. p.161.
40 ibid. p.163.
41 Tracey and Morrison (1979) op. cit. p.15.
42 ibid. p.18.
43 Whitehouse (1977) op. cit. pp.82–3; Whitehouse (1982) op. cit. p.175; and Tracey and Morrison (1979) op. cit. p.18.
44 Tracey and Morrison (1979) op. cit. p.20.
45 Whitehouse (1982) op. cit. p.235.
46 ibid. p.238.
47 Devlin, Lord P. (1959) *The Enforcement of Morals*, Oxford: Oxford University Press.
48 Whitehouse (1982) op. cit. p.137.
49 Tracey and Morrison (1979) op. cit. p.137.
50 Whitehouse (1977) op. cit. p.235.
51 ibid. p.72.
52 Caulfield (1975) op. cit. p.17.
53 Whitehouse (1977) op. cit. p.228.
54 Whitehouse, M. (1970) 'Promoting Violence', Royal College of Nursing Professional Conference "The Violent Society", 5 April 1970.
55 Whitehouse (1977) op. cit. p.230.
56 Welsby, Canon P.A. (1984) *A History of the Church of England*, Oxford: Oxford University Press, p.113.
57 Whitehouse (1977) op. cit. p. ??.
58 Wallis, R. and Bland, R. (1979) 'Purity in Danger: A Survey of Participants in a Moral-Crusade Rally', *British Journal of Sociology* 30: 188.
59 ibid. p.189.
60 Letter from Lyndon Bowring, Chairman of NFoL/CARE, 1983.
61 This account is taken from Cliff, D. (1979) 'Religion, Morality and the Middle Class', in King, R. and Nugent, N. (eds) *Respectable Rebels*, London: Hodder & Stoughton.
62 The Responsible Society (undated) 'An Invitation to Join'.
63 ibid.
64 Youth Concerned (undated) 'Saying NO isn't always easy...!'
65 ibid.
66 Becker (1963) op. cit.
67 Gusfield, J.R. (1963) *Symbolic Crusade: Status Politics and the American Temperance Movement*, Urbana: University of Illinois Press.
68 Gusfield (1963) op. cit., quoted in Wallis, R. (1977) 'A Critique of the Theory of Moral Crusades as Status Defence', *Scottish Journal of Sociology* 2: 196.
69 Zurcher, L.A., Kirkpatrick, R.G., Cushing, R.G. and Bowmar, C.K. (1973) 'Ad-hoc Anti-pornography Organisations and their Active Members: A Research Summary', *Journal of Social Issues* 29.

70 Gusfield (1963) op. cit., quoted in Clarke, A. (1987) 'Moral Protest, Status Defence and the Anti-Abortion Campaign', *British Journal of Sociology* 38 (2).
71 Cf. Wallis (1977) op. cit.; Tracey and Morrison (1979) op. cit.
72 Wallis (1977) op. cit. p.197.
73 ibid.
74 Tracey, M. and Morrison, D. (undated) 'The Jericho People: Mary Whitehouse and the National Viewers' and Listeners' Association', Report to the SSRC.
75 Wallis, R. (1976) 'Moral Indignation and the Media: An Analysis of the NVALA', *Sociology* 10.
76 ibid. p.292.
77 Watney, S. (1987) *Policing Desire: Pornography, AIDS and the Media*, Comedia, p.43.

3 The Wolfenden Report and legislative change

1 Wildeblood, P. (1957) *Against the Law*, Harmondsworth: Penguin.
2 Hyde, H.M. (1970) *The Other Love*, London: Heinemann, and Weeks, J. (1977) *Coming Out: Homosexual Politics from the Nineteenth Century to the Present*, London: Quartet (revised and updated 1990).
3 Hyde (1970) op. cit. p.213.
4 ibid. p.214.
5 *Hansard* HC debs vol. 251 col. 1298; quoted in Hyde (1970) op. cit.
6 Wolfenden, J. (1976) *Turning Points*, London: Bodley Head.
7 Church of England Moral Welfare Council (1952) *The Problem of Homosexuality*, Church Information Board.
8 *New Statesman and Nation*, 10 April 1954, quoted in Hyde (1970) op. cit.
9 Wolfenden (1976) op. cit. p.130.
10 Smart, C. (1981) 'Law and the Control of Women's Sexuality', in Hutter, B. and Williams, G. (eds) *Controlling Women: The Normal and the Deviant*, Croom Helm.
11 Report of the Committee on Homosexual Offences and Prostitution, Cmnd. 247 para.1 (The Wolfenden Report).
12 ibid. para.229.
13 Wolfenden (1976) op. cit. pp.141–2.
14 R.A. Butler, *Hansard* HC debs vol. 598 col. 1271.
15 R. v. Webb (1964) 1 Q.B. 357.
16 Greenwood, V. and Young, J. 'Ghettos of Freedom', in National Deviancy Conference (eds) (1980) *Permissiveness and Control*, London: Macmillan.
17 Hutter and Williams (eds) (1981) op. cit.
18 In Hutter and Williams (eds) (1981) op. cit.
19 Cmnd. 247, para.355.
20 ibid. para.124.
21 Church of England Moral Welfare Council (1956) *Sexual Offenders and Social Punishment*, Information Board, pp.40–1.
22 Cmnd. 247, para.67.
23 ibid. para.71.
24 ibid.
25 ibid. para.97.
26 ibid.

27 Hopkins, H. (1963) *A Social History of the Forties and Fifties in Britain*, London: Martin Secker & Warburg.
28 Hyde (1970) op. cit. pp.235–6. The signatories included: Lord Attlee, the Bishops of Birmingham and Exeter, Professors A.J. Ayer, Isaiah Berlin and Julian Huxley, Sir Robert Boothby MP, J.B. Priestley, Bertrand Russell and Barbara Wootton.
29 *Hansard* HC debs vol. 596 col. 365.
30 *Hansard* HC debs vol. 596 col. 369.
31 *The Times*, 27 November 1958.
32 *The Times*, 26 November 1958.
33 *Hansard* HC debs vol. 596 col. 437.
34 *The Times*, 11 May 1965.
35 *Hansard* HC debs vol. 738 col. 1077.
36 *Hansard* HL debs vol. 738 col. 1108–9.
37 *Sunday Telegraph*, 14 August 1966.
38 *Daily Telegraph*, 22 July 1967.
39 Warner, N. (1983) 'Parliament and the Law', in Galloway (1983).
40 *Hansard* HC debs, 19 December 1966, col. 1120.
41 Knuller v. DPP (1973) AC 436 at p.457. Quoted in Galloway (1983) op. cit. p.87.
42 Numerous well documented examples of discrimination in all these areas can be found in Galloway (1983) op. cit.
43 The information for this section was largely based on an article by Roy Walmsley, 'Indecency between Males and the Sexual Offences Act 1967', *Criminal Law Review* (1978).
44 *Daily Telegraph*, 22 July 1967.
45 Cmnd. 247 op. cit. para.61.
46 Quoted in Devlin (1959) op. cit. p.3.
47 ibid.
48 Mill, J.S. (1859) *On Liberty* (London: George Routledge & Sons) and Stephens, J.F. (1873) *Liberty, Equality, Fraternity* (London: Macmillan).
49 Hart, H.L.A. (1963) *Law, Liberty and Morality*, Oxford: Oxford University Press.
50 ibid. p.4.
51 ibid.
52 ibid. p.6.
53 ibid. pp.6–7.
54 ibid. p.9.
55 ibid. p.11.
56 Cmnd. 247 op. cit. para.13.
57 Devlin (1959) op. cit. p.13.
58 ibid. p.15.
59 ibid. p.23.
60 Hart (1963) op. cit. p.4.
61 Cmnd. 247 op. cit., quoted in Hart (1963) op. cit. p.14.
62 ibid. p.31.
63 ibid. p.34.
64 Quoted in Mitchell, B. (1967) *Law, Morality and Religion in a Secular Society*, Oxford: Oxford University Press.
65 ibid. p.22.

4 Obscenity and the law: the permissive years?

1 Johnson, P. Hansford (1967) *On Iniquity*, London: Macmillan, p.17.
2 Whitehouse, M. (1977) *Whatever Happened to Sex?*, London: Hodder & Stoughton, pp.180–1.
3 R. v. Sedley (1663) 1. Sid. 168.
4 R. v. Hicklin (1868) L.R. 3 Q.B. 360; 27 LJMC 89; 18 L.T. 395.
5 (1868) L.R. 3 Q.B. 360, at. p.371.
6 Robertson, G. (1979) *Obscenity*, London: Weidenfeld and Nicolson, quotes Mr Asquith, the future PM, and then an eager junior prosecuting counsel, as saying that he had spent 'the best part of a fortnight in the long vacation, with scissors and a pot of paste at hand, in a diligent quest for the most objectionable passages in M. Zola's voluminous works'.
7 Havelock Ellis (1936) *Sexual Inversion*, New York: Random House.
8 R. v. Reiter (2954) 2 Q.B. 16.
9 Werner Laurie Ltd had been prosecuted two months previously for publishing *Julia* by Margot Bland, and had pleaded guilty.
10 *New Statesman*, 10 July 1954.
11 Robertson (1979) op. cit.
12 R. v. Secker & Warburg (1954) 2 All E.R. 683; (1954) 1 WLR 1138, at pp.1139–1142.
13 6 November 1954.
14 *Guardian*, 18 September 1954; quoted in Street, H. (1982) *Freedom, the Individual and the Law*, Harmondsworth: Penguin, p.122; St John Stevas, N. (1956) *Obscenity and the Law*, London: Martin Secker & Warburg, p.116; and Robertson (1979) op. cit. p.42.
15 ibid.
16 *The Times*, 19 and 21 May 1954.
17 Leader 7 March 1954, quoted in St John Stevas (1956) op. cit. p.117.
18 "Literature and the Law", 5 June 1954, and continued almost every day until 19 June 1954.
19 *The Times*, 28 October to 5 November 1954.
20 Bertrand Russell, Harold Nicolson, Compton Mackenzie, J.B. Priestley, H.E. Bates, Somerset Maugham and Philip Gibbs.
21 A useful list of major articles written at the time is provided by St John Stevas, N. (1956) op. cit. p.120.
22 The first president of the committee was Sir Alan Herbert, the second Sir Gerald Barry. The other members were: Walter Allen, H.E. Bates, David Carver, Prof. Guy Chapman, W.B. Clowes, W.A.R. Collins, Joseph Compton, Rupert Hart-Davis, C.R. Hewitt, R. Jenkins MP, Denys Kilham Roberts, A.D. Peters, V.S. Pritchett, John Duchey, Sir Herbert Read, N. St John Stevas, W.E. Williams.
23 *The Times*, 3 Feb. 1955.
24 A copy of the draft Bill is contained in appendix II of St John Stevas, N. (1956) op. cit. and *Criminal Law Review* (1955) 218.
25 St John Stevas (1956) op. cit.
26 See article by Kingsley Martin in the *New Statesman* 25 Sept. 1985, and general discussion in Pearson, G. (1984) *Hooligan: A History of Respectable Fears*, London: Macmillan.
27 *Hansard* vol. 537 col. 1089–90.

28 *Hansard* vol. 537 col. 1122.
29 *Hansard, House of Commons Official Report* vol. 538 Nos 60–63.
30 The Children and Young Persons (Harmful Publications) Act 1955.
31 Barker, M. (1984) *A Haunt of Fears: The Strange History of the British Horror Comics Campaign*, London: Pluto.
32 ibid. p.182.
33 24 March 1955.
34 The Committee's membership included: Sir Peter Agnew, Mr Ede, Mr Hugh Fraser, Sir Lancelot Joynson-Hicks, Mr Roy Jenkins, Mr Elwyn Jones, Viscount Lambton, Mr Nigel Nicolson, Sir Leslie Plummer, Mr Robinson, Mr Simon, Sir Spencer Summers, Mr Turton, Mr Younger.
35 Minutes of Evidence taken before the Select Committee on the Obscene Publications Bill in session 1956–7 (HC 123).
36 Sir John Nott-Bower KCVO Commissioner of Police of the Metropolis, Mr T. MacD. Barker, CBE, Solicitor to the Metropolitan Police Force and Inspector D. McLeod.
37 Minutes of evidence, p.89 and *The Spectator*, 26 August 1960.
38 *Hansard* vol. 597 col. 1021.
39 *Hansard* vol. 597 col. 1030.
40 *The Times*, 3 December 1958.
41 Sir Alan Herbert (1970) *APH; His Life and Times*, London: Heinemann, pp.213–14. For a brief account by APH, see *Daily Telegraph*, 27 July 1959.
42 Sir Alan Herbert (1970) op. cit. p.214.
43 R. v. Hicklin (1868) L.R. 3 Q.B. 360; 27 LJMC 89; 18 L.T. 395.
44 Robertson (1979) op. cit. p.54.
45 R. v. Martin Secker & Warburg (1954); WLR 1138.
46 *Solicitor's Journal*, 20 November 1959.
47 The Obscene Publications Bill, 1955.
48 *The Author*, Spring 1955, p.56.
49 Whitehouse (1977) op. cit. p.172.
50 Herbert (1970) op. cit. p.238.
51 Booker, C. (1970) *The Neophiliacs*, London: Collins, p.195.
52 Whitehouse (1977) op. cit. p.181.
53 *The Times* 20 August 1960.
54 17 August 1960.
55 18 August 1960.
56 8 August 1960.
57 Rolph, C.H. (1961) *The Trial of Lady Chatterley*, Harmondsworth: Penguin, p.19.
58 ibid. p.20.
59 ibid. p.29.
60 Levin, B. (1972) *The Pendulum Years*, London: Pan Books, p.287.
61 A full list is included in Rolph (1961) op. cit.
62 Bernard Levin (1972) op. cit. Pan Books 1972 p.287, quoted in Robertson (1979) op. cit. p.133.
63 *The Times*, 3 November 1960.
64 *News of the World*, 6 November 1960.
65 *The Times*, 4 November 1960 and 3 February 1961.
66 *The Times*, 9 November 1960.
67 *The Spectator*, 26 August 1961.

68 Whitehouse (1977) op. cit. p.182.
69 Robertson (1979) op. cit. p.213.
70 Home Office (1959) Cmnd. 247 op. cit. para.102.
71 *The Times*, 8 August 1960.
72 Shaw v. DPP (1962) A.C. 220.
73 *Daily Telegraph*, 22 September 1960.
74 ibid.
75 *The Times*, 14 December 1960.
76 *The Times*, 15 and 22 December 1960.
77 Robertson, G. (1974) *Whose Conspiracy?* NCCL, p.18.
78 Shaw v. DPP 1961 2 All E.R. 446 at p.452, quoted in Robertson (1974) op. cit. p.18.
79 ibid.
80 Robertson (1974) op. cit. p.22.
81 O'Higgins, P. (1972) *Censorship in Britain*, London: Nelson, quoted in Spicer, R. (1981) *Conspiracy*, London: Lawrence and Wishart, p.85.
82 13 May 1961.
83 *Sunday Times*, 7 May 1961.
84 A list of interesting articles is provided by Robertson (1974) op. cit.
85 See Hyde, H.M. (1964) *A History of Pornography*, London: Heinemann, p.97.
86 Robertson (1979) op. cit. p.25.
87 *The Times*, 8 November 1963.
88 Hyde, H.M. (1964) op. cit. p.209.
89 Kennedy, L. (1964) *The Trial of Stephen Ward*, London: Victor Gollancz, p.23.
90 *Guardian*, 11 February 1964.
91 Roy Jenkins in *The Observer*, 16 February 1964.
92 Robertson (1979) op. cit. p.106.
93 *Hansard*, 7 July 1964, col. 358 (Mr Rees-Davis).
94 Hewitt, P. (1982) *The Abuse of Power*, Oxford: Martin Robertson, p.100, and Robertson (1979) op. cit.
95 *The Spectator*, 21 February 1964.
96 *Sunday Times*, 15 December 1963.
97 See above p.90. O'Higgins suggests that the use of the common law conspiracy charge was a method of avoiding stringencies of the criminal law, and it is difficult to see how one could deny that this argument fits the *Fanny Hill* case.
98 *Sunday Telegraph*, 16 February 1964.
99 ibid.
100 ibid.
101 C.M. Woodhouse, *Hansard* vol. 695 col. 1143.
102 *Hansard* vol. 695 cols 1164–65.
103 *Hansard* vol. 695 col. 1159.
104 *Hansard* vol. 695 col. 1192.
105 Sutherland, J. (1982) *Offensive Literature*, Junction Books, p.46.
106 Gosling, R. (1965) 'The Trial', *New Society*, 30 December, p.21.
107 R. v. Calder and Boyars (1969) I Q.B. 151 at p.165.
108 *Hansard* HC debs vol. 730 col. 1751. Also quoted in Tribe, D. (1973) *Questions of Censorship*, London: George Allen & Unwin, p.104 and *The Queen* 4 January 1967 p.26.
109 Marion Boyars, Dr Lindsay Neustatter, Edward Lucie-Smith, Dr Lionel Tiger, Bryan Magee, Robert Burgess, Peter Fryer, John Calder.

110 H. Montgomery Hyde, Robert Pitman, Sir Basil Blackwell, Dr Ernest Clayton, Robert Maxwell MP, Professor George Catlin, Fielden Hughes, David Holloway.
111 Peter Fryer in the *New Statesman*, 16 December 1966.
112 1 December 1967.
113 Foreword in *Last Exit to Brooklyn*, London: Calder and Boyars (1966) p.13.
114 *The Times*, 2 December 1967.
115 Whitehouse (1977) op. cit. p.182.
116 Arts Council of Great Britain (1969) *The Obscenity Laws*, London: Andre Deutsch Ltd, p.11.
117 The Committee members were: Chairman: John Montgomerie. Members: Professor Frank Kermode, John Mortimer QC, R.G. Davis-Poynter, T.A. Joy, John Calder, Kathleen Nott, Dorothy Morland, Benn Levy, T.E. Callander, J.E. Morpurgo, Clifford Simmons, Tony Smythe, R.H. Code-Holland, F.J. Warburg, C.R. Hewitt (C.H. Rolph), Howard Loxton, Ronald Harwood, Wiliam Gaskill.
118 *The Times*, 1 August 1969.
119 They cite the Vagrancy Acts of 1824 and 1838.
120 Arts Council of Great Britain (1969) *The Obscenity Laws* op. cit. p.37.
121 Quoted in NCCL (1972) *Against Censorship*, p.37.
122 Arts Council of Great Britain (1969) *The Obscenity Laws* op. cit.
123 ibid. p.39.
124 21 July 1969 and 19 July respectively.
125 16 July 1969.
126 16 July 1969.
127 18 July 1969.
128 *The Times*, 16 July 1969.
129 *The People*, "Freedom for Filth", 20 July 1969.
130 ibid.
131 *Daily Mirror*, 21 July 1969.
132 ibid.
133 *Hansard* 24 July 1969, 787. The motion was backed by sixty other MPs.
134 'MPs press to kill obscenity laws', *Sunday Times*, 6 July 1969.
135 *Hansard* vol. 787 col. 2109.
136 *Books and Bookmen*, October 1971, pt 1 pp.32–3.

5 Obscenity and the law: backlash?

1 Lord Longford (1974) *The Grain of Wheat*, London: Collins.
2 *Evening News*, 31 July 1972, p.10.
3 ibid.
4 Watney, S. (1987) *Policing Desire: Pornography, AIDS and the Media*, Comedia.
5 *Observer*, 17 September 1972.
6 *Pornography: The Longford Report*, Coronet (1972) p.12.
7 *Sunday Times*, 27 January 1974.
8 *Spectator*, 4 September 1971.
9 *Sunday Times*, 27 January 1974.
10 ibid.

11 *Spectator*, 4 September 1971.
12 *Sunday Times*, 29 August 1971.
13 September 1972.
14 27 and 30 August 1971.
15 *The Longford Report* op. cit. pp.383–5.
16 Dworkin, R. quoted in NCCL (1972) *Against Censorship*, pp.33–4.
17 *The Longford Report* (1972) op. cit. p.428.
18 S. Binney, D. Delderfield, J. Murray Brown, Cliff Richard, Jimmy Savile.
19 *The Longford Report* (1972) op. cit. pp.218–19.
20 ibid. p.221.
21 ibid. p.214.
22 ibid. p.218.
23 ibid. p.308.
24 ibid. p.309.
25 ibid. pp.313–14.
26 ibid. p.332.
27 ibid. p.343.
28 ibid. p.339.
29 ibid. p.348.
30 ibid. p.357.
31 *Sunday Times*, 24 September 1972.
32 *Daily Telegraph*, 21 September 1972.
33 *The Times*, 21 September 1972.
34 *Daily Telegraph*, 21 September 1972.
35 ibid.
36 *The Times*, 21 September 1972.
37 *Daily Telegraph*, 21 September 1972.
38 *The Times*, 21 September 1972.
39 *Daily Telegraph*, 21 September 1972.
40 *The Times*, 22 September 1972.
41 *Daily Telegraph*, 21 September 1972.
42 ibid.
43 *The Longford Report* (1972) op. cit. p.278.
44 *The Times*, 23 September 1972.
45 *The Times*, 26 October 1972.
46 *Guardian*, 26 September 1972.
47 *Observer*, 24 September 1972.
48 Society of Conservative Lawyers (1971) 'Pollution of the Mind'.
49 *Economist*, 18 December 1971.
50 John Calder (Publications) Ltd. v. Powell (1965) 1 Q.B. 509.
51 *The Longford Report* (1972) op. cit. p. 313.
52 Shaw v. DPP (1962) A.C. 220 quoted in NCCL (1972) op. cit. p.17.
53 Robertson (1979) op. cit. p.216.
54 ibid.
55 Quoted in the *Guardian*, 11 November 1970.
56 Sutherland (1982) op. cit. p.108.
57 Quoted in Robertson (1979) op. cit. p.108.
58 *The Times*, 16 March 1971.
59 Tribe, D. (1979) op. cit. p.136.

60 Quoted in Palmer, T. (1971) *The Trials of OZ*, London: Blond and Briggs, pp.25–6.
61 *OZ* no. 28 'Schoolkids' Issue' p.5.
62 ibid.
63 Palmer (1971) op. cit. p.35.
64 Robertson (1979) op. cit. p.126.
65 R. v. Calder and Boyars (1969) I Q.B. 151.
66 Palmer (1971) op. cit. p.96.
67 ibid. p.119.
68 *The Times*, 3 July 1971.
69 *The Times*, 3 July 1971.
70 *The Times*, 6 July 1971.
71 *Daily Telegraph*, 20 July 1981; *The Times*, 23 July 1971.
72 *The Times*, 21 July 1971.
73 Palmer (1971) op. cit. p.252; *Guardian*, 28 July 1971.
74 ibid. p.257.
75 Quoted in Michael, R. (1972) *The ABZ of Pornography*, Panther, pp.117–18 and Robertson (1979) op. cit. p.133.
76 *Daily Telegraph* leader 29 July 1971, quoted in Palmer (1971) op. cit. p.262.
77 Quoted in Palmer (1971) op. cit. p.263.
78 *Guardian*, 6 August 1971.
79 *Daily Telegraph*, 6 August 1971.
80 ibid.
81 *The Times*, 6 August 1971.
82 *Evening Standard*, 5 August 1971.
83 *The Times*, 6 July 1971.
84 ibid.
85 *The Times*, 6 July 1971.
86 *The Times* 7 August 1971, from: Bruce Page, Tony Delano, John Pilger, Phillip Knightley, Derek Porter, Murray Sayle and Clive James.
87 *Sunday Telegraph*, 8 August 1971.
88 *Observer*, 8 August 1971.
89 *Sunday Times*, 8 August 1971.
90 *The Times*, 10 August 1971.
91 *Guardian*, 13 August 1971.
92 *The Times*, 4 November 1971.
93 R. v. Anderson (1971) 3 All ER at p.1160 quoted in Robertson (1979) op. cit. p.49.
94 *Daily Telegraph*, 6 November 1971.
95 R. v. Anderson (1971) 3 All ER at p.1161.
96 (1971) 3 WLR 939 at p.950; Robertson (1979) op. cit. p.135.
97 *Daily Telegraph*, 6 November 1971.
98 Hansen, S. and Jensen, J. (1971) *The Little Red Schoolbook*, Stage One Publishers.
99 ibid. p.29.
100 ibid. p.52.
101 ibid. p.95.
102 ibid.
103 ibid. p.127.
104 *The Times*, 30 June 1971.

105 *The Times, The Daily Telegraph,* 30 June 1971.
106 *The Times,* 2 July 1971.
107 *Daily Telegraph,* 2 July 1971.
108 *The Times,* 4 July 1971.
109 *Guardian,* 12 July 1971.
110 Tracey and Morrison (1979) op. cit.
111 Whitehouse, M. (1977) op. cit. p.235.
112 *Freethinker,* 10 July 1971.
113 *Evening Standard,* 29 October 1971.
114 Appeal of Richard Handyside, Inner London Crown Court, 29 October 1971 and Robertson, G. (1979) op. cit. pp.292–3.
115 Separate opinion of Judge Mosles, European Court of Human Rights, Handyside Case 7 December 1976.
116 *Sunday Times,* 28 January 1973.
117 Cox, B. (1975) Civil Liberties in Britain, Harmondsworth: Penguin.
118 In NDC (eds) (1980) op. cit.

6 A woman's right to choose?: Abortion and the law in post-war Britain

1 Professor McLaren's response to the passing of the 1967 Act was to say: "There'll be nobody murdering little babies in Birmingham", *The Listener,* 7 February 1980.
2 Simms, M. (1978) 'Forty Years Back – Abortion in the Press', in *Abortion: Ten Years On,* Birth Control Trust and (1981) 'Abortion: The Myth of the Golden Age', in Hutter, B. and Williams, G. (eds) *Controlling Women: The Normal and the Deviant,* Kent: Croom Helm.
3 Hindell, K. and Simms, M. (1971) *Abortion Law Reformed,* Peter Owen, p.13.
4 ibid. p.73.
5 Quoted in Potts, M., Diggory, P. and Peel, J. (1977) *Abortion,* Cambridge: Cambridge University Press.
6 R. v. Bourne (1939) 1 K.B. 687.
7 Jenkins, A. (1961) *Law for the Rich,* London: Victor Gollancz, p.67.
8 Jenkins, A. (1961) op. cit. p.76.
9 Brookes, B. (1988) *Abortion in England,* 1900–67, Kent: Croom Helm.
10 ibid.
11 ibid. p.144.
12 Smith, L.J.F. (1980) 'The Abortion Controversy, 1936–77', unpublished PhD Thesis, University of Edinburgh.
13 Brookes (1988) op. cit. p.152.
14 *Hansard* vol. 270 col. 1168.
15 RCOG 'Report on Legalised Abortion', *British Medical Journal,* 2 April 1966.
16 RCOG, op. cit. p.852.
17 *Hansard* vol. 732 col. 1074.
18 *Hansard* vol. 732 col. 1075.
19 *Hansard* vol. 732 col. 1103.
20 Hindell and Simms (1971) op. cit.
21 Greenwood, V. 'The Theft of the Body: The Sociology of the Abortion Law', unpublished MA Thesis, University of Sheffield.

22 Hindell and Simms (1971) op. cit. p.167.
23 ibid., p.170.
24 ibid. p.177.
25 ibid. p.178.
26 ibid. p.7.
27 ibid. p.185.
28 *Hansard* vol. 747 col. 464.
29 Hoggett, J.C. (1968) 'The Abortion Act 1967', *Criminal Law Review*.
30 Marsh, D. and Chambers, J. (1981) *Abortion Politics*, Junction Books.
31 Lovenduski, J. and Outshoorn, J. (1986) *The New Politics of Abortion*, London: Sage, and Francome, C. (1984) *Abortion Freedom*, London: George Allen & Unwin.
32 *Hansard* vol. 750 col. 1372, and quoted in part in, Hindell and Simms (1971) op. cit. pp.201–1.
33 Francome (1984) op. cit. p.159.
34 *Daily Telegraph* 14 February 1970.
35 Potts, Diggory and Peel (1977) op. cit. p.313.
36 ibid. p.324.
37 Litchfield, M. and Kentish, S. (1974) *Babies for Burning*, Serpentine Press.
38 ibid. p.148.
39 ibid. p.149.
40 Potts, Diggory and Peel (1977) op. cit. p.325.
41 Lovenduski, J. (1986) 'Parliament, pressure groups, networks and the women's movement: the politics of abortion law reform in Britain (1967–83)', in Lovenduski and Outshoorn (eds) (1986) op. cit.
42 Marsh and Chambers (1981) op. cit. p.141.
43 Simms, M. (1974) 'Abortion Law and Medical Freedom', *British Journal of Criminology* 14.
44 Hindell and Simms (1971) op. cit. p.8.
45 See e.g. Potts, Diggory and Peel (1977) op. cit. Ch. 9 or Greenwood, V. and Young, J. (1976) *Abortion in Demand*, Pluto Press.
46 Brookes (1988) op. cit. p.156.
47 *Hansard* HC debs vol. 732 col. 1074.
48 Brookes (1988) op. cit. p.163.
49 ibid. p.163.
50 ibid.
51 ibid.

7 Morality, the law and contemporary social change

1 Watney, S. (1987) Policing Desire: Pornography, AIDS and the Media, London: Methuen.
2 Cf. Hall (1979) 'Reformism and the Legislation of Consent', in National Deviancy Conference (1980) *Permissiveness and Control: The Fate of Sixties Legislation*, London: Macmillan.
3 Pearson, G. (1983) *Hooligan: A History of Respectable Fears*, London: Macmillan.
4 Hall (1979) op. cit.
5 McCabe, C. (1988) 'Is Television About to Enter the Dark Ages?' *The Listener*, 11 February.

6 Gittens, D. (1985) *The Family in Question*, London: Macmillan.
7 Quoted in Weeks, J. (1981) *Sex, Politics and Society*, London: Longmans.
8 Quoted in Smart, C. (1984) *The Ties that Bind*, London: Routledge & Kegan Paul.
9 Briggs, A. (1961) *Seebohm Rowntree*, London: Longmans.
10 Abrams, M. (1959) 'The Home-centred Society', *The Listener*, 26 November, quoted in Winship, J. (1981) 'Woman Becomes an Individual: Femininity and Consumption in Women's Magazines 1954–69', Centre for Contemporary Cultural Studies, *Special Paper no.65*, p.15.
11 ibid.
12 Birmingham Feminist History Group (1979) 'Feminism as Femininity in the 1950s', *Feminist Review* 3: 49–50.
13 Smart, C. (1981) 'Law and the Control of Women's Sexuality', in Hutter, B. and Williams, G. (eds) (1981) *Controlling Women: The Normal and the Deviant*, Kent: Croom Helm.
14 Smart (1984) op. cit. p.29.
15 Bouchier (1983) *The Feminist Challenge: The Movement for Women's Liberation in Britain and the United States*, London: Macmillan.
16 Hutter, B. and Williams, G. (1981) 'Controlling Women: The Normal and the Deviant', in Hutter and Williams (eds) (1981) op. cit.
17 MacInnes, C. (1959) *Absolute Beginners*, London: Allison & Busby, p.6, quoted in Frith, S. (1983) *Sound Effects: Youth, Leisure and the Politics of Rock and Roll*, London, Constable, p.182.
18 Pearson (1983) op. cit.
19 Abrams, M. (1959) *The Teenage Consumer*, London: Routledge & Kegan Paul, p.9.
20 Clarke, Hall, Jefferson and Roberts (1976) 'Subcultures, Cultures and Class', in Hall and Jefferson (1976) *Resistance through Rituals*, London: Hutchinson.
21 Dunning, E.G., Murphy, P. and Williams, J. (1988) *The Roots of Football Hooliganism*, London: Routledge & Kegan Paul.
22 Hebdige, for example, has argued that

> as the 50s wore on, [the] negative consensus uniting cultural critics of all persuasions began to settle around a single term: Americanisation. References to the pernicious influence of American popular culture began to appear whenever the 'levelling down' process was discussed...By the early 1950s, the very mention of the word 'America' could sum up a cluster of negative associations.

Quoted in Hillier, B. (1983) *The Style of the Century*, Herbert Press, p.146.
23 Tony Jefferson (1975) argues that, as a style, it evolved from an initial attempt to buy status, using Edwardian upper class dandies as a mode, to a personal expression of solidarity (in the face of upheaval in the post-war working class community) and masculinity. For a fuller explanation cf. also Cohen, P. (1972) 'Subcultural Conflict and Working Class Community', *Working Papers in Cultural Studies* no.2, Centre for Contemporary Cultural Studies: University of Birmingham.
24 Pearson (1983) op. cit. p.15.
25 Dunning *et al.* (1988) op. cit.
26 Parkin, F. (1968) *Middle-Class Radicalism*, Manchester: Manchester University Press, quoted in Muncie, J. (1984) *The Trouble With Kids Today*, London: Hutchinson, pp.111–12.

27 Whitehouse (1977) *Whatever Happened to Sex?*, London: Hodder & Stoughton, p.239.
28 Cf. Goldthorpe, J., Lockwood, D., Bechofer, F. and Platt, J. (1969) *The Affluent Worker in the Class Structure*, Cambridge: Cambridge University Press, or Zweig, F. (1961) *The Worker in an Affluent Society*, London: Heinemann.
29 Gillis, J. (1981) *Youth and History: 1977 to the Present*, London: Academic Press, p.187.
30 Gillis (1981) op. cit.
31 ibid. p.187.
32 Tanner, J.H. (1962) *Growth at Adolescence*, Oxford: Blackwell.
33 Gillis (1981) op. cit. p.190.
34 Robinson, J.A.T. (1963) 'The Debate Continues', in Edwards, and Robinson, J.A.T. (eds) *The Honest to God Debate*, SCM Press.
35 ibid. p.246.
36 Quoted in Welsby, Canon, P.A. (1984) *A History of the Church of England: 1945–80*, Oxford: Oxford University Press, p.113.
37 Booker, C. (1970) *The Neophiliacs*, London: Collins, pp.194–5.
38 Heron, A. (ed) (1963) *Towards a Quaker View of Sex: An Essay by a Group of Friends*, Friends Home Service Committee.
39 Whitehouse (1971) *Who Does She Think She Is?*, London: New English Library, p.45.
40 McIntyre, A. (1967) *Secularisation and Moral Change*, Oxford: Oxford University Press, p.57.
41 Hall (1980) op. cit.
42 ibid.
43 Quoted in Greenwood, V. and Young, J. (1980) op. cit.
44 *Daily Telegraph*, 22 July 1967.

8 Postscript: Thatcherism and the politics of morality

1 Report of the Committee on Obscenity and Film Censorship, Cmnd. 7772 p.iv.
2 ibid. 9.36.
3 Quoted in Simpson, A.W.B. (1983) *Pornography and Politics*, Waterlow Publishers Ltd, pp.63–4.
4 ibid. p.58.
5 NFoL (1980) *Observations on the Committee on Obscenity and Film Censorship*.
6 *Daily Star*, 24 November 1983.
7 Barker, M. (ed) (1984) *The Video Nasties: Freedom and Censorship in the Media*, Pluto Press.
8 *Daily Mail*, 24 November 1983.
9 Brown, B. (1986) 'Exactly What We Wanted', in Barker, M. (1984) op. cit. p.68.
10 ibid. p.79.
11 Barker, M. (1984) 'Nasty Politics or Video Nasties?' in Barker, M. (1984) op. cit. p.13.
12 *Guardian*, 8 March 1984.
13 See for example the collected readings on this political development in Levitas, R. (ed) (1986) *The Ideology of the New Right*, Polity Press.

14 Altman, D. (1986) *AIDS and the New Puritanism*, Pluto Press.
15 Watney, S. (1989) 'Taking Liberties', in Carter, E. and Watney, S. (eds) *Taking Liberties*, Serpents Tail.
16 Quoted in Watney, S. (1989) op. cit. p.39.
17 Quoted in Weeks, J. (1990) *Coming Out*, revised and updated edn, London: Quartet, p.245.
18 Watney, S. (1989) op. cit.
19 Quoted in Lumsden, A. (1986) 'New Bill, Old Values', *New Statesman*, 28 February.
20 Cf. Watney, S. (1987) *Policing Desire: Pornography, AIDS and the Media*, Comedia, Chapter four.
21 Quoted in David, M. (1986) 'Moral and Maternal: The Family in the Right', in Levitas (1986) op. cit.
22 Shapiro, R. (1985) 'Britain's Sexual Counter-Revolutionaries', *Marxism Today*, February.
23 Cf. Berger, B. and Berger, P. (1984) *The War Over the Family*, Harmondsworth: Penguin.
24 For example, in the eleven years in which Mrs Thatcher was in power the percentage of births outside marriage rose from 10.9% to 27% (*Social Trends* 1990).
25 Cf. discussion in Weeks, J. (1985) *Sexuality and its Discontents*, London: Routledge & Kegan Paul, especially Chapters 2 and 8.

Bibliography

Abrams, M. (1959) *The Teenage Consumer*, London, Routledge & Kegan Paul.

Adam, B.D. (1989) 'The State, Public Policy and AIDS Discourse', *Contemporary Crises* 13: 1–14.

Adam, R. (1977) *A Woman's Place*, New York, Norton.

Adams, M. (1968) *Censorship: The Irish Experience*, Dublin, Scepter Books.

Aldridge, T.M. (1977) *The Criminal Law Act, 1977*, Kent, Butterworths.

Alston, J.P., and Tucker, F. (1973) 'The Myth of Sexual Permissiveness', *Journal of Sex Research* 9 (1).

Altman, D. (1986) *AIDS and the New Puritanism*, Pluto Press.

Archbishop of Canterbury's Group (1966) *Putting Asunder: A Divorce Law for Contemporary Society*, London, SPCK.

Arran, Lord (1972) 'The Sexual Offences Act', *Encounter*, March.

Arts Council of Great Britain (1969) *The Obscenity Laws*, London, Andre Deutsch Ltd.

Ashdown-Sharp, P. (1975) 'Abortion: How We Won the Battle and Nearly Lost the War', *Nova*, October.

Banks, O. (1981) *Faces of Feminism*, Oxford, Martin Robinson.

Barber, D.F. (1972) *Pornography and Society*, Charles Skilton.

Barker, D. and Allen, S. (1976) *Sexual Divisions and Society: Process and Change*, London, Tavistock.

Barker, M. (1984) *A Haunt of Fears: The Strange History of the British Horror Comics Campaign*, Pluto Press.

Barker, M. (ed.) (1984) *The Video Nasties: Freedom and Censorship in the Media*, Pluto Press.

Barlow, G. and Hill, A. (eds) (1985) *Video Violence and Children*, London, Hodder & Stoughton.

Barr, J. (1967) 'The Abortion Battle', *New Society*, 9 March.

Becker, H. (1963) *Outsiders: Studies in the Sociology of Deviance*, Free Press.

Beloff, M. (1972) 'Onwards from *OZ* ', *Encounter*, March.

Benedicius, D. (1975) 'Defeated Youth', *Sunday Times*, 8 June.

Bennion, F. (1977) 'Account of the "Libertine" Trial in Leicester', *New Statesman*, 18 February.

Berger, B. and Berger, P. (1984) *The War Over the Family*, Harmondsworth, Penguin.

Birmingham Feminist History Group (1979) 'Feminism as Femininity in the 1950s', *Feminist Review* 3.

Blackwell, T. and Seabrook, J. (1985) *A World Still to Win: The Reconstruction of the Post-War Working Class*, London, Faber & Faber.

Blanchard, J. (1982) 'Prostitution and the Social Control of Female Sexuality', unpublished MA thesis, University of Leicester.

Bland, R. and Wallis, R. (1977) 'Comment on Wilson and Zurcher's Status Inconsistency and Participation in Social Movements', *Sociological Quarterly* 18 (3).

Bland, L., McCabe, T. and Mort, F. (1979) 'Sexuality and Reproduction: Three 'Official' Instances', in Barrett, M., Corrigan, P., Kuhn, A. and Wolff, J. *Ideology and Cultural Reproduction*, Kent, Croom Helm.

Bloch, I. (1958) *Sexual Life in England, Past and Present*, Corgi Books.

Blom-Cooper, L. and Drewry, A. (eds) (1976) *Law and Morality*, London, Duckworth.

Bogdanor, V. and Skildelsky, R. (1970) *Age of Affluence*, London, Macmillan.

Booker, C. (1969) *The Neophiliacs*, London, Collins.

Boston, R. (1966) 'On Magistrate Leo Gradwell', *New Society*, November.

Bouchier, D. (1983) *The Feminist Challenge: The Movement for Women's Liberation in Britain and the United States*, London, Macmillan.

Bourne, A. (1962) *A Doctor's Creed*, London, Gollancz.

Bowlby, J. (1963) *Child Care and the Growth of Love*, Harmondsworth, Penguin.

Boyle, K., Hadden, T. and Hillyard, P. (1975) *Law and State*, Oxford, Martin Robertson.

Brake, M. (1980) *The Sociology of Youth Culture and Youth Subcultures*, London, Routledge & Kegan Paul.

Brake, M. (ed) (1982) *Human Sexual Relations*, Harmondsworth, Penguin.

Briggs, A. (1961) *Seebohm Rowntree*, London, Longmans.

British Council of Churches (1966) *Sex and Morality*, London, SCM Press.

British Medical Association (1955) *Homosexuality and Prostitution*, London, BMA.

Brookes, B. (1988) *Abortion in England, 1900–67*, Kent, Croom Helm.

Brophy, J. and Smart, C. (1981) 'From Disregard to Disrepute: The Position of Women in Family Law', *Feminist Review*, October.

Brownmiller, S. (1975) *Against Our Will*, London, Martin Secker & Warburg.

Burns, A. (1972) *Deprave and Corrupt*, Davis-Poynter.

Calder, J. (1970) 'A Reply to Pamela Hansford Johnson', *Encounter*, April.

Carter, A. (1988) *The Politics of Women's Rights*, London, Longmans.

Carter, E. and Watney, S. (1989) *Taking Liberties: AIDS and Cultural Politics*, Serpents Tail.

Caulfield, M. (1975) *Mary Whitehouse*, Mowbrays.

Chandos, J. (ed) (1962) *To Deprave and Corrupt*, London, Souvenir Press.

Charney, M. (1981) *Sexual Fiction*, New Accents.

Chesler, P. (1979) *About Men*, London, Women's Press.

Church of England Moral Welfare Council (1952) *The Problem of Homosexuality*, Church Information Board.

Church of England Moral Welfare Council (1956) *Sexual Offenders and Social Punishment*, Church Information Board.

Clarke, A. (1970) 'Abortion Act: Inquiry or Farce?' *Humanist News*, October.

Clarke, A. (1970) 'The Abortion Act Vindicated', *Humanist*, April.

Clarke, A. (1987) 'Moral Protest, Status Defence and the Anti-Abortion Campaign', *British Journal of Sociology* 38 (2).

Clarke, A. (1987) 'Moral Reform and the Anti-Abortion Movement', *Sociological Review* 35.

Clarke, J., Hall, S., Jefferson, T. and Roberts, B. 'Subcultures, cultures and class – a theoretical overview', in S. Hall and T. Jefferson (1976).

Cliff, D. (1979) 'Religion, Morality and the Middle Class', in King, R. and Nugent, N. *Respectable Rebels: Middle-class Campaigns in Britain in the 1970s*, London, Hodder & Stoughton.

Cohen, P. (1972) 'Subcultural Conflict and Working Class Community', *Working Papers in Cultural Studies* no. 2, Centre for Contemporary Cultural Studies, University of Birmingham.

Cohen, S. (1980) *Folk Devils and Moral Panics*, Oxford, Martin Robertson.

Coote, A. and Campbell, B. (1982) *Sweet Freedom*, London, Picador.

Coser, L. (1978) 'The Bridling of Affect and the Refinement of Manners', *Contemporary Sociology* 7.

Court, J.H. (1977) 'Pornography and Sex Crimes: A Re-evaluation in the Light of Recent Trends Around the World', *International Journal of Criminology and Penology* 5.

Court, J.H. (1980) *Pornography: A Christian Critique*, IVCF.

Court, J.H. (undated) 'Pornography, Harm and Williams', NVALA.

Cousins, M. and Hussain, A. (1984) *Michel Foucault*, London, Macmillan.

Coward, R. (1978) 'Sexual Liberation and the Family', *M/F* 1.

Cox, A. (1975) *Civil Liberties in Britain*, Harmondsworth, Penguin.

Craig, A. (1962) *The Banned Books of England*, London, George Allen & Unwin.

Currie, A. and Gilbert, D. (1972) 'Religion', in Halsey, A.H. *Trends in British Society Since 1900*, London, Macmillan.

David, M. (1986) 'Moral and Maternal: The Family in the Right', in Levitas, R. (ed.) *The Ideology of the New Right*, Polity Press.

Davies, C. (1975) *Permissive Britain*, London, Pitman.

Davis, K. (1937) 'The Sociology of Prostitution', *American Sociological Review*, 2.

Devlin, P. (1959) *The Enforcement of Morals*, Oxford, Oxford University Press.

Dhavan, R. and Davies, C. (1978) *Censorship and Obscenity*, Oxford, Martin Robertson.

Dickens, B.M. (1966) *Abortion and the Law*, London, MacGibbon & Kee.

Dickson, D.T. (1968) 'Bureaucracy and Morality: An Organisational Perspective on a Moral Crusade', *Social Problems* 16.

Diggory, P.L.C. and Simms, M. (1970) 'Two Years After the Abortion Act', *New Scientist* 48.

Dominian, J. (1971) *The Church and the Sexual Revolution*, SCM.

Driberg, T. (1964) *The Mystery of Moral Re-armament*, London.

Dunning, E., Murphy, P. and Williams, J. (1988) *The Roots of Football Hooliganism: An Historical and Sociological Study*, London, Routledge & Kegan Paul.

Durkheim, E. (1970) *Suicide*, London, Routledge & Kegan Paul.

Durkheim, E. (1964) *The Division of Labour in Society*, New York, Free Press.

Dworkin, A. (1981) *Pornography: Men Possessing Women*, London, The Women's Press.

Edgar, D. (1987) 'The Morals Dilemma', *Marxism Today*, October.

Edwards, S. (1981) *Female Sexuality and the Law*, Oxford, Martin Robertson.

Elias, N. (1978) *The Civilizing Process*, Oxford, Basil Blackwell.

Elias, N. (1978) *What is Sociology?*, London, Hutchinson.

Elias, N. (1982) *State-Formation and Civilization*, Oxford, Basil Blackwell.
Elias, N. (1987) 'The Changing Balance of Power Between the Sexes – A Process-Sociological Study: The Example of the Ancient Roman State', *Theory, Culture and Society* 4.
Ellis, H. (1936) *Sexual Inversion*, New York, Random House.
Eysenck, H.J. (1970) 'Obscenity – Officially Speaking', *Penthouse*, vol. 4.
Eysenck, H.J. and Nias, D.K.B. (1980) *Sex, Violence and the Media*, Paladin.
Farren, M. and Barker, E. (1972) *Watch Out Kids*, London, Open Gate Books.
Faust, B. (1981) *Women, Sex and Pornography*, Harmondsworth, Penguin.
Ferman, J. (1976) 'On "Deep Throat"', *New Statesman*, 16 July.
Ferguson, M. (1983) *Forever Feminine: Women's Magazines and the Cult of Femininity*, London, Heinemann.
Findlater, R. (1967) *Banned! – A Review of Theatrical Censorship in Britain*, MacGibbon & Kee.
Foucault, M. (1971) 'Orders of Discourse', *Social Science Information* 10.
Foucault, M. (1981) *The History of Sexuality*, Harmondsworth, Pelican.
Foucault, M. (1987) *The Use of Pleasure*, Harmondsworth, Penguin.
Fountain, N. (1988) *Underground: The London Alternative Press, 1966–74*, Comedia.
Friedenberg, E.Z. (1963) 'The Image of the Adolescent Minority', *Dissent* 10.
Francombe, C. (1984) *Abortion Freedom: A Worldwide Movement*, London, George Allen & Unwin.
Frith, S. (1983) *Sound Effects: Youth, Leisure and the Politics of Rock and Roll*, London, Constable.
Fryer, P. (1966) *Private Case – Public Scandal*, London, Martin Secker & Warburg.
Fryer, P. (1967) 'A Map of the Underground', *Encounter*, October.
Fryer, P. (1967) 'To Deprave and Corrupt', *Encounter*, March.
Fryer, P. (1968) 'Censorship at the British Museum', *Encounter*, October.
Gagnon, J.H. and Simon, W. (1967) *Sexual Deviance*, New York, Harper & Row.
Gale, G. (1972) Review of *The Longford Report*, *Spectator*, September.
Galloway, B. (ed) (1983) *Prejudice and Pride: Discrimination Against Gay People in Modern Britain*, London, Routledge & Kegan Paul.
Gay Left Collective (1980) *Homosexuality: Power and Politics*, London, Allison & Busby.
Gilbert, A.D. (1980) *The Making of Post-Christian Britain*, London, Longman.
Gillie, O., Wallace, M., Ashdown-Sharp, P., and Zimmerman, L. (1975) 'Abortion Horror Tales Revealed as Fantasies', *Sunday Times*, 30 March.
Gillis, J.R. (1981) *Youth and History*, London, Academic Press.
Girodias, M. (1966) 'The Erotic Society', *Encounter*, February.
Gittens, D. (1985) *The Family in Question*, London, Macmillan.
Gleichmann, P.R., Goudsblom, J. and Korte, H. (1977) *Human Figurations*, Amsterdams Sociologisch Tijdschrift.
Goldthorpe, J., Lockwood, D., Bechofer, F. and Platt, J. (1969) *The Affluent Worker in the Class Structure*, Cambridge, Cambridge University Press.
Goodhart, A.L. (1961) 'The Shaw Case: The Law and Public Morals', *The Law Quarterly Review* 77, October.
Gosling, R. (1962) *Sum Total*, London, Faber & Faber.
Gosling, R. (1966) 'On the Trial of "Golden Convulvulus"', *New Society*, March.
Greenwood, V. (1973) 'The Theft of the Body: The Sociology of the Abortion Law', unpublished MA thesis, University of Sheffield.

Greenwood, V. and Young, J. (1976) *Abortion in Demand*, Pluto Press.

Greenwood, V. and Young, J. (1980) 'Ghettos of Freedom', in National Deviancy Conference (eds) *Permissiveness and Control*, London, Macmillan.

Grey, A. (1975) 'Homosexual Law Reform', in Frost, B. (ed.) *The Tactics of Pressure*, Stainer and Bell.

Gummer, J. Selwyn (1971) *The Permissive Society*, London, Cassell & Co.

Gusfield, J.R. (1963) *Symbolic Crusade: Status Politics and the American Temperance Movement*, Urbana, University of Illinois Press.

Hall, S. (1979) 'Drifting into a Law and Order Society', Cobden Trust Human Rights Day Lecture.

Hall, S. (1980) 'Reformism and the Legislation of Consent', in National Deviancy Conference (eds) *Permissiveness and Control*, London, Macmillan.

Hall, S., Clarke, J., Critcher, C. and Roberts, B. (1978) *Policing the Crisis*, London, Macmillan.

Hall-Williams, J.E. (1961) 'The *Ladies' Directory* and Criminal Conspiracy', *Modern Law Review* 24.

Hansen, S. and Jensen, J. (1971) *The Little Red Schoolbook*, Stage One.

Harris, P. (1980) *An Introduction to Law*, London, Weidenfeld & Nicolson.

Hart, H.L.A. (1963) *Law, Liberty and Morality*, Oxford, Oxford University Press.

Hart, H.L.A. (1967) 'Social Solidarity and the Enforcement of Morality', *University of Chicago Law Review* 35.

Hazell, R. (1974) 'Conspiracy and Civil Liberties', *Occasional Papers on Social Administration*, Social Administration Research Trust.

Hebdige, D. (1979) *Subculture: The Meaning of Style*, New Accents.

Heron, A. (ed), *Towards a Quaker View of Sex: An Essay by a Group of Friends*, Friends' Home Service Committee.

Hewison, R. (1986) *Too Much!: Art and Society in the Sixties, 1960–75*, London, Methuen.

Hewitt, P. (1982) *The Abuse of Power*, Oxford, Martin Robertson.

Hill, D. (1960) 'The Habit of Censorship', *Encounter*, September.

Hill, J. (1986) *Sex, Class and Realism: British Cinema, 1956–63*, London, British Film Institute.

Hillier, B. (1983) *The Style of the Century, 1900–80*, Herbert Press.

Hindell, K. and Simms, M. (1961) 'The Law Relating to Therapeutic Abortion', *Law Society's Gazette* 58 (9).

Hindell, K. and Simms, M. (1968) 'How the Abortion Lobby Worked', *Political Quarterly* 39 (3).

Hindell, K. and Simms, M. (1971) *Abortion Law Reformed*, Peter Owen.

Hoggett, A.J.C. (1968) 'The Abortion Act, 1967', *Criminal Law Review*, May, pp. 247–58.

Holbrook, D. (1972) On 'Oh! Calcutta!', *Spectator*, 5 February.

Holbrook, D. (1972) *The Pseudo-Revolution*, Willmer Bros. Books.

Hollander, X. (1972) *The Happy Hooker*, Tandem.

Home Office (1945–75) *Criminal Statistics for England and Wales*, HMSO.

Home Office (1957) Report of the Committee on Homosexuality and Prostitution, Cmnd. 247, HMSO.

Home Office (1974) The Working Party on Vagrancy and Street Offences: Working Paper, HMSO.

Home Office (1979) Report of the Committee on Obscenity and Film Censorship, Cmnd. 7772, HMSO.

Hopkins, H. (1963) *The New Look*, London, Martin Secker & Warburg.
Hopkins, H. (1963) *A Social History of the Forties and Fifties in Britain*, London, Martin Secker & Warburg.
Hordern, A. (1971) *Legal Abortion: The English Experience*, Oxford, Pergamon Press.
Hudson, K. (1983) *Dictionary of the Teenage Revolution and its Aftermath*, London, Macmillan.
Hughes, D.A. (ed) (1970) *Perspectives on Pornography*, London, Macmillan.
Humphries, S. (1981) *Hooligans or Rebels?: An Oral History of Working-class Childhood and Youth, 1889–1939*, Oxford, Blackwell.
Hunt, A. (1978) *The Sociological Movement in Law*, London, Macmillan.
Hutter, B. and Williams, G. (1981) *Controlling Women: The Normal and the Deviant*, Beckenham, Croom Helm.
Hyde, H.M. (1964) *A History of Pornography*, London, Heinemann.
Hyde, H.M. (1970) *The Other Love*, London, Heinemann.
Inglis, B. (1965) *Private Conscience Public Morality*, Four Square.
Ingram, I.M. (1971) 'Abortion Games: An Inquiry into the Working of the Act', *Lancet* ii, 1197.
Irving, C., Wallington, J. and Hall, R. (1964) *Scandal 63: The Profumo Sensation Complete*, Mayflower Dell.
Jefferson, T. (1975) 'Cultural Responses of the Teds', *Working Papers in Cultural Studies* nos 7/8.
Jeffreys, S. (1990) *Anticlimax: A Feminist Perspective on the Sexual Revolution*, London, The Women's Press.
Jenkins, A. (1961) *Law for the Rich*, London, Victor Gollancz.
Jenkins, D. (Bishop of Durham) (1985) 'A Theology for the Liberation of Tomorrow's Britain', *Guardian*, 15 April.
Jenkins, R. (1959) *The Labour Case*, Harmondsworth, Penguin.
Jenkins, R. (1959) 'Obscenity, Censorship and the Law', *Encounter*, October.
Johnson, P. Hansford (1970) 'Peddling the Pornography of Violence', *Encounter*, April.
Johnson, P. Hansford (1967) *On Iniquity*, London, Macmillan.
Jowell, R., Witherspoon, S. and Brook, L. (eds) (1988) *British Social Attitudes: The 5th Report* SCPR, London, Gower.
Kennedy, L. (1987) *The Trial of Stephen Ward*, London, Gollancz.
Kinsey, A., Pomeroy, W.A. and Martin, C.E. (1948) *Sexual Behaviour in the Human Male*, Saunders and Co.
Kirkup, J. (1976) On 'The Love That Dares To Speak Its Name', *Observer*, 17 July.
Kronhausen, E. and Kronhausen, P. (1967) *Pornography and the Law*, Kent, New English Library.
Lambert, J.W. (1967) 'The Folly of Censorship', *Encounter*, 29.
Leavis, F.R. (1961) 'The New Orthodoxy', *Spectator*, 19 February.
Lee, S. (1986) *Law and Morals: Warnock, Gillick and Beyond*, Oxford, Oxford University Press.
Leigh, D. (1979) 'Sex Offenders and the Chemical Cure', *Evening Standard*, 7 February.
Leiser, B.M. (1986) *Liberty, Justice and Morals*, New York, Macmillan.
Levin, B. (1972) *The Pendulum Years*, London, Pan Books.
Levitas, R. (ed) (1986) *The Ideology of the New Right*, Polity Press.

Litchfield, M. and Kentish, S. (1974) *Babies for Burning*, Serpentine Press.

Longford, Lord (1972) *Longford Report on Pornography*, Coronet Books.

Longford, Lord (1974) *The Grain of Wheat*, London, Collins.

Lovenduski, J. and Outshoorn, J. (eds) (1986) *The New Politics of Abortion*, London, Sage.

Lukes, S. (1975) *Emile Durkheim: An Historical and Critical Study*, Peregrine.

Lumsden, A. (1982) 'Gay News Blasphemy Trial: It Looks Like the End of the Road', *Gay News* 242, 10–23 June.

Lumsden, A. (1986) 'New Bill, Old Values', *New Statesman*, 28 February.

McCabe, C. (1988) 'Is Television About to Enter the Dark Ages?' The South Bank Lecture 1988, *The Listener*, 11 February.

McGlashen, A. (1963) 'Sex on these Islands', *Encounter*, July.

McGregor, O.R. (1972) 'Equality, Sexual Values and Permissive Legislation: The English Experience', *Journal of Social Policy* 28.

Macinnes, C. (1962) 'Experts on Trial', *Encounter*, March.

Macinnes, C. (1980) *Absolute Beginners*, London, Allison & Busby.

MacIntyre, A. (1967) *Secularisation and Moral Change*, Oxford, Oxford University Press.

MacIntyre, A. and Edwards, D. (eds) (1963) *The Honest to God Debate*, SCM Press.

McKie, D. and Cook, C. (1972) *The Decade of Disillusion: British Politics in the Eighties*, London, Macmillan.

Marcuse, H. (1966) 'Pornotopia', *Encounter*, August.

Mark, Sir R. (1978) *In the Office of Constable*, London, Collins.

Mark, Sir R. (1977) *Policing in a Perplexed Society*, London, George Allen & Unwin.

Marsh, D. and Chambers, J. (1981) *Abortion Politics*, Junction Books.

Martin, B. (1983) *A Sociology of Contemporary Cultural Change*, Oxford, Basil Blackwell.

Martin, K. (1954) 'Sadism for Kids', *New Statesman and Nation* 25, September.

Marwick, A. (1982) *British Society Since 1945*, Harmondsworth, Penguin.

Masters, B. (1985) *The Swinging Sixties*, London, Constable.

Melly, G. (1972) *Revolt into Style: The Pop Arts in Britain*, Harmondsworth, Penguin.

Merton, R. (1957) *Social Theory and Social Structure*, New York, Free Press.

Michael, R. (1972) *The ABZ of Pornography*, Panther.

Midgley, T.S. (1975) 'The Role of Legal History', *British Journal of Law and Society* 2 (2).

Mills, C.W. (1959) *The Sociological Imagination*, London, Oxford, Oxford University Press.

Ministry of Labour (1955–63) *The Labour Gazette*, London, HMSO.

Mishan, E.J. (1972) 'Making the World Safe for Pornography', *Encounter*, March.

Mitchell, B. (1967) *Law, Morality and Religion in a Secular Society*, Oxford, Oxford University Press.

Montgomerie, J. (1970) 'Pornography and Violence: A Reply to Pamela Hansford Johnson', *Encounter*, 34.

Mort, F. (1987) *Dangerous Sexualities: Medico-Moral Politics in England Since 1830*, London, Routledge & Kegan Paul.

Muncie, J. (1984) *The Trouble With Kids Today*, London, Hutchinson.

National Council for Civil Liberties (1972) *Against Censorship*, London, NCCL.

National Deviancy Conference (1980) *Permissiveness and Control: The Fate of Sixties Legislation*, London, Macmillan.

National Viewers and Listeners Association (undated) 'Comments on Some Aspects of the Report of the Committee on Obscenity and Film Censorship', NVALA.

National Viewers and Listeners Association (undated) 'Comments on the Williams Report', NVALA.

National Viewers and Listeners Association (undated) 'Pornography: A Matter of Taste?' NVALA.

Nationwide Festival of Light (1978) 'Obscenity, Indecency and Violence in Publications and Film Censorship', NFoL.

Nationwide Festival of Light (1980) 'Observations on the Report of the Committee on Obscenity and Film Censorship', NFoL.

Neville, R. (1972) 'Never Trust Anyone Over Thirty!' *OZ* 40.

Neville, R. (1971) *Playpower*, London, Paladin.

New Musical Express (1983) 'Knockabout: Knocked About and Nearly Knackered', 12 March.

Norman, E. (1970) 'Establishment Versus Radicals', *Spectator*, 12 December.

Nuttall, J. (1970) *Bomb Culture*, London, Paladin.

Office of Population, Censuses and Surveys (1965–90) *Social Trends*, London, HMSO.

O'Higgins, P. (1972) *Censorship in Britain*, Nelson.

Ollman, B. (1979) *Social and Sexual Revolution*, Pluto Press.

Ossowska, M. (1986) *Bourgeois Morality*, London, Routledge & Kegan Paul.

OZ, issues 1–30.

Palmer, T. (1971) *The Trials of OZ*, London, Blond & Briggs.

Parkin, F. (1968) *Middle-Class Radicalism*, Manchester, Manchester University Press.

Parsons, T. (1951) *The Social System*, London, Routledge & Kegan Paul.

Passas, N. (1988) 'Anomie and Social Change: The Case of Abortion', unpublished paper delivered at the British Sociological Association Conference, Edinburgh.

Pawling, C. (1984) *Popular Fiction and Social Change*, London, Macmillan.

Pearson, G. (1983) *Hooligan: A History of Respectable Fears*, London, Macmillan.

Peckham, M. (1966) 'Pornotopia', *Encounter*, July.

Peel, J. and Potts, M. (1969) *A Textbook of Contraceptive Practice*, Cambridge, Cambridge University Press.

Perrin, N. (1970) *Dr Bowdler's Legacy. A History of Expurgated Books in England and America*, London, Macmillan.

Phelps, G. (1975) *Film Censorship*, London, Gollancz.

Playfair, G. (1969) *Six Studies in Hypocrisy*, London, Martin Secker & Warburg.

Plummer, K. (1981) *The Making of the Modern Homosexual*, London, Hutchinson.

Polsky, N. (1961) 'The Village Beat Scene: Summer 1960', *Dissent* VIII.

Port, K.A. (1960) 'A Wreath for the Gamekeeper', *Encounter*, February.

Potts, M., Diggory, P. and Peel, J. (1977) *Abortion*, Cambridge, Cambridge University Press.

Pratt, J.D. (1982) 'The Sexual Landscape: Repression or Freedom?' *Theory, Culture and Society*.

Pratt, J.D. and Sparks, R. (1987) 'New Voices From the Ship of Fools', *Contemporary Crises* 2.

Pym, B. (1974) *Pressure Groups and the Permissive Society*, David & Charles.

Rapp, R. (1979) 'Examining Family History', *Feminist Studies* 5.

Rembar, C. (1969) *The End of Obscenity*, London, Andre Deutsch.

Richards, P.G. (1972) Parliament and Conscience, London, George Allen & Unwin.

Robertson, G.R. (1974) *Whose Conspiracy?*, London, NCCL.

Robertson, G.R. (1976) *Reluctant Judas*, Temple Smith.

Robertson, G.R. (1979) *Obscenity*, London, Weidenfeld and Nicolson.

Robertson, G.R. (1980) 'The Future of Film Censorship', *British Journal of Law and Society* 7.

Robertson, G.R. (1980) 'Frightening the Horses', *Media, Law and Practice* 1.

Robertson, G.R. (1985) 'How Scum Draws a Line for the Censors', *Guardian*, 15 April.

Robinson, J.A.T. (1963) *Honest to God*, SCM Press.

Robinson, J.A.T. (1970) *Christian Freedom in a Permissive Society*, SCM Press.

Robinson, P. (1976) *The Modernisation of Sex*, London, Paul Elek.

Rock, P. and Cohen, S. (1970) 'The Teddy Boys', in V. Bogdanor, and R. Skidelsky (eds) (1970) *Age of Affluence*, London, Macmillan.

Rolph, C.H. (1959) 'Obscene Publications: The New Act', *Solicitor's Journal*, 20 November.

Rolph, C.H. (ed) (1961) *Does Pornography Matter?*, London, Routledge & Kegan Paul.

Rolph, C.H. (1961) *The Trial of Lady Chatterley*, London, Penguin.

Rolph, C.H. (1965) 'Wolfenden Revived', *New Statesman*, 21 May.

Rolph, C.H. (1973) 'The Uses of Conspiracy', *New Statesman*, 3 August.

Rubin, J. (1970) *Do It!*, New York, Simon & Schuster.

Ryder, J. and Silver, H. (1970) *Modern British Society*, London, Methuen.

St John Stevas, N. (1955) 'Obscenity and Law Reform', *Spectator*, 4 February.

St John Stevas, N. (1955) 'The Obscene Publications Bill, 1955', *The Author*, Spring, no. 3.

St John Stevas, N. (1956) *Obscenity and the Law*, London, Secker & Warburg.

Selby, Jr, H. (1966) *Last Exit to Brooklyn*, London, Calder & Boyars.

Sennett, R. (1975) *The Fall of Public Man*, London, Faber & Faber.

Shapiro, R. (1985) 'Britain's Sexual Counter-revolutionaries', *Marxism Today*, February.

Simms, M. (1969) 'The Abortion Act – One Year Later', *British Journal of Criminology*, July.

Simms, M. (1970) 'Abortion Law Reform: How the Controversy Changed', *Criminal Law Review*, October.

Simms, M. (1973) 'How Do We Judge the Abortion Act? Reflections on the Lane Committee and the 1967 Abortion Act', *Public Health, London* 87.

Simms, M. (1974) 'Abortion Law and Medical Freedom', *British Journal of Criminology* 14.

Simms, M. (1975) 'The Progress of the Abortion (Amendment) Bill', *Family Planning* 24.

Simms, M. (1978) 'Forty Years Back – Abortion in the Press', in *Abortion: Ten Years On*, Birth Control Trust.

Simms, M. (1981) 'Abortion: The Myth of the Golden Age', in Hutter, B. and Williams, G. (eds) *Controlling Women: The Normal and the Deviant*, Beckenham, Croom Helm.

Simpson, A.W.B. (1983) *Pornography and Politics: The Williams Committee in Retrospect*, Waterlow Publishers.

Sion, A.A. (1977) *Prostitution and the Law*, London, Faber & Faber.

Sked, A. (1987) *Britain's Decline*, Oxford, Basil Blackwell.

Sklair, L. (1970) *The Sociology of Progress*, London, Routledge & Kegan Paul.

Smart, C. (1979) 'The New Female Criminal: Reality or Myth?' *British Journal of Criminology* 19.

Smart, C. (1981) 'Law and the Control of Women's Sexuality', in Hutter, B. and Williams, G. (eds) *Controlling Women: The Normal and the Deviant*, Beckenham, Croom Helm.

Smart, C. (1984) *The Ties that Bind: Law, Marriage and the Reproduction of Patriarchal Relations*, London, Routledge & Kegan Paul.

Smith, L.J.F. (1980) 'The Abortion Controversy 1936–77: A Case Study in the Emergence of Law', unpublished PhD thesis, University of Edinburgh.

Smoker, B. (1971) 'Big Blue Schoolboy at Lambeth', *Peace News*, 9 July.

Society of Conservative Lawyers (1971) 'The Pollution of the Mind', unpublished.

Sparrow, J. (1962) 'R. v. Penguin Books Ltd. An Undisclosed Element in the Case', *Encounter*, 18.

Spicer, R. (1981) *Conspiracy: Law, Class and Society*, London, Lawrence & Wishart.

Stanworth, M. (1987) *Reproductive Technologies: Gender, Motherhood and Medicine*, Polity Press.

Steel, D. (1968) 'Reflections on the Abortion Act', *Medical Tribune* 31, October.

Steiner, G. (1966) 'Pornography and the Consequences', *Encounter*, March.

Stevens, I.N. and Yardley, D.C.M. (1982) *The Protection of Liberty*, Oxford, Basil Blackwell.

Stockwood, M. (1971) 'The Prurient and the Puerile', *Books and Bookmen*, October.

Street, H. (1982) *Freedom, the Individual and the Law*, Harmondsworth, Pelican.

Sutherland, J. (1982) *Offensive Literature: Decensorship in Britain 1960–82*, Junction Books.

Taylor, I. (1987) 'Violence and Video: For a Social Democratic Perspective', *Contemporary Crises* 2.

Tolson, A. (1975) 'The Family in a Permissive Society', *Occasional Papers in Cultural Studies*, Centre for Contemporary Cultural Studies, University of Birmingham.

Toynbee, P. (1981) 'On the Williams Report', *Guardian*, 30 October.

Tracey, M. and Morrison, D. (undated) 'The Jericho People: Mary Whitehouse and the National Viewers' and Listeners' Association', Report to the Social Science Research Council.

Tracey, M. and Morrison, D. (1979) *Whitehouse*, London, Macmillan.

Trevelyan, J. (1960) 'The Censor's Reply', *Encounter*, September.

Trevelyan, J. (1973) *What the Censor Saw*, London, Michael Joseph.

Trevor-Roper, H. (1968) 'The Philby Affair', *Encounter*, April.

Tribe, D. (1973) *Questions of Censorship*, London, George Allen & Unwin.

Van Stolk, B. and Wouters, C. (1987) 'Power Changes and Self-Respect: A Comparison of Two Cases of Established–Outsider Relations', *Theory, Culture and Society* 4.

Wallis, R. (1972) 'Dilemma of a Moral Crusade', *New Society*, 13 July.

Wallis, R. (1976) 'Moral Indignation and the Media: An Analysis of the NVALA', *Sociology* 10.

Wallis, R. (1976) 'Processes in the Development of Social Movements: Goal

Displacement and the Routinisation of Charisma in the Nationwide Festival of Light', *Scottish Journal of Sociology* 1 (1).

Wallis, R. (1977) 'A Critique of the Theory of Moral Crusades as Status Defence', *Scottish Journal of Sociology* 1 (2).

Wallis, R. and Bland, R. (1978) 'Five Years On: Report of a Survey of Participants in the Nationwide Festival of Light in Trafalgar Square, London, 25 September 1976', Report to the Social Science Research Council.

Wallis, R. and Bland, R. (1979) 'Purity in Danger: A Survey of Participants in a Moral Crusade Rally', *British Journal of Sociology* 30.

Walmsley, R. (1978) 'Indecency between Males and the Sexual Offences Act, 1967', *Criminal Law Review*, July pp. 400–7.

Walmsley, R. and White, K. (1978) 'Sexual Offences, Consent and Sentencing', *Home Office Research Study*, London, HMSO.

Walter, N. (1977) 'Blasphemy in Britain: The Practice and the Punishment of Blasphemy and the Trial of Gay News', Rationalist Press Association.

Wandor, M. (1987) *Look Back in Gender: Sexuality and the Family in Post-War British Drama*, London, Methuen.

Warner, N. (1983) 'Parliament and the Law', in B. Galloway (ed) *Prejudice and Pride: Discrimination Against Gay People in Modern Britain*, London, Routledge & Kegan Paul.

Watkins, A. (1969) 'On the Trial of *My Secret Life*', *New Statesman*, 14 February.

Watney, S. (1987) *Policing Desire: Pornography, AIDS and the Media*, Comedia.

Watney, S. (1989) 'Taking Liberties', in Carter, E. and Watney, S. (eds) *Taking Liberties: AIDS and Cultural Politics*, Serpents Tail.

Weeks, J. (1977) *Coming Out: Homosexual Politics in Britain from the Nineteenth Century to the Present*, London, Quartet Books (revised and updated 1990).

Weeks, J. (1981) *Sex, Politics and Society: The Regulation of Sexuality Since 1800*, London, Longman.

Weeks, J. (1985) *Sexuality and its Discontents*, London, Routledge & Kegan Paul.

Weiner, B. (1981) 'The *Romans in Britain* Controversy', *The Drama Review* 25 (1).

Welsby, P.A. (1984) *A History of the Church of England 1945–80*, Oxford, Oxford University Press.

Wertham, F. (1954) *Seduction of the Innocent*, Reinhart & Co. Ltd.

Whitehouse, M. (1967) *Cleaning-up TV*, Blandford.

Whitehouse, M. (1971) 'Backlash', *Books and Bookmen*, October.

Whitehouse, M. (1971) *Who Does She Think She Is?*, Kent, New English Library.

Whitehouse, M. (1977) *Whatever Happened to Sex?*, London, Hodder & Stoughton.

Whitehouse, M. (1982) *A Most Dangerous Woman?*, Lion Publishing.

Whiteley, C. and Whiteley, W. (1967) *Sex and Morals*, London, Batsford.

Wildeblood, P. (1957) *Against the Law*, Harmondsworth, Penguin.

Williams, D.G.T. (1964) 'Sex and Morals in the Criminal Law 1954–63', *Criminal Law Review*, April, pp. 253–67.

Williams, G. (1961) 'Conspiring to Corrupt', *Listener*, 24 August.

Williams, G. (1966) 'Authoritarian Morals and the Criminal Law', *Criminal Law Review*, March.

Williams, R. (1961) 'The Law and Literary Merit', *Encounter*, September.

Wilson, E. (1977) *Women and the Welfare State*, London, Tavistock.

Wilson, E. (1980) *Only Halfway to Paradise: Women in Post-war Britain 1945–68*, London, Tavistock.

Winship, J. (1981) 'Woman Becomes an Individual: Femininity and Consumption in Women's Magazines 1954–69', *Special Paper no. 65*, Centre for Contemporary Cultural Studies, University of Birmingham.

Wistrich, E. (1978) *I Don't Mind the Sex, It's the Violence*, London, Marion Boyars.

Wistrich, E. (1980) 'Review of the "Report of the Williams Committee on Obscenity and Film Censorship" Pertaining to Film Censorship', *Media, Law and Practice* 1.

Wolfenden, J.F. (1960) 'The Homosexual and the Law: Ahead of Public Opinion?' *New Statesman*, 25 June.

Wolfenden, J.F. (1976) *Turning Points: Memoirs*, London, Bodley Head.

Wood, M. and Hughes, M. (1984) 'The Moral Basis of Moral Reform: Status Discontent vs. Culture and Socialisation as Explanations of Anti-pornography Social Movement Adherence', *American Sociological Review* 49.

Wootton, G. (1978) *Pressure Group Politics in Contemporary Britain*, Massachusetts, Lexington Books.

Worsthorne, P. (1973) 'Thoughts After Longford', *Encounter*, May.

Wouters, C. (1977) 'Informalisation and Civilising Processes', in Gleichmann, P. *et al. Human Figurations*, Amsterdams Sociologisch Tijdschrift.

Wouters, C. (1986) 'Formalisation and Informalisation, Changing Tension Balances in Civilising Processes', *Theory, Culture and Society* 3.

Wouters, C. (1987) 'Developments in the Behavioural Codes between the Sexes: The Formalisation of Informalisation in the Netherlands, 1930–85', *Theory, Culture and Society* 4.

Young, W. (1963) *The Profumo Affair: Aspects of Conservatism*, Harmondsworth, Penguin.

Zack, D. (1969) 'Smut for Love, Art, Society', *Art and Artists*, December.

Zellick, G. (1971a) 'Films and the Law of Obscenity', *Criminal Law Review*, March, pp. 126–50.

Zellick, G. (1971b) 'Two Comments on Search and Seizure under the Obscene Publications Act', *Criminal Law Review*, September, pp. 504–14.

Zinner, M. (1978) 'Michel Foucault: La Volonté de Savoir', *Telos* 36.

Zurcher, L.A., Kirkpatrick, R., Cushing, R.G. and Bowmar, C.K. (1973) 'Ad-hoc Anti-pornography Organisations and their Active Members: A Research Summary', *Journal of Social Issues* 29 (3).

Zweig, F. (1961) *The Worker in an Affluent Society*, London, Heinemann.

Index

what has happened / interpret the effects of
liberal vs coercive legislation
is it behind or not?

other cultures.